Ethical Practice and the Abuse of Power
in Social Responsibility

Ethical Practice and the Abuse of Power in Social Responsibility

Leave No Stone Unturned

Edited by Helen Payne and Brian Littlechild

Jessica Kingsley Publishers
London and Philadelphia

First published in the United Kingdom in 2000 by
Jessica Kingsley Publishers Ltd,
116 Pentonville Road, London
N1 9JB, England
and
325 Chestnut Street,
Philadelphia PA 19106, USA.

www.jkp.com

© Copyright 2000 Jessica Kingsley Publishers

British Library Cataloguing in Publication Data
Ethical practice and the abuse of power in social responsibility : leave no stone unturned
1. Social service – Great Britain 2. Social service – Moral and ethical aspects
I. Payne, Helen II. Littlechild, Brian
361.3'0941

Library of Congress Cataloging in Publication Data
A CIP catalog record for this book is available from the Library of Congress

ISBN 1 85302 743 X

Printed and Bound in Great Britain by
Athenaeum Press, Gateshead, Tyne and Wear

Contents

CHAPTER I

Introduction

Helen Payne

This book offers a documentation of the problem of abuse of power in social responsibility, not necessarily solutions. Ethical practice in professions of social responsibility to date has not recognised the extent of institutional or professional abuse. We trust that those professionals who read this book will listen and not react defensively to the content. It is hoped those involved in policy making will take account of these chapters in their considerations.

Service users will find *Ethical Practice and the Abuse of Power in Social Responsibility* revealing and we hope supportive, particularly where there is an experience with which they can identify. If you work in or have had involvement in the social services, family judiciary, community development, children and family services, courts and legal services then this book is essential reading for you. It is hoped the volume will be read by front-line workers, policy makers, directors of social and mental health services, local authorities, the judiciary, government departments on families, voluntary organisations concerned with children and mental health service users, community development bodies, trainers and parents.

The idea for the book came from a vision of a heavy stone being over-turned revealing to the light a patch of darkness and creepy crawlies. The 'overturning' related to several phenomena in my life, both personal and professional. One was those glimpses and insights I was receiving from my work as a therapist with clients. Over many years they had disclosed numerous examples of questionable practice by professionals from a range of disciplines and institutions.

At the same time I was also in contact with some psychotherapy and counselling colleagues who were particularly concerned with the abuse of power and socially responsible practice. In the light of these two 'nudges' and the original vision, I knew I was called to facilitate the voicing of concerns about 'institutional abuse' or 'system abuse' (see Sue Amphlett, Chapter 10) in the professionalised area of social responsibility. This refers to the way, for example, bias, prejudice, personal values and opinions or religious/cultural beliefs are projected onto/into procedures or policies/decisions by those in positions of power. Those working in professional institutions are empowered by their role to make decisions which may significantly damage people's lives. When conscious/unconscious content is acted out in work intended to help or treat others it may be particularly abusive and harmful for the victim. For example, Mary Neville, in her story (Chapter 11), illustrates how such abuse can lead to a complete breakdown of trust in state health provision. The title of the book was originally *Leave No Stone Unturned*, which was a reflection of the fact that the stories of professional or institutional abuse appear to be one of the last taboos in society. This may be because we are looking at our own workers – those meant to be caring, ethical practitioners. The taboo on self-reflection as practitioners has been longstanding. Why should professionals look at their own practice? After all, don't we know best, aren't we the experts, trained, experienced, neutral/independent, etc? In claiming that we are caring for people, whether children, those in poverty, those challenged with learning difficulties or mental health problems, or separating parents we need to be careful we are not simply exerting power over them in the guise of acting in their best interests.

Some of the chapters of this book have been sought through calls to many organisations (see List of Organisations), and pressure groups, and some through personal contacts in the professional world. There were numerous telephone calls from service users wishing to tell their story. I personally had lengthy discussions on the telephone with people who told of horrific experiences in situations such as mental health, medicine, social services, the legal services and business. Not all those who wished to contribute could.

Despite our attempts to cover all perspectives in this book we are aware that a blank perspective from service users is missing. Proposals from such groups were not forthcoming. This could be due to a number of factors. We continue to believe that such views are essential to inform policy and practice.

We had a very clear brief and book length. Some of the telephone calls were extremely distressing. People were frightened of identification and/or of retribution or legal ramifications. They were concerned about anonymity and confidentiality. They have been courageous to speak out despite their reservations, for example surrendering their copyright. Some have relived their abusive experiences as they wrote their chapters. For some, hurt and pain were restimulated and they have had to face further conflicts in voicing their stories. They have become exposed in their own grief but nonetheless felt moved to share their experiences, distressing though they were, in the hope that in so doing they may help others still suffering abuse and not able to speak out. A number of people writing have experienced repeated disbelief from professionals. Some people may have been angry at decisions going against them and could have been vengeful because of criticism. However, this would not account for all the responses. Unless the screams of pain are witnessed how do you ever recognize the abuse being perpetrated?

We also had many letters from people who had stories of abuse by professionals in the above fields. There followed a process of inviting potential contributors to write a short outline. Colleagues and others expressed an interest in contributing. Those eventually selected to write for the book fell into two broad categories: the service user and the professional. We wanted to combine these contributions in one book in order to facilitate a dialogue between them in the readership. The seemingly prevalent institutional or system abuse urgently needs addressing. We felt that by offering both perspectives (whether by choice or not) – those from the professions and those using their services – would help to provide a third perspective to the reader in developing, for example, policies, procedures or innovative systems in areas such as accountability, independent advocacy, ethical codes of practice, confidentiality, complaints processes and so on.

We selected those service users who could speak about their own experiences of abuses of power and make recommendations for changes in policy and practice as a result. We also selected contributions from professionals who had insights into the abuse of power in the systems/institutions either because of their own experiences or because they offered a more participative approach to working with people. Chapter 9, by Peter Beresford and Anne Wilson, combines the perspectives of the service user and the professional.

The dark side of professional practice is sinister to contemplate. Access to vulnerable people is obvious. Structures are all in place, training developed. Surely we can be trusted not to abuse our powerful positions. We do not need an outside body to monitor them as they only do 'good' – we can monitor ourselves. But can we? Do we involve those at the receiving end of our practice in evaluation or decision making in order for our work to be more effective?

From my experience in my own field, some professionals in social responsibility are confused about the purpose and nature of counselling and psychotherapy. At times these 'helping' relationships have been used as a form of social control. I have heard of a judge recommending a person to undertake psychotherapy with an objective of changing their attitudes about a specific injustice.

Prescribing therapy for someone with a view to forcing acceptance of a particular scenario is not only abusive, it denies that person's free will. Therapists and counsellors fortunately would not accede to such prescriptive objectives, particularly where there has been an injustice. Social workers have been known to make recommendations to 'victims' of sexual abuse, for example, that they enter psychotherapy to 'come to terms with the experience'. Others are referred to 'come to terms' with their housing problem, drug problem or loss of a child. Counsellors and psychotherapists are not generally in the business of supporting particular belief systems or professionals' views of what clients need to 'come to terms with' (whatever that phrase means).

If we were to take on board those objectives, counsellors would be working with the starving populations of the world to 'help' them come to terms with their plight, instead of recognising that many problems are out there in the world and cannot be addressed in the consulting room alone. Socio-political factors cannot be ignored whenever clients are referred by the legal, mental health or social services. These professionals have begun to view counselling as a way of managing so-called 'difficult' people, such as those who will not accept an unjust legal decision, those campaigning for human rights and others who are disturbing the status quo.

Using therapy to force people to adapt is unethical, or at best misguided. The appalling conditions in some people's outer worlds need to be addressed by those in positions of power. Counselling clients to 'accept' their lot in life may be a political act in itself. It would also be supporting the professionals who have deemed the client in need of counselling.

What happens when human nature, with all its prejudices and preconceptions, is set free in the inner sanctums of power? There have been numerous high profile instances of the kind of abuse which results. We work in social and economic structures many of which do not operate in a constructive way for the 'service users'. Some people have been severely damaged and wounded by the very institution which says it aims to help them; for example the mental health service. Part of the professionals' responsibility is listening to patients/clients: this book is a loud shout to those who have hitherto closed their ears.

Luckily in my profession we have the notion of countertransference, which helps us to recognise the ways our bias/prejudice can influence our decisions and processes with clients. In addressing our countertransference we can guard against inflicting our belief system on clients and thus against any harmful effects. Along with our insistence on supervision for all practising counsellors and psychotherapists, it is part of our normal practice to undertake our own therapy. This enables us to explore our own feelings, projections, judgements and interpretations in a safe environment. Our desires and motivations are uncovered, we attend to our responses to clients and inquire into what they mean in terms of the relationship. All this is held within a value base of the 'three Rs': responsibility, respect for self and respect for others. This is a sound basis for ethical practice. We need ethics to guide us in our practice if we are to engage with the phenomenological worlds of others. The deepest currents of meaning and knowledge take place within the individual through the senses, perceptions, beliefs and judgements. It is these deep currents which need to be explored if professionals working with service users are to respond ethically.

We know that the experiences of looked after children are good or bad depending on whether the professionals working with them listen and respond to the voices of the young people themselves. Too often the care system is unresponsive to those who should not have to be 'shouting' to be heard (Voice for the Child in Care 1998).

This book documents views from both professionals and users of the mental health, family judicial and social services which seriously question the way in which people are experiencing these systems.

There has been a mind-set which places professionals who may decide on life-changing action above any kind of accountability. Judges, in particular, appear to have an attitude that they are neutral, above bias and prejudice (see Lee Heal, Chapter 4). This is an arrogance that must be addressed. All judges have personal opinions. The bias or interest may not be intentional or conscious – that is precisely why it needs to be noticed and confronted. We all have blind spots, even psychotherapists who have had years of personal therapy. None of us is fully aware all of the time, even those with many years of self-awareness training.

It is hoped that by reading this book those working in the legal, social and mental health professions will be challenged to explore the bias, vested interest and prejudice in themselves and in the system as a whole. Currently it appears they either deny it or ignore it. The methodology employed in these great institutions presupposes a strict causal determinism. A model which uses relative indeterminism, people having their own autonomy and with self-determinism is far better suited to an explanation of human behaviour. Often these systems attempt to explain human behaviour in a manner which suits the interventions and procedures already in place, usually a cause-and-effect approach to problems which becomes more part of the problem than the solution (see Peter Beresford and Anne Wilson, Chapter 9).

Many procedures disempower people's thinking ability, as experienced by the expert witness in family hearings (see Sue Williscroft, Chapter 5; Judith Trowell and Lois Colling, Chapter 6; and Maria Pozzi, Chapter 7). In these procedures it appears that the structure and rules outweigh the content and processes to such an extent that group dynamics become completely unconscious, to the detriment of all involved, but particularly to those whose lives are to be severely affected by the outcomes. For example, if one group thinks it has the right answer they automatically believe the other has the wrong answer. That then becomes oppressive and it is a very small step from there to persecution. I was struck by the amount of triangulation and cross-validation between these independently written chapters.

The use of deception by professionals in, for example, retaining information which does not coincide with their view of what the outcomes should be, can be very harmful to those who know that this was done, particularly since there is no recourse to redress such omissions.

Knowledge is power, as we are all aware. In being marginalised, people caught up in one of these systems are then excluded from the processes of knowledge creation (see Sue Williscroft, Chapter 5). If on the other hand they were included (as recommended by Lee Heal, Chapter 4) in the production of knowledge their position is likely to improve.

The psychodynamics of social responsibility and the legal system have been explored by Judith Trowell and Lois Colling (Chapter 6) with reference to the family judicial system. They comment on the profound effect these psychodynamics have on social care practice and law implementation. If we are to begin to understand the process of social care then the study of the psychodynamics of social responsibility must be our starting point. Peter Beresford and Anne Wilson (Chapter 9) have illustrated some of the underlying processes at work in the mental health system which result in abusive 'care' for patients. These need addressing. Uncritical acceptance of existing ideology condemns us to deepening the malaise which is currently sweeping our culture and institutions.

To do this, though, we will need to look at those ugly, dark, unknown parts of ourselves (and inevitably the system as a whole contains them too), often manifested in our day-to-day practice and in the procedures we set up together. It is not pleasant to see these parts; they are usually hidden under a familiar, known part like the stone. Often we will want to replace the 'stone' quickly to blot out what is viewed. We need to acknowledge that there could be something else besides the known surface, something deeper and more sinister, hidden below but ever hard at work doing what it does. Maybe when we open this part to the light of examination and exploration we can begin to sharpen the blunt and outdated instruments professional institutions currently function with and within.

Section 3 of the 1998 government White Paper *Modernising Social Services (Services for Children)* outlines key themes including:

1. New, stronger systems for the protection of children.

2. Quality protects: the importance of quality for all children's services.

3. Better health and education for those in care.

4. More and better help for young people leaving care.

Brian Littlechild (Chapter 3) and Maggie Lane (Chapter 8) have much to say on these key themes. The document goes on to recommend that outcomes required should be stated in advance and an assessment of whether they have been achieved implemented. This needs to be a matter of policy on all decisions concerning children, since children grow and develop, families grow and change, and circumstances alter. This book would be helpful to those involved in family policy. The institutional abuse of children is receiving a great deal of concern recently. All children have a right to the best possible care. Therefore it is crucial that those children (whether looked after or not) let down by a parent or professional responsible for their day-to-day care can speak out. To do this they need quick access to processes through which their concerns and complaints about, say, quality of care, contact or residence can be listened to attentively, scrutinised properly, examined fairly and responded to. In some circumstances if the parent/professional carer continues to oppress/abuse the child the initiation of legal proceedings is a more appropriate way for children to challenge decisions made about their care.

It appears that looked after children have this right already. A child in care may have a request for different contact arrangements with parent(s) or sibling(s) that has been ignored or denied. Recourse to the courts is the only option for this child. This right needs to be extended to the child living with a parent who, say, refuses to consider the child's wishes for contact.

All children need to be given a right of access to independent advocacy if they have complaints about their care, wherever they live and whatever their age. In the absence of such a legal safeguard many children may become significantly damaged adults, underfunctioning and with low self-esteem and/or poor relationship skills.

It appears from news items and the literature that many children today do not have their voices heard and are often in the very situations in which they most need to be able to speak out. Professionals need to have more respect for what children say and to respond as a matter of urgency rather than just paying lip service to the 'views of the child'. To ignore or deny them their rights is another form of institutional abuse and a denial of their right under Article 12 of the United Nations Convention of the Rights of the Child. This states they have a right to have their views given due weight and to be 'provided with the opportunity to be heard in any judicial and administrative proceedings affecting [them] either directly or through a representative or appropriate body'.

Roger Green and Andy Turner (Chapter 2) address ways in which anti-poverty programmes as currently practised disempower the people workers set out to work with to overcome poverty and disadvantage. The chapter describes community development at grass roots level becoming a way through poverty for families. In an illuminating case study they describe how on an inner-city estate the community itself is developing strategies for combatting poverty and creating community facilities. This has resulted in self-worth and enthusiasm as well as respect for the community as a place which can become self-empowered.

There appears to be the beginning of a sea change in the culture of social services and the judiciary, as evidenced in recent news reports. Professionals are beginning to see the need for developing forms of public life that are friendly towards children and their families rather than the old alienating systems. Promoting friendly environments needs more than a willingness to take action. Resources are required and tradition needs to be deconstructed to promote family life. Finally, if we are to believe these reports, social work and the judiciary are to be open to public scrutiny and more pressure for accountability appears inevitable. As this book was being conceived a publication by Cannon and Warren (1996) explored a community development approach using social action for child and family welfare. More recently the Lord Chancellor has said the judiciary will become accountable and judges will be reviewed in the light of their performances, to be assessed by an independent body.

The book has a major theme for a more participatory approach from those involved in social responsibility, in which the needs, wishes, feelings and experiences of those who are vulnerable and disempowered can be attended to. Abuse of power in social responsibility may be defined as top down and non-participatory systems in poverty-action (Roger Green and Andy Turner, Chapter 2) or as denying the basic rights of people who have mental health problems to participate in decision-making processes which affect them (Peter Beresford and Anne Wilson, Chapter 9).

Social agency systems appear to define social responsibility as the translation of their legal and executive functions into the process of protecting the child from abuse (Brian Littlechild, Chapter 3). How can such systems be made more participatory for the service users?

It seems that there is a positive note on which to end. This book can be received, as it was conceived, as a need to look at what is hidden from superficial view. In doing this we will continue to learn about human beings and what informs their behaviour. We hope readers will experience the book as a constructive way forward for our society in developing policies and practices in our social and legal institutions which are both effective and ethical.

References

Cannon, C. and Warren, C. (eds) (1996) *Social Action With Children and Families*. London: Routledge.

Government White Paper (1998) Social Services Consultation Document *Modernising Social Services*. Section 3: *Services for Children*. London: HMSO.

Voice for the Child in Care (1998) *Shout to be Heard – Stories from Young People in Care*. Unit 4, Pride Court, 80-82 White Lion Street, London N1 9PF.

CHAPTER 2

Challenging the Power of Professionals

Involving the Community in Tackling Poverty

Roger Green and Andy Turner

Washing one's hands of the conflict between the powerful and the powerless means to side with the powerful, not to be neutral. (Freire 1970)

Introduction

This chapter will show how communities who experience poverty, in all its many forms, can themselves be directly involved in finding solutions.

The chapter is located within the context of the Kingsmead Kabin Project and its work with residents of the Kingsmead Estate, in Hackney, East London, one of the most socially and economically deprived areas in England (DETR 1998). We argue that an organic bottom-up approach to working with communities experiencing poverty should be the cornerstone of any antipoverty strategy. Such an approach, we will argue, encompasses and celebrates the participation of people in the process of tackling their poverty.

This will be set against the more traditional antipoverty approaches historically undertaken by both central government and local authorities, which utilise a top-down approach to devising and implementing antipoverty strategies. Such strategies result in communities often being disempowered by professionals in a process which excludes them from the very policies and locally based strategies which aim to combat their poverty.

The challenge that we pose is that the voice of the community often goes unheard in this 'professional' approach – that antipoverty programmes planned and developed by this approach therefore run the risk of further marginalising poor communities experiencing the corrosive effects of poverty in all its many forms.

Drawing on the work of a number of authors we challenge this 'top-down' approach by arguing that community-based projects working with the poor need to 'take sides' with the residents of communities.

The chapter will conclude with the lessons which are being learnt from this community development approach to poverty on the Kingsmead Estate, thereby offering a new way forward for professionals employed by local authorities and other agencies who are involved in the antipoverty field.

Uncritical dependence on professionals: central government and local government responses to tackling poverty at the community level

Central government and local government antipoverty policies and strategies in the UK have traditionally adopted top-down approaches to addressing poverty at the community level since the rediscovery of poverty in the 1960s (Abel-Smith and Townsend 1965).

From the launch in 1969 of the Community Development Projects as part of the Conservative government's attack on socio-economically deprived inner-city areas urban policy has, as Colenutt and Cutten (1994) note, zigzagged from one set of initiatives to another.

Mrs Thatcher's ill-fated Action for Cities initiative in 1987, with her promise to 'help' people living in the inner cities, is but one example. Visions of her marching across a derelict site in a northern city for a photocall session are all that remain.

The latest in such initiatives was the announcement by Peter Mandelson, the then new Labour government's Minister without Portfolio, in August 1997 at a Fabian Society summer lecture (Mandelson 1997) of the creation of a special Social Exclusion Unit. Chaired by the Prime Minister, Tony Blair, the unit is set up to co-ordinate action across government departments in response to the growing so-called underclass and to tackle poverty and social exclusion. This initiative had the familiar 'top-down' ring to it.

At the local level, antipoverty work since the 1980s has been directed by central government programmes such as Inner City Partnerships, Urban Development Corporations and City Challenge. As Alcock et al. (1995) have noted, these have been focused on economic investment and growth with the aim of attracting inward private investment.

This agenda, set by Conservative governments throughout the 1980s, paid marginal interest to people and communities, instead focusing on property and physical regeneration.

The introduction of the Single Regeneration Budget (SRB) in 1993 heralded a new co-ordinated approach to urban funding (Nevin and Shiner 1995). Whilst retaining its emphasis on local economic regeneration, and the involvement of the business and private sector, it includes within its aims 'concern with social conditions, the built environment, crime and the quality of life, and the promotion of local community involvement' (Alcock *et al.* 1995, p.37).

The Labour government has now recently announced a new programme called a 'New Deal for Communities' (Social Exclusion Unit 1998; Thompson and Holman 1998). This provides funding to regenerate some of the most deprived neighbourhoods in the country. Seventeen pilot areas have been selected based on the severity of their problems with the aim of analysing the needs of that neighbourhood and drawing up a plan involving local people.

Whilst this could be seen as an attempt to involve and engage communities, it is yet another 'top-down' regeneration initiative in this long line of such inner-city programmes.

The experience in Hackney

Hackney is the fourth most deprived local authority district in England according to the index of local deprivation (Social Exclusion Unit 1998). The council in the London Borough of Hackney has, following a lengthy eighteen-month consultation process, recently published its strategy to tackle poverty and social exclusion (London Borough of Hackney 1998). Despite having a foreword by Professor Peter Townsend and its claim that some fifty agencies in Hackney were involved in developing the strategy, it still lacked the authentic 'voice' of the poor. This came as no surprise as the strategy was underpinned by a comprehensive profile of poverty in Hackney (Griffiths 1996) which totally ignored people's daily experiences of poverty. Whilst it was an excellent piece of research in its own right, the use of secondary data throughout this profile with some supporting case studies only fed in to the perception that the poor themselves were not part of this process.

The launch of the Hackney strategy in a community centre on a council estate at which only 'professionals' and others involved in the strategies' working parties were invited further highlighted this exclusion.

Our experience therefore is that the development of the antipoverty strategy placed great importance and prestige on being seen to be 'power sharing', 'working in partnership' and led by the community. In reality, however, the strategy has been led and staffed by professionals, whose aim has been to retain power and control, limiting the opportunity for profound and dynamic change, and involvement, at the grass-roots community level.

Similar to this experience has been the Single Regeneration Budget (SRB) Challenge fund bid by the London Borough of Hackney in 1996 for Hackney Wick, a geographical area in Hackney in which the Kingsmead Estate is situated. The bid, when published, was a 25 page document (London Borough of Hackney 1996) which included such 'community friendly' sections as Synergy and Opportunity, Maximising Leverage, Linkages and Funding, and Delivery and Outputs.

The most significant element in the bid/programme was the Pathways to Employment, with its 'targeting' of residents on three estates where there was a concentration of unemployment and disadvantage; this included the Kingsmead Estate. Yet with 39 signatures and a substantial list of organisations participating, only four were tenant groups and the bid document was wholly written and conceived by the local authority. Ownership by local communities was not on the agenda.

Residents on the Kingsmead Estate are unaware of the Single Regeneration Budget (SRB), the European Social Fund, or Objectives 1, 2, 3 or 4 (Government and European Social Funding Programmes) and the opportunities they may present for them. Only recently has the establishment of a community forum, mentioned in the Hackney Wick SRB bid and ensuing programme three years ago, been given attention with the appointment of a community development worker.

Sited in the middle of the Hackney Wick SRB area the Kingsmead Estate has now become congested with new expensive cars. Parking for those few residents who own a car has become a problem. They now have to compete with consultants and professional experts buzzing about the estate, eager for a slice of the regeneration cake.

In the mid-1990s, during the first three years of the Kingsmead Kabin, both local employment support projects and education resources such as the community college were approached and invited to establish crucially needed outreach work and small-group work on the estate. Neither, though, were prepared to visit or undertake any development work on Kingsmead. Now, with SRB monies available, they are parked outside and moving in – bringing their ideas, agendas, expertise and assumptions. They appear prepared to move on when the money moves elsewhere.

From our experience the structure and culture of antipoverty strategies and programmes such as SRB implicitly and explicitly prevent involvement and ownership by small grass-root projects and residents.

With SRB, emphasis is placed on scoring. Regeneration is reduced to output measurements. The more outputs, the more funding, with outputs being measured through a somewhat crude and bureaucratic scoring system. These measures rarely take into account the subtleties or complexities of social exclusion, poverty and disadvantage in a community such as the Kingsmead Estate.

Arguably it would appear the system itself, its language and bureaucracy, seems to shake off most community projects at the first hurdle. If they have enough money to match the needed SRB fund then they will be able to proceed. The truth is that the larger, more significant the project, the more likely a larger outside agency, with its funding secure, will be able to success-fully bid, move in and deliver the project to the exclusion of the community's ideas and their needs.

Given these circumstances it becomes opportunistic for larger organ-isations to ignore the often quiet voices of those people in the community, who know at length the strength and subtlety of the problems and have innovative and creative ideas locked away which can help bring answers.

In our experience, dynamic, committed grass-root projects, managed and run by those living in the area (round the corner, in touch, accessible) where they are delivering the service (and on the receiving end), are best placed to deliver vibrant community-led development projects. Single Regeneration Boards, like the local authorities or the Housing Association which has taken over as landlord of the Kingsmead Estate, are not structured to achieve this.

In Hackney, and it would seem with many other local authorities and urban regeneration schemes, there exists a strong culture of investing money into presentation, for example, 'communicating achievements', public relations, expensive glossy reports, and manipulative use of the local press and media. Projects in need of positive 'public relations' or funding face enormous pressure to collude and promote themselves. In this context 'being seen' often means seeing and promoting ideas. The results, for residents living in the situation, may simply not be there.

Power of the professionals

Within this process professionals leading antipoverty initiatives, whether at central government or at the local community level, must run the risk of creating passive clientèle especially when they, as Illich *et al.* (1977) stress, they presume to diagnose and to prescribe. The absence of participatory approaches with the needs of communities defined and agreed by common consent remains the norm and with it continued professional dominance. It is this professional legitimacy which excludes communities. A further criticism is that professionals run the risk of placating poor communities rather than liberating them from their poverty. Communities have things done to them rather than determining their own futures. Indeed, as Popple (1995) has noted, professionalism is an élitist activity – people are employed by agencies and work on their behalf not on behalf of the local community and marginalised groups.

Similarly, professionalism is concerned with the control of knowledge. For although their practice is centred on helping and benefiting clients, the power relationship between professional and client is such that, as Foucault (1972) argues, it results in using that knowledge in a way which asserts power over them. This in our view is an abuse of power.

Therefore we would argue that professional-led antipoverty initiatives which promote self-help often control by status and ideology, and become oppressive by their practice.

Bob Holman (1996) takes this further by arguing that one of the main problems of socially deprived communities is that very few professionals live in these communities nor spend their salaries there. This, in his view, has a negative economic effect on the local economy in addition to reinforcing poor communities' lack of choices.

It appears that we have developed a tradition in the UK, over the past twenty-five years or so, of ignoring people living in poverty by denying them a voice. They have been effectively silenced with top-down initiatives imposed on them and driven by the political whims of government ministers and ideas from senior civil servants. These have often been supported by the captains of industry and executives from some of the charities with household names brought in to give credibility to the initiative.

Grounding such initiatives in the actual experiences of people living in the most disadvantaged housing estates and communities in the country, listening to their ideas for tackling their poverty, and involving them in the processes and structures of change have been noticeable by their absence.

The Kingsmead Kabin Project from its outset has attempted to address this 'professionalism', this dominating 'power', as Witz (1992) notes, this failure to consult with and fully involve people, and has challenged people's experience of being compliant in their acceptance of remaining uninvolved.

Involving the community in tackling poverty: the Kingsmead Kabin Project

The King and Queen in visiting the King's Mead Housing Estate at Hackney Marsh yesterday, saw some of the most up-to-date features of any flats in the country. (North London Record 1939)

A brief history of the Kingsmead Estate

Built in the mid-1930s by the London County Council for people affected by slum clearance in the old boroughs of Stepney and Bethnal Green, the estate is situated in the London Borough of Hackney. The estate consists of sixteen five-storey walk-up blocks of flats, with over 900 dwellings housing almost 3000 people (Kingsmead Community Trust 1995).

The estate passed to the Greater London Council (GLC) in 1964 and then to the London Borough of Hackney in 1982 following the transfer of the GLC's housing stock to the London Boroughs with the demise of the GLC (Jarvis 1986).

From its earliest days the estate was given a 'garden city' image by the press, '... the L.C.C.'s great new King's Mead housing estate, built like a village, with its green and trees on the marshes' (*News Chronicle* 1939).

This image still prevailed through to the early 1950s, and photographs of the estate from this period show a 'cosy' postwar living room scene with children happily playing and doing their homework in front of a blazing fire, (Mander and Golden 1991).

However by the 1970s it was being labelled a 'dump' estate, a community which had lost its traditional East End social cohesion. This was blamed on the GLC's policy of housing people onto the estate from all over London, many with existing problems:

If this is your address, you will probably find it more difficult to get goods on hire purchase or to get a job, because of the reputation of being filled with 'problem families' ... there are many one parent families ... have history of rent arrears ... there are families with low income and many children ... (*Guardian* 1973, p.4)

The term 'island' also began to be used by some writers to describe the estate and its decline and physical isolation from other neighbouring Hackney communities (Murphy and Fearon 1985):

This continued and from the mid 1980's through to the 1990's the estate's image had changed to that of a slum. There is no other word than slum for the Kingsmead Estate in Hackney, North East London. Here they all are, the visual clichés of the genre: the blocks of grimy brick, five stories high, with urine-soaked stairways and bleak passages running along their backs; the shattered windows; the empty flats blinded and gagged by steel shutters; the sordid yards with their rusted discarded fridges and washing machines; and cars with shattered windscreens and flat tyres. (Barwick: 1991, p.26)

The estate's public image sunk to a further low with the killing of a teenage runaway in a homosexual orgy at a flat on the estate in 1985.

The fear of crime increasingly began to haunt the estate which suffered from high levels of crime, particularly domestic burglaries, and street robberies, which the local authority Housing Department called, 'gangs of youths "steaming" on Kingsmead Estate ie committing robberies in gangs' (Crime Concern 1993, p.14).

From the 1980s onwards the estate began to be seen by sections of the media as a manifestation of the breakdown of civil society and law and order (Pearce 1993).

It was not until 1993 that the council in a joint strategy with the police used civil rather than criminal law in obtaining civil injunctions against a number of young residents and their families involved in criminal activities on the estate (Parry-Davies 1993; Tendler 1993; Katz 1993). Repossession orders were used to evict 'persistent troublemakers' including one family which had threatened violence against anyone on the estate reporting their criminal activities (Duce 1993).

As a result the number of burglaries on the estate, which had made up for a quarter of all burglaries dealt with by Hackney Police, fell dramatically (Osborn and Shaftoe 1995).

These initiatives, coupled with the setting up in 1993 of an estate community trust, the Kingsmead Community Trust, began to attract resources onto the estate (London Borough of Hackney 1994).

The estate still, however, continued to be labelled by the local press as a 'problem estate' (*Hackney Gazette* 1994, p.10) and journalists continued to use the estate as a benchmark to illustrate inner-city urban decay, particularly council estates in decline – so-called 'sink' estates (Bowcott 1996, p.6).

The most recent chapter in the estate's history began in 1998 when, in a close vote, residents voted to transfer to Kingsmead Homes, part of the Shaftsbury Housing Association, rather than remain with the London Borough of Hackney as their landlord. Kingsmead Homes have promised to invest £39 million over the next five years in modernising flats on the estate and promoting some limited social and economic regeneration. However, as Durston (1997) noted in a recent report, poverty will still remain an issue: 'Physical regeneration alone will not solve the problems on this estate ... poverty is one such problem' (Durston 1997, p.7).

Poverty on the estate

In 1996 a community needs poverty profile was undertaken on the estate (Green 1997). It was underpinned by a participatory research approach which listened to residents and recorded their experiences of what it is like being unemployed, managing on a low income, receiving inadequate benefits, and the exclusion from areas of communal life and social activities that these phenomena bring.

It was a bottom-up attempt to understand, collate, and articulate ways forward for the community to begin to get organised in taking forms of action aimed at re-empowering themselves.

The findings made bleak reading. Children hungry on the estate; some travelled to the local school in winter in slippers; many had never had a holiday. The elderly fared no better. Many were living on a reduced state pension only, unaware that they might be entitled to additional benefits such as Income Support and the Disability Living Allowance, highlighted graphically by one elderly resident who admitted to living on cornflakes and biscuits.

Almost half the estate was in long-term rent arrears with many of the households owing £1000 or more. Resident access to credit via banks or building societies was restricted because of the estate's 'poor' reputation.

Debts of £2000 to £3000 to catalogue companies, loan sharks and hire purchase agreements were commonplace.

Over 50 per cent of adults were unemployed, and the majority of tenants did not own a car or have a telephone in their flat. The sense of social isolation brought about by poverty, particularly for the elderly and lone parents with small children, was all too evident.

However, in spite of these problems residents, when asked what ideas and strategies they had themselves for tackling poverty on the estate, voiced a number of possibilities based on their daily experiences.

These ranged from the need for decent paid, permanent part-time and full-time employment, access to skills training, retraining and education for real jobs, the availability of locally based, affordable, child care facilities, better quality housing, sufficient money to live on and increased choices or opportunities in their lives. What tenants wanted more than anything was a say in their future.

Their 'voices' called for locally based community action and the development of more 'creative partnerships' with the local council and other statutory and voluntary bodies. Specific antipoverty strategies voiced by residents centred on income maximisation through targeted benefit take-up campaigns, expanding welfare rights/money advice and information work on the estate, and the setting up of a credit union and a local exchange trading system (LETS) scheme designed to foster and introduce new skills and create job opportunities.

The residents and community groups similarly saw the need to tackle the problems faced by specific groups on the estate such as children and their families, the unemployed and asylum seekers. Equally they were not short on ideas for the need for further research on the impact of poverty on, for example, pensioners (Green 1997).

The origins and development of the Kingsmead Kabin Project

The idea for the Kingsmead Kabin Project was developed out of Christchurch on the Mead, an Anglican Church meeting on Kingsmead, and born of numerous cups of tea in front rooms on the estate and houses in the surrounding streets of Hackney.

Slowly between 1991 and 1994 a handful of Kingsmead residents, an eclectic mix of people and ideas, became organised and formed a steering group. One meeting became many meetings, minutes were recorded and written up, a three-year grant from a charity was obtained and the Kabin, a shop-front community development project, opened on the estate in October 1995.

This was not some central government or local authority imposed scheme, a project popping up and buoyed along by a convenient stash of funding or government subsidy. Nor was it an organisation shipped in, imported onto the estate to get the people 'back on their feet', which many of the residents had experienced in recent years.

This wasn't a 'fly by night' outfit staffed by professionals, commuting in from outside the borough, from Essex or across the Thames river in Kent.

A number of things made it different from the more professionally led agencies often associated with community regeneration. First, the Kabin had taken four years to become a reality. The growth, development and change from cups of tea and informal, irregular steering group meetings, to funding for a worker, a building and a management committee was slow but profound. Second, and more importantly, it was resident resourced.

No monitoring forms. No outputs. No leverage. The emphasis was on the subjective, and areas of work often difficult to quantify or measure. Needs such as for residents to experience consistency and presence, to build relationships and develop trust, were met. The need for listening and the development of interest and ideas were also met.

People's potential to see the possibilities of real change is critical in the work of the Kabin, as is their commitment to become involved in the process of making this change happen.

Meeting needs with such an approach is very different from more 'traditional' 'top-down' strategies. It is not attractive for professionals who require instant results or clever stories for an upbeat annual report. But then whoever said building relationships, establishing trust and developing authentic community involvement was a quick and easy task?

So cups of tea, lingering conversation, purposeful interaction and relationships are critical. This is the glue which involves residents and holds the various projects within the Kabin together.

Fighting poverty from the bottom up

Since its inception the Kabin's objectives have been threefold:

1.   To work with residents to achieve their economic, educational, social and spiritual potential.

2. To develop project work that tackles poverty, prejudice and powerlessness.

3. To develop appropriate services to meet the needs of Kingsmead tenants by working with individuals, community groups, statutory services and the private sector.

These objectives are met in the following ways. In tackling poverty and the social exclusion experienced by residents, the Kabin is working with people on developing useful purposeful activities – work that usually evolves out of dialogue and discussion. Nothing is set in stone. Some ideas and projects work, some do not. People matter. Listening is important. Purposeful, thoughtful action is very important.

The Kabin is developing a safe space for people to play with ideas, imprinting their style and uniqueness onto a project which has evolved from them. All the projects are concerned with making a difference and bringing about change. For residents to feel able to become involved, the Kabin must feel like a safe place in which to make a mistake, to fail with a project. A place where critical reflection and learning are important.

Take one example of how projects develop. A community meal, organised by the Kabin, which brought together those with power and privilege (poverty professionals, doctors, social workers, teachers) with residents (pensioners, mums, dads, unemployed, young people) gave a resident, Dawn, the idea for a children's clothing project.

From a simple idea, a project based in the Kabin's premises that sold the best in new and nearly new children's clothes, toys, books and games was discussed. Dawn knew it was a good idea because she knew of the difficulty in getting access to these products. With London's East End manufacturers on the doorstep, letters to retailers and a network of Church links, the idea of Kidstuff began to emerge. Today Kidstuff is a weekly shop, where residents can also enjoy a cup of tea or coffee and a biscuit, put their feet up and talk about their week. All the money raised is recycled into trips, events and days out planned and programmed by the residents.

A lively team of volunteer residents staff the project and thousands of clothes, games, toys and books have been sold or distributed free via networks with locally based health visitors.

Kidstuff is a small but profoundly important project. Involvement is multifaceted and arguably it has led to many women on the estate establishing new contacts and supportive networks, regaining confidence and feeling good about themselves.

In disadvantaged communities experiencing the rough edge of social policy, such 'organic' ideas from the street which become action truly enable people to re-empower themselves. Using this approach the Kabin has successfully developed a number of other community-led projects, such as the 'Bus Run', a weekly minibus shuttle to one of the local supermarkets; and an advice service which opens twice a week for residents seeking advice on debt problems, benefits advocacy or general advice and information. An important part of this service is income maximisation. Other projects include a Homework Club for primary school children; the Stompers Parent Toddler Club which has almost one hundred parents participating, and the twice-weekly Drop-In session which provides a supportive environment for residents.

The Kabin's community development role is currently working with residents to set up a credit union, a food co-operative and an employment and outreach training base. Such developments have grown 'organically' from residents to address their needs in tackling the corrosive effects of poverty they experience daily on the estate.

Since this transfer of the estate to Kingsmead Homes the estate is still periodically visited by journalists from the 'broadsheets' and television film crews looking for a suitable location for their newspaper story or documentary. Recent examples have included interviews with parents of young children concerning poverty and nutrition, and what has become known as 'food deserts' (*Independent* 1998). Whilst residents have agreed to be interviewed the aftermath is often feelings of powerlessness and hopelessness when they are shared in the Kabin's drop-in session.

These feelings following visits to the estate by professionals simply reinforce the residents' poverty-bound situation. Newspaper articles using residents' daily experiences of poverty offer no solutions. Rees (1991) comments that when people living in poverty are asked to talk about the experience(s) they are facing and events over which they have little or no control this can be disempowering.

Lessons from below: the way forward

Involving people

By listening to the voices of those experiencing poverty on a daily basis, their needs and their ideas for tackling poverty, the participatory community development approach is emphasised leading to solutions which are missing from so much of antipoverty work.

As Skinner (1997) has shown, residents, community groups and community organisations of social and economically excluded communities can play a major part in the regeneration of their neighbourhoods. Through capacity-building which emphasises the development of participative structures and processes within a community infrastructure people can reclaim their collective voice and begin to challenge the power of agencies and their professional staff.

Nowhere was it deemed important by the residents of the Kingsmead Estate to ask the government to set up a Whitehall-based Social Exclusion Unit for 'tackling the scourge and waste of social exclusion' (Mandelson 1997, p.6). Indeed, as Stewart (1997) has noted, co-ordination across government departments may indeed be important but much more important are co-ordinated strategies at the local level between community and tenant organisations, local authority departments, voluntary sector projects, health bodies and local people.

If the New Labour government and local authorities are really serious about including the individuals, families and communities who have been systematically socially excluded during the years of successive Conservative governments then they need to begin to listen to and involve them.

As Helen Dent (1997) reminds us, in gathering evidence for the NCH Action for Children report on cities which she co-chaired, the working group held public hearings around the country and listened to people about their concerns and ideas of how to solve some of their problems.

Similarly Beresford and Croft (1995) have argued that the participation of poor people in the poverty debate is crucial, but poverty experts, whether they be academics or professionals themselves, have a role to play in achieving this aim. The new Social Exclusion Unit then, as the 'new experts' in the poverty discourse, likewise could have a role to play in this developing process.

Zena Peatfield, a member of the Social Exclusion Unit, has echoed this view by stating that tackling poverty is not just about relying on the experts, but also including in the debate the 'users of services' (Peatfield 1997, p.5), presumably meaning people in poverty and the socially excluded. A year later, however, a major report from the Social Exclusion Unit (1998) has unfortunately omitted those 'users of services' in its analysis and action plans.

What is clear in this debate is that without the consent and ownership of antipoverty initiatives by residents living in deprived, poverty-ridden communities, any progress may be limited and short-lived.

Using community research to tackle poverty

Both historically and currently, research on poverty has followed traditional lines and has been concerned with measuring poverty and its distribution and causes, often highlighting its effects on families and the community (Rees and Rees 1980; Bradshaw and Holmes 1989; Peak District Rural Deprivation Forum 1993; Alcock 1993; Kempson 1996).

Underpinned by top-down agendas which tend to stress the need for new strategies in tackling poverty, such research has now also begun to take account of wider factors such as globalisation or changes in the labour market (Oppenheim 1998). However, the voice of the poor has largely been absent from such writings. They have been spectators. Similarly the growing field of poverty profile research has also tended to exclude their voice (BMRB 1994; Costello, Cousins and Hewitt 1995; Edwards and Flatley 1996; Griffiths 1996).

Poverty research that does exist and has as its starting point people's experiences of poverty is limited in that although it explores the world of the welfare recipient or the family on a low income it fails to engage them in ways forward. An example of this is Berrick's (1997) otherwise excellent qualitative study of women and their children in the USA.

We see community-based research as redressing this imbalance by playing a significant part in involving residents of poverty-ridden communities through undertaking a poverty profile of their locality. A community needs a profiling approach (Green 1996) to community development with marginalised groups. It is an approach which seeks to give people the opportunity to voice their needs and speak of how they experience poverty (Green 1998).

This aims to break what Freire (1970) has called the 'culture of silence', with its oppressive and passive acceptance of the status quo. It also attempts to give what Hardcastle, Wencour and Powers (1997) call a 'hearing' by listening to people, recording their needs and – importantly – looking at ways forward by initiating a community development process.

By using such a research approach key findings can emerge, such as:

- providing evidence that poverty exists over and beyond a lack of income
- listening to marginalised groups and seeking out their 'felt' needs

- maximising the 'voice' of people by gathering data through a range of research methods, in effect triangulating the data

- providing localised information to local authorities and other community service providers on the needs of people and their communities

- offering bottom-up community development initiatives based on evidence and need; and finally

- challenging the notion that the poor are powerless and without ideas.

In offering these the approach underpins and supports a culture of inclusion not exclusion.

Taking sides

Work with residents on the estate has adopted the 'community social worker' model which Bob Holman originally pioneered on a local authority housing estate in Bath during the late 1970s (Holman 1981). This involves working alongside residents and understanding and articulating their needs as part of a community development process (Clarke 1996; Hadley *et al.* 1987). The model also argues the importance of having a working knowledge of a community (Mayo 1998) and has been informed by the work of Mullaly (1993) with his concept of 'structural social work'. The emphasis here is on 'transformation' – that is, working with people in a learning process which is mutually reciprocal rather than disempowering by simply providing expertise.

Instead of acting as neutral 'community filters' of local state antipoverty policies and Single Regeneration Budget programmes we see community participation in the battle against poverty as being people and community led. Involvement by people, as Beresford and Croft (1993) note, prefigures action.

We have taken sides against the long history of the 'neutral' tradition within community development work. O'Malley (1977) identified this tradition as being one that views working-class communities and their organisations as lacking sufficient organisational ability, and one which attempts to remain above conflicts by using the language of objectivity and consensus.

Similarly Filkin and Naish (1982) argue that community development workers and community social workers need a vision of the society and community in which they are working and that the notion of change is fundamental to this vision. An integral part is the redistribution of resources, which challenges the 'neutral' tradition of simply bringing people together in community groups.

We would argue that although antipoverty professionals are the new front-line workers against poverty, they have an underpinning ideology of consensual community development work which is both a controlling and deconflictualising force in communities lacking 'people power'.

Similarly, whilst so-called 'poverty experts' and 'professionals' continue to highlight and discuss the meaning of poverty, the causes of poverty, and the costs of poverty (Oppenheim 1998), there are existing examples of communities taking action themselves in establishing community organisations and activities (Holman 1997; Townsend et al. 1996) which community development and social workers can build on.

Antipoverty work does not necessarily need to be centrally funded or national in scope. Localised bottom-up community-led initiatives might increase the effectiveness of funding whilst also providing maximum engagement with people. There is an argument, in our experience, that communities experiencing poverty are more likely to spend funding efficiently and more effectively than 'poverty professionals'.

Investing in people and their communities, giving them the power and control of regeneration and antipoverty projects in their own areas should be the objective of our work.

As the Kingsmead Kabin experience demonstrates, there is no shortage of ideas nor determination amongst residents to be the architects of their own solutions.

Acknowledgements

The authors wish to thank residents of the Kingsmead Estate, particularly Alec Watson, for their ideas and experiences which have contributed to the. writing of this chapter.

References

Abel-Smith, B. and Townsend, P. (1965) *The Poor and the Poorest.* London: Bell.

Alcock, P. (1993) *Understanding Poverty.* London: Macmillan.

Alcock, P., Craig G., Dalgleish, K. and Pearson, S. (1995) *Combating Local Poverty. The Management of Antipoverty Strategies by Local Government.* Luton: Local Government Management Board.

Barwick S.(1991) 'Still a slum.' *The Spectator,* 11 May.

Beresford, P. and Croft, S. (1993) *Citizen Involvement: A Practical Guide for Change.* London: Macmillan.

Beresford, P. and Croft, S. (1995) 'It's our problem too! Challenging the exclusion of poor people from poverty discourse'. *Critical Social Policy 15,* 44/45, 75–93.

Berrick J.D. (1997) *Faces of Poverty. Portraits of Women and Children on Welfare.* New York: Oxford University Press.

BMRB (1994) *Breadline Greenwich Report.* London: BMRB/London Borough of Greenwich.

Bowcott, O. (1996) 'Council estates in downward spiral'. *Guardian,* 13 February.

Bradshaw, J. and Holmes, H. (1989) *A Study of the Living Standards of Families on Benefit in Tyne and Wear.* London: Child Poverty Action Group.

Clarke, S. (1996) *Social Work as Community Development.* London: Avebury.

Colenutt, B. and Cutten, A. (1994) 'Community empowerment in vogue or vain'. *Local Economy 9,* 3, 236–250.

Costello, J., Cousins, C. and Hewitt, M. (1995) *Wellfield Report.* Hatfield: Wellfield Trust/University of Hertfordshire.

Crime Concern (1993) *Youth Crime in Hackney – Analysis and Options.* Swindon: Crime Concern.

Dent, H. (1997) 'Local government is key to solving problems'. *Community Care,* 13–19 November.

Department of the Environment, Transport and Regions (DETR) (1998) *1998 Index of Local Deprivation: Regeneration Summary no.15.* London: Department of the Environment, Transport and Regions.

Duce, R. (1993) 'Council uses civil court to end family's terror reign'. *The Times,* 12 March.

Durston, S. (1997) *The Kingsmead Kabin. An Independent Evaluation.* London: Hackney, unpublished.

Edwards, P. and Flatley, J. (1996) *The Capital Divided. Mapping Poverty and Social Exclusion in London.* London: London Research Centre.

Filkin, E. and Naish, M. (1982) 'Whose side are we on? The damage done by neutralism'. In G. Craig, N. Derricourt and M. Loney (eds) *Community Work and* the State. *Community Work Eight*. London: Routledge and Keegan Paul/Association of Community Workers.

Foucault, M. (1972) *The Archaeology of Knowledge and the Discourse on Language*. New York: Pantheon.

Freire, P. (1970) 'Cultural action and conscientization'. *Harvard Educational Review* 40, 3, 452–477.

Green, R. (1996) *Marginal Inclusion? A Survey of Refugees in the London Borough of Redbridge 1996*. London: Redbridge Refugee Forum.

Green, R. (1997) *Community Action Against Poverty. A Poverty Profile of the Kingsmead Estate in Hackney*. London: Kingsmead Kabin.

Green, R. (1998) 'Why New Labour's Social Exclusion Unit is in danger of getting it wrong'. *Benefits. A Journal of Social Security Research, Policy and Practice* 22, 38–40.

Griffiths, S. (1996) *The Challenge. A Profile of Poverty in Hackney*. London: London Borough of Hackney.

Guardian (1973) 'The people on Kingsmead are drawn mainly from lists of nominees from boroughs all over London'. *Guardian*, 8 August.

Hackney Gazette (1994) 'Estate's clean up sets fine example'. *Hackney Gazette*, 12 December.

Hadley, R., Cooper, M., Dale, P. and Stacey, G. (1987) *A Community Social Worker's Handbook*. London: Tavistock.

Hardcastle, D.A., Wencour, S. and Powers, P.R. (1997) *Community Practice. Theories and Skills for Social Workers*. New York: Oxford University Press.

Holman, B. (1981) *Kids at the Door*. Oxford: Basil Blackwell.

Holman, B. (1996) 'Self help in action'. In P. Townsend, P. Leith, S. Tumin. and J. Verma (eds) (1996) *The Great, The Good and the Dispossessed. The Report of the Channel 4 Commission on Poverty*. London: Channel 4 Television.

Holman B. (1997) *FARE Dealing. Neighbourhood Involvement in a Housing Scheme*. London: Community Development Foundation.

Illich, I., Zola, I.K., McKnight, J., Caplan, J. and Shaiken, H. (1977) *Disabling Professions*. London: Marion Boyars.

Independent (1998) 'Just a single orange in the fridge: The facts of life in a "food desert"'. *Independent*, 16 October.

Jarvis, G.D. (1986) *The Early History of the Kingsmead Estate, E9*. London: Kingsmead Kabin, unpublished.

Katz, I. (1993) 'Rough justice for tearaways divides crime-hit estate'. *The Times*, 22 June.

Kempson, E. (1996) *Life on a Low Income*. York: Joseph Rowntree Foundation.

Kingsmead Community Trust (1995) *Annual Report 1994–1995*. London: Kingsmead Community Trust.

London Borough of Hackney (1994) *Putting the Heart Back into Kingsmead Estate*. London: London Borough of Hackney Press Release.

London Borough of Hackney (1996) *Hackney Wick. Another Piece in the Stratford Regeneration Jigsaw*. Single Regeneration Budget Challenge Fund Bid. London: London Borough of Hackney.

London Borough of Hackney (1998) *Tackling Poverty in Hackney. A Strategy to Challenge Poverty and Social Exclusion*. London: London Borough of Hackney.

Mandelson, P. (1997) *Labour's Next Steps: Tackling Social Exclusion*. Fabian pamphlet 581. London: Fabian Society.

Mander, D. and Golden, J. (1991) *The London Borough of Hackney in Old Photographs*. London: Alan Sutton.

Mayo, M. (1998) 'Community work'. In R. Adams, L. Dominelli and M. Payne (eds) *Social Work: Themes, Issues and Critical Debates*. London: Macmillan.

Mullaly, R.P. (1993) *Structural Social Work: Ideology, Theory and Practice*. Toronto: McClelland and Stewart.

Murphy, J. and Fearon, M. (1985) *Devils Island*. London: Marshalls.

Nevin, B. and Shiner, P. (1995) 'Community regeneration and empowerment: A new approach to partnership'. *Local Economy 9*, 4, 308–322.

News Chronicle (1939) 'Bottle of beer for the King'. *News Chronicle*, 31 March.

North London Record (1939) 'What the King and Queen saw'. *North London Record*, 31 March.

O'Malley, J. (1977) *The Politics of Community Action*. London: Spokesman.

Oppenheim, C. (1998) (ed) *An Inclusive Society. Strategies for Tackling Poverty*. London: Institute for Public Policy Research.

Osborn, S. and Shaftoe, H. (1995) *Safe Neighbourhoods? Successes and Failures in Crime Prevention*. London: Safe Neighbourhoods Unit.

Parry-Davies, B. (1993) 'An end to estates of siege?'. *The Times*, 29 June.

Peak District Rural Deprivation Forum (1993) *Low Income in the Peak National Park*. Derbyshire: Peak District Rural Deprivation Forum.

Pearce, E. (1993) 'Commentary: Hackney's terror estate finding a cure'. *Guardian*, 12 June.

Peatfield, Z. (1997) 'Caught on the edge'. *Guardian*, 12 December 1997.

Popple, K. (1995) *Analysing Community Work. Its Theory and Practice*. Buckingham: Open University Press.

Rees, G. and Rees, T.L. (1980) (eds) *Poverty and Social Inequality in Wales*. London: Croom Helm.

Rees, S. (1991) *Achieving Power. Practice and Policy in Social Welfare*. Sydney: Allen and Unwin.

Skinner, S. (1997) *Building Community Strengths. A Resource Book on Capacity Building*. London: CDF Publications.

Social Exclusion Unit (1998) *Bringing Britain Together: A National Strategy for Neighbourhood Renewal*. Report by the Social Exclusion Unit. London: HMSO.

Stewart, M. (1997) 'Tackling social exclusion: A history of failure'. *Poverty 98*, 3–4.

Tendler, S. (1993) 'Hackney initiative cuts crime on estate'. *The Times*, 12 June.

Thompson, A. and Holman, B. (1998) 'New Labour, big deal?'. *Community Care*, 13–19 August, 16–18.

Townsend, P., Leith, P., Tumin, S. and Verma, J. (1996) *The Great, The Good and the Dispossessed. The Report of the Channel 4 Commission on Poverty*. London: Channel 4 Television.

Witz, A. (1992) *Professions and Patriarchy*. London: Routledge.

CHAPTER 3

The Rights of Children in Statutory Decision Making

Brian Littlechild

Introduction

The nature of social responsibility in relation to child protection has changed dramatically in the latter half of the twentieth century. Within current social and political formations, 'social responsibility' is essentially the translation of agencies' legal and executive functions into the processes of protecting children and young people from abuse, however that is defined at any point in time. This has not always been the case. At the end of the last century and the beginning of this, the majority of child welfare and protection work was the domain of voluntary and philanthropic agencies such as Barnardos and the National Society for the Prevention of Cruelty to Children. The state has more recently continually passed legislation determining the focus of work in this area, and issued formal guidance to the local government agencies responsible for child welfare and protection. The most recent manifestation of this trend is the government's unprecedented announcement in 1998 that they are to take control centrally in order to monitor and regulate local authorities' services to young people accommodated by them (*Guardian* 1998), and the subsequent proposals for independent inspection of their services through central government regional organisations (Department of Health 1998). The majority of social work practice in relation to child care is now centred upon child protection work, not the preventative work of previous years. This theme is explored further in Sue Amphlett's chapter in this book (Chapter 10). There is a great emphasis on following agency procedures which can lead to less creativity in work with families and young people (Parton 1998). This field of work can now claim to be one of the most highly regulated in any area of social care.

In Chapter 9, Peter Beresford and Anne Wilson describe an interpretation of social responsibility which has led to legal and agency systems which deny the basic rights of individuals who have mental health problems to participate in the decision-making processes which affect them. The paternalistic, bureaucratic and frequently patronising approaches of many agencies have led to further disempowerment and oppression. The same concerns apply to children, who have little opportunity to have their views taken into account and represented as of right within the child protection enterprise, with particular lack of attention to the requirements of minority ethnic group children (Abdullah 1998) and children with disabilities (Morris 1998). An additional difficulty for children is that they are nearly always wholly dependent upon adults to have their views directly represented in potentially supportive and protective arenas.

This chapter will examine how social work and advocacy procedures can help promote the rights of children within the quasi-legal child protection system, and in the court system in terms of preparation for appearance as a witness. Whilst the points raised in this chapter apply mainly to child protection social workers, and to some extent judges, they also have relevance to the work of court welfare officers and guardians ad litem. Throughout the chapter, the terms 'young person' and 'child' are used to denote children and young people under the age of 18 years, as the terms are often used interchangeably in different contexts.

Focusing on the needs of the child

The formal systems of the courts and social work agencies can replicate the disempowerment and abuse of the child which may have originally brought the child into that system. Sue Amphlett (Chapter 10) elaborates upon one form of such system abuse. The challenge for agencies and individual professionals is to produce a system which:

- is sensitive to the views and needs of the children who may require some degree of protection, including issues of ethnicity, gender and disability
- employs methods of working which give justice to the child's needs and views, and ensures that these are taken into account in any decision-making processes which may affect their future

- is sensitive to the needs of the child's carer(s) and
- is sensitive to the difficulties and support needs of other parties involved, including the social workers attempting to operate that system.

Lord Justice Butler-Sloss stated in her influential Cleveland child protection inquiry report: 'the child is not an object of concern' (Butler-Sloss 1988). I will argue that agencies and courts can improve matters for young people by recognising their vulnerabilities and problems in fully participating in child protection and court procedures, and taking as a benchmark for further practice and policy developments the United Nations Convention on the Rights of the Child (hereinafter referred to as the Convention). To achieve this, agencies will need to develop policies and procedures to support social workers in ensuring young people are placed at the centre of procedures as valued human beings and not as objects of concern. Equally, the increasing use of the courts by clients to sue social services departments may lead to agencies emphasising risk assessments which are based on avoiding legal liability rather than on promoting the best interests of the child (Carson 1996; Cooper 1998; Guthrie 1998; Inman 1998). As a result, policy and practice often focus on the management and monitoring of abstract factors deemed liable to produce risk for young people, and not on the representation of the young person's interests by way of a direct face-to-face relationship with them. Such a model attempts to ensure risk elimination, failing to appreciate the 'central characteristic of child welfare policy and practice in terms of pervasiveness of uncertainty' (Parton 1998, p.6). Such denial of the problems puts additional strain on workers and clients, and provides a disincentive for social workers to encourage the consideration of an individual child's or young person's needs and difficulties within the context of his or her development and circumstances.

Very few published works have relevance to young people's rights within social work practice. Butler-Sloss (1988), Barford and Wattam (1991), Newell (1991), The United Nations (1994), Joseph (1995) and Fox Harding (1996) do begin to address these issues. It is not the intention here to undertake a comprehensive review of the concept of competing models of children's rights. Fuller discussions of the different models, such as liberationalist and protectionist stances, can be found in the works of Franklin (1995) and Fox Harding (1996). Briefly, liberationist stances take the view that young people should be liberated from the oppressive and discriminating adult constructed world of childhood, whilst the alternative viewpoint is the protectionist perspective which recognises that young people require special consideration due to their relative immaturity and their powerless position within society. Within the protectionist model, young people are also seen to be in need of special protection from the law, and within legal processes. This chapter argues from a protectionist stance which at the same juncture promotes the young person's right to real and substantive participation in decision making as required by the Convention and the Children Act 1989 in relation to child protection and court proceedings.

The United Kingdom does not have an unblemished record in its implementation of the Convention's requirements. The UN Monitoring Committee on the Rights of the Child criticised the United Kingdom in 1995 for not emphasising Article 12 in official guidance to statutory agencies and court (Lansdown 1995). Government, social workers and their employing agencies need to re-examine how they to put into operation the Children Act 1989 in the light of duties laid down within the Convention. For example, social workers and courts are required to take into account the wishes of children, and make the welfare of the child paramount. Social workers need to consider further how this duty fits with their professional values and skills in relation to preparing children for their part in the process and dealing with their fears and worries in an open, honest and informative manner. Whilst social workers and other professionals cannot immediately change agency policies or legal procedures, they can influence policy and practice developments. They can also develop their skills and networking capabilities in order to promote the full participation of children whilst they are within their area of influence. There are some small signs of change. Central government, for example, has recently started to require social services departments to have regard to the Convention's statements on children's participation, although it provides no guidance on how this might operate in practice (Audit Commission 1994; Department of Health Local Authority Circular 1995; Department of Health 1995).

Participation by young people? Current practice

Agencies and professionals are stumbling in uncharted territory in attempting to give a voice to young people where this has not been part of wider societal or agency culture. Agency systems and courts were not set up for young people and certainly not with the primacy of their welfare in mind

(Spencer and Flyn 1993). This is also true for social work agency policy and procedures and social work theory and practice.

Barford and Wattam's (1991) study focused on the experiences of four adolescent young people from initial referral through to the child protection conference, and suggests that two of the most important elements to be developed in practice and policy are (a) the effective dissemination of information and (b) the establishment of recognisable channels of communication for young people. All of the young people in the study stated that they found the initial contact to be ambiguous, contradictory and confusing, and the subsequent case conference did not shed any further light on their confusion. One of the girls, Ruth, aged 14, stated: 'there was a meeting about us once but we were not allowed to go. We weren't even allowed to know what was said in it. They should have the meeting but we could get told afterwards but we didn't.' The researchers concluded that the young people's experiences and participation could have been enhanced with better preparation including explanation of the role of the conference, the identification of participants and a more relaxed atmosphere with the absence of jargon in favour of more understandable language.

Shemmings (1996) examined young people's attendance and participation at child protection conferences from parents', professionals' and young people's perspectives. The study, based on two local authorities, involved 34 young people, 121 professionals and 23 parents. Shemmings viewed the young people's and their parents' responses as generally positive. The professionals in the main believed that the young person's attendance led to beneficial effects including 'no secrets', 'to demystify the whole thing', and 'increased trust for the child' (Shemmings 1996, p.15).

Shemmings did find, however, that professionals found it difficult to give painful, critical information or perceptions about the family situation or their views to the parents and young people, and might try and minimise this or avoid it altogether. He concluded that 'the most effective ways of involving children can only be discovered when each individual child's needs, wishes and feelings are identified and then analysed ... with the child as a partner' (Shemmings 1996, p.39).

Schofield and Thoburn (1996) note that there is a very poor history of young people's views and wishes being given attention within either the private sphere of family life, or the public protection, court and care systems. They conclude that the most important element in aiding participation is proper information given within a trusted relationship to the child or young person. Supplied with the knowledge of the possible outcomes and what the demands on them might be at the different stages within the process, the young person then has some control over their participation. They also found that the child's participation helped the child begin the process of healing from often very disempowering, abusive relationships where they had not felt they or their views had been of importance at all. The court process frequently fails to help in this process, as it continues the feelings of disempowerment and lack of respect involved in the original abuse. Lansdown (1995) also puts forward the argument that it is important for children to learn to negotiate with others as part of a mutually respectful relationship. A genuinely participative approach in the child protection and court process can help to achieve this through modelling respect for the child and her or his views.

Rights of children: national statutes and worldwide conventions

In order to challenge the abuse of power within agency systems and social work practice, it is necessary to understand the relevant legislation and Conventions, and how these can define and affect practice and policy developments. In this section, I will consider both the Children Act 1989 and the UN Convention on the Rights of the Child.

First, the Children Act 1989 unified many different pieces of legislation in relation to children, and was also radical and reforming. It introduced the requirement that seeking to prevent significant harm is the basis for all statutory agency intervention into children's lives. The Act's welfare checklist, in section 1 (3) (a), states that regard must be given to 'the ascertainable wishes and feelings of the child concerned (considered in the light of his age and understanding)' where she/he may be separated from parents.

There is a duty laid down by the Act to ascertain and have regard to the child's wishes before making any decision with respect to a child whom they are looking after or may be proposing to look after (section 22 (4) (a) and (5) (a), taking into account their age and understanding. This duty also applies to the wishes of parents and others involved, but should be viewed within the context of the child's best interests being paramount. In addition, the cultural and linguistic background, religious persuasion and racial origin of the child must be taken into account by agencies and social work practitioners (section 22 (5) (c). Within the many volumes of guidance and regulations attached to the Children Act, this duty is constantly reiterated.

The Act's section 1 (1) partially reflects the UN Convention in that it states that courts must give the child's welfare paramount consideration when determining any question relating to his or her upbringing. However, the Convention requires 'in all actions concerning children, whether undertaken by public or private social welfare institutions, courts of law, administrative authorities or legislative bodies, the best interests of the child shall be of primary consideration' (UN Convention on the Rights of the Child, art. 3, para. 1). The elements of 'social welfare' and 'administrative authorities', the latter of which refers to social services departments and their procedures, are not specifically covered in the Act.

The faltering movement towards giving children basic human rights had arguably its most important impetus when the United Kingdom signed the Convention in December 1991. The Convention had been signed by 177 countries by 1995, an unprecedented level of support for a United Nations Convention. It has been ratified by countries comprising nearly every religion and language in the world. Article 12 states that:

> The States Parties shall assure to the child who is capable of forming his or her own views the right to express those views freely in all matters affecting the child, the views of the child being given due weight in accordance with the age and maturity of the child.

> And, for this purpose, the child shall in particular be provided the opportunity to be heard in any judicial and administrative proceedings, affecting the child either directly or through a representative or an appropriate body in a manner consistent with the procedural rules of national law. (UN Convention on the Rights of the Child 1990, art. 12)

In this context, 'administrative proceedings' include child protection conferences.

Once the basic needs of children are met – such as the right to life, to thrive physically, to a home and a roof over their head – there then comes the issue of abuse and neglect within care situations. The Convention requires that signatory states ensure that all the rights in the Convention apply to all children equally whatever their race, sex, religion, language, disability, opinion or family background (art. 2).

Schofield and Thoburn (1996) argue for the Convention to be employed to underpin all policy and practice in relation to child protection case conferences and court processes, and that this may require independent advocacy for the child. They also argue that the evidence from their study demonstrates that children and young people often do not want the burden of deciding matters but do want their views to be taken into account. They consider that the best way to achieve this is by the employment of a model where the presence of the child, and/or an advocate who has no other role or vested interest in the proceedings, ensures that the child's views and wishes are effectively represented. They argue that local authority social workers are seen as having roles to play other than being pure advocates for the child, and have to balance different areas of interests and wishes from amongst the different parties involved, and therefore are not the best advocates purely for the child's views and wishes.

Schofield and Thoburn found in their review of the research that child protection conferences rarely had an item on the agenda specifically relating to children's wishes. Where there was such an agenda item, it was usually wishes of parents and children, and that the parent's wishes almost always predominated (Schofield and Thoburn 1996). This demonstrates an inherent resistance to promoting the child's voice in proceedings.

Lansdown (1995) examines concerns that participation by children would reduce the rights of parents, and she and Schofield and Thoburn (1996) argue that this need not necessarily be the case. Children can feel ambivalent just as adults can about their situation. Lansdown argues that the important thing is that children feel that their views have been represented when the decision is made, not that their view is necessarily the sole determinant. Lansdown also makes the point that social workers should not try to compel a child or a young person to participate. Attempting to force children in any way in such circumstances is generally unhelpful and unjust. She argues that the child's level of competence in the courts and in other decision-making forums which affect them, in relation to child protection investigations, should be seen in the same way as medical assessments in English law as resolved in the Gillick finding (*Gillick v West Norfolk and Wisbech Area Health Authority* 1986). There it was determined that if a young person is deemed to be of sufficient age, maturity and understanding, she/he should have the final say in relation to their participation in medical decisions.

The court process

In relation to court proceedings, Schofield and Thoburn (1996) state that they found in their research that solicitors quite often do not see the child alone and in confidence, and this may be a problem in children getting their wishes and views heard. Spencer and Flyn (1993) and the Bridge Child Care Development Service (1998) set out in detail the further abuse and disempowerment suffered by children who have to give evidence in court against alleged abusers in criminal proceedings, which has no statutory minimum age or level of understanding proviso. This makes for an anomaly, where children giving evidence in care or family proceedings have still to satisfy a competence requirement (Spencer and Flyn 1993; Bainham 1998).

Two areas in particular affect children who may have to appear as witnesses in court. First, Home Office and Department of Health guidance (1992) concerns the interviewing of children who may have been abused, where criminal proceedings may follow. In order not to fall foul of current legal requirements on standards of proof and gathering of evidence, the process runs counter to what we know about how children begin to tell of abuse, and the trust which needs to be built up to facilitate disclosure. Video tapes must be made in special suites set up specifically for this purpose, and there are strict rules which have to be complied with concerning the number of permissible interviews, and the types and methods of questioning. This process is disempowering and potentially frightening for young people, who may perceive a pressure to come up with allegations in the absence of support of counselling or therapy, which is normally precluded for the young person at this stage on legal advice as it may be seen by the court to have been a form of coaching of the young person, and/or 'contaminating' evidence. Alternatively it may lead to the evidence required to convict an abuser remaining undisclosed. Agencies' concerns about the legal ramifications as a result of their child protection duties provide uncertainty and ambivalence for social workers in how they should represent the views of, and provide supportive work for, the children with whom they are working (Spencer and Flyn 1993), and there would seem to be a need for an independent advocate for the young person because of this dilemma. Hallett (1995) argues that there is too great an emphasis on evidence gathering, driven by the requirements of the law, and that this detracts from a focus being kept on the psychological and emotional needs of the young person, and can be viewed as a type of secondary abuse in itself.

Second, this process is the precursor to the child's attendance at court, where the problems of such child witnesses within the adult-centred criminal court have been recognised for some time. Some improvements have been made. The Home Office Report on Video Evidence, referred to as the Pigot Committee (Home Office 1989), reported several areas of concern, including the importance of ensuring perpetrators are brought to justice, and the court's requirement for reliable evidence. The report stated that the inability of the traditional court to meet the needs of child victims, and the stress this causes, can lead to the child's demeanour suggesting that she/he is an unreliable witness, unable to recall and describe events reliably. This may then lead to the court misjudging and discounting the child's evidence (Home Office 1989).

Upon application, the court may allow children to give evidence by live video link, but the defending barrister can still cross-examine the child. A barrister will often try to get the witness to seem idiotic, deceitful or incompetent. This is very easy for a barrister to do with a vulnerable child who is already feeling fearful, possibly guilty for the abuse and its effects, has a poor self-image and low self-confidence. It will be particularly difficult for her/him if the perpetrator is a member of their own family or a close family friend. Children are often well aware that they and their competence and truthfulness are on trial. The long-term effects of such secondary abuse and where she/he experiences the apparent disbelief of the courts can be devastating.

Laura: Child-centred projective identification

In order to fully appreciate the issues of the abuse of power in relation to the court and agency processes involved in trying to protect children from abuse, the reader might try to put themselves into the position of Laura. This case study is based on several real life situations melded together to protect confidentiality.

Laura is 12 years old, with all of the uncertainties, hopes and fears of a young person of this age. Laura lives with her mother, 8-year-old brother and stepfather.

Laura had reported to her mother that her stepfather had been sexually abusing her. She was fearful whether she would be believed or not, what action might result, and how this might affect her, the rest of her family and the alleged perpetrator. Her mother said that she would deal with the matter. However, the abuse continued, and Laura was afraid of what her mother's reaction would be if she raised it again. Laura confided in a friend at school, who persuaded her to talk to a teacher. The social services department became involved following a telephone call from the teacher. This left Laura in an extremely vulnerable position in her discussions with the social worker, and concerned how the authorities might handle matters. When confronted by social workers and the police the mother became angry and upset. The stepfather was evasive about exactly what had happened, but did agree to leave the home while investigations continued.

One method of keeping the child's perspective paramount is the use of projective identification, which is more proactive a concept than empathy. The importance of attempting to see matters from the point of view of the child is made by Trowell (1995). If the different professionals and agencies were required to demonstrate and record how they had viewed the situation as if they were the abused child, and how from this understanding they could ensure the child's fullest participation within the constraints of the current paradigms of social responsibility, this would cut through some of the defensive and adult-centred methods and procedures currently employed. This would ensure that an attempt had been made to examine issues such as:

- What would Laura's feelings, uncertainties, anxieties, fears, and hopes be within her experiences of the situation she finds herself in?

- How would Laura be feeling about her mother and her brother?

- What would Laura's thoughts, hopes, anxieties and fears be about the alleged perpetrator?

- What would Laura be considering in relation to what she had – or had not – told professionals, and in relation to what had happened and what she hoped would now happen?

- Can social workers help Laura with these problems to allow her to tell her story and participate in that way?

There would then need to be a structured and planned examination of the situation, recorded and accounted for, which demonstrates what issues the social workers and, possibly, court personnel had taken into account in relation to the power dynamics involved within the family situation and the agency interventions, such as:

- What would the workers' thoughts be about the potential for further conflict and difficulties in this situation, between whom? What procedures and practices could be put into place to deal with these and reassure Laura about her participation? How would these deal with the issues identified for the different parties?

- Will there be comebacks, from whom and towards whom, from further disclosures, if for example the stepfather had to leave?

- What issues are there concerning Laura being subjected to care proceedings, or for the stepfather to be made subject to criminal proceedings? For example, will Laura be made out to be deceitful or unreliable in some ways, and how can this be avoided/addressed?

- How can it be ensured that Laura's wishes and views are kept in focus by all involved, in the different meetings and reports?

- How does the brother feel about the events?

- How will the procedures and individual professionals involved plan for these possibilities with all involved, including Laura, and provide support to help overcome them?

- How does the mother feel about the events? How might this affect her feelings and attitudes towards Laura, and their long-term relationship?

Laura was at the centre of a set of relationships which were uncertain, and the future unpredictable. The social worker was trying to ensure that the trauma from Laura's abuse was dealt with. However, in her work with Laura and her mother, she then became aware that the stepfather was visiting the home in the evenings and overnight. The mother made it clear that if it came to the choice, she wished to have her partner in the home and not Laura. This revelation shattered Laura's, and her brother's, worlds.

Laura was placed in a children's home where she had to come to terms with the consequent isolation, loneliness and rejection. In addition, Laura had to attend court in relation to the criminal proceedings which ensued. The stepfather said that there had been a close and physical, but not a sexual, relationship with Laura. Laura felt abused and rejected by the system. The social worker felt she had let Laura down because she had not been able to improve matters for her, and had been part of possibly making matters worse, in that Laura had lost the relationship with her mother; whether this was worse than her previous situation became a nagging doubt for the worker. Trowell (1995) notes that the young person in such a situation may wish for the abuse to stop, but to remain within the family.

For the social worker there was the issue of how she balanced all the different pressures. In one way she wished for Laura not to have to give evidence. On the other hand this was one of the few ways in which Laura could be vindicated. If the stepfather were to be convicted this would demonstrate that others believed her. It also would have been important as gaining a conviction would help restrain the stepfather from possibly abusing in other situations. However, if he were found not guilty, Laura would appear to be fabricating the situation.

What becomes important for Laura and others in such situations is to be able to discuss the possibilities and the ramifications openly and honestly, with an impartial person, based on information on what would be likely to happen in meetings, conferences and the court. Helping children develop court-craft skills, as do social workers and other professionals, then becomes a possibility, though it would be important given current rules of evidence to ensure that it could not be construed that this was coaching the child in the evidence she/he was to give. Projective identification is a useful tool for the social worker to help prepare for this work. This requires workers who are trained and supported in direct work with children in such settings, with a full understanding of the complexities and difficulties of such work within the current systems, and the effects on the professional relationship with Laura and her family. It also requires determining means whereby the young person can access counselling and therapy which can aid them in overcoming the potential stress and traumas of the events. If the agency does not ensure this, it is failing its workers and failing its clients.

Supporting professionals to support children

Social workers in this field can 'suffer from low morale, from feelings of vulnerability and isolation, from a perceived lack of support and from the increasing and persistent denial of their expertise' (Spicer 1995, p.14). Trowell notes that professionals experience difficulties when trying to 'resolve conflicts between the needs and feelings of children and the responsibilities of adults in the complex situations of abused children and their families' (Trowell 1995, p.64). The complex and distressing work which results from involvement in such power relationships and abuse increases the demands and stresses involved when trying to work them through agency and court systems. This can create considerable emotional demands and stresses on the children and workers (Brock 1995).

Agency support systems are often lacking for social workers carrying out what is professionally and emotionally demanding work. Social workers have been known to pay for private counselling to help them cope with these stresses. Those who work with the most complex and difficult cases are often expected to work with consultation, but not with detailed and skilled supervision. This can be seen as an agency abuse when the issues that need to be addressed are ignored, resulting in disempowering procedures and decisions for young people.

One of the problems for supervisors, social workers and other professionals trying to operate within this system is that they believe they have to ensure they are following very strict bureaucratic government and agency procedures. They fear that if they do not follow the bureaucratic procedures and something goes 'wrong', they will be blamed for any tragedy, and this detracts from creative and helpful practice to the child and family.

Embedding children's participation into practice and procedures in such a climate requires careful and skilful supervision to enable the worker to stay with the pain and the anger expressed by clients which are inevitable concomitants of such situations, to help the child think through what is happening to them, and provide full and clear information in terms of the legal requirements and demands there might be placed upon them as participants, and possibly as witnesses.

The government's Social Services Inspectorate (1998) emphasised that supervision must be made a priority for social workers to be able to carry out their duties effectively. They found in their inspections of social services departments' practice that many social workers told them that they do not have the confidence or skills to find out children's wishes and feelings (Social Services Inspectorate 1998). This is particularly true for children from ethnic minority groups (Abdullah 1998), and for children with disabilities (Kennedy 1995; Morris 1998). Schofield and Thoburn (1996) also consider that the disempowerment of children can be aggravated by workers not having the confidence and skills to adequately engage with them. Similar concerns are raised by Lord Justice Butler-Sloss (1988). Supervision needs to include consideration of the emotional effects of being caught up in the type of work involved in Laura's situation, in order to help maintain a focus on the child's interests and difficulties.

It is clear, then, that such work requires skilled and comprehensive supervision (see for example, Department of Health 1988; Brock 1995). Iwaniec sees supervision as a key element in ensuring effective practice in all areas of child protection work, as workers experience anxiety and stress on a daily basis. 'Crises, setbacks, hostility of the care givers (and at times of other agencies), uncertainties as how to manage difficult situations, facing the misery of children and breaking up of families, all create stress and pressure' (Iwaniec 1995, p.208). She goes on to say that the work can be draining physically and psychologically, and can lead to reactive rather than proactive responses or passive neglect. The experiences of the child might stir memories of a worker's own abuse, for example, or the worker may experience transference or countertransference which will lead to inappropriate assessment and intervention. Workers who deal with abuse which has echoes of their own experiences of abuse also need to ensure that they gain appropriate support for their assessments and interventions to remain objective as far as possible, and for their own well-being (Doyle 1990).

Lack of focused supervision has been noted as a contributory factor in a number of child abuse death inquiries (Department of Health 1991). What then becomes important in social work practice and procedures is that social workers are given the support to deal with the conflicts inherent in such work, and to bear the child's ambivalence and ambiguity of the pain and possible loss. Children and young people will have swings of mood and views within such complex family situations; this can also be true for professionals. Social workers need to have a sound training and support procedures to understand and manage such conflict-ridden sets of relationships.

Participation in the preparation for formal proceedings

The problems for young people who attend child protection meetings and who are victims appearing in court as witnesses are compounded by the nature of the processes which they have to experience in addition to their other difficulties. There are several key areas to systematically address in developing effective procedures for children and young peoples' participation within the current paradigm of social responsibility in this area. Workers, managers and policy makers may wish to ask themselves these questions in relation to practice and policy development within their agencies. By putting themselves in the positions of the young people involved, they may be more able to understand their fears, ambivalence and motivations and why they are reacting as they are, and this may result in the development of strategies to overcome barriers to participation.

The following suggestions can be used by local authority social services departments, legal personnel and court officers in relation to child protection meetings, planning meetings, and court hearings. All considerations should also include an appreciation of the particular child's personality and developmental stage, and any cultural, religious, ethnic background, and gender or disability issues:

- Use approaches which allow the young person to tell their story from their own perspective and to have an appreciation of how the information disclosed will be used.

- Clarify what may happen to them and their family as a result of giving that information and version of events, before they disclose. Ensure that they understand it is not confidential. Lansdown (1995) believes that it is valuable to ensure that information is given verbally and in writing in language which is appropriate to a child or young person's age, maturity and understanding. This may be by way of play techniques, drawings, use of puppets, toys, dolls and dolls houses, as well as the use of speech.

- Develop skills which make the young person feel that their views are being heard and respected. This would include skills in clarifying the limitations about what can be done with information received, and how much effect it can have on the outcome, and why. Young people need to be shown that they are respected for their views even if these cannot always be paramount at that point in time.

- Design channels of communication to inform the child/young person of the process, the possible outcomes, and any demands these may make on them.

- Consider the systematic use of projective identification as a means of taking into account the viewpoint of the young person as they might be experiencing the power and control inherent within the court and agency processes.

- Provide the young person with clarity as to the limits of confidentiality; what the professional may have to say to whom, why, and what may happen to the information they give, and any consequences for them.

- Ensure the young person is given full information about the system they are entering, including practical details of who will support them and how. However, it is important not to coach too far otherwise evidence might later be rejected, for example in court proceedings.

- Provide details of the process of any meetings or hearings the young person will participate in. Who will transport him/her to the meeting if needs be, when? Has she/he seen the setting with a trusted adult in order to have some familiarisation with the reception areas, rooms to be used, and met with those who will have some input, e.g. receptionist, chair of the meeting, etc.? Do they know the agenda for the meeting, how it will operate, how their part will fit in and be dealt with? Have they been assured about arrangements for meeting – or avoiding – others involved in the meeting about whom they may have concerns, e.g. parents/carers, certain workers?

- Ensure that any information provided by the professional is appropriate to the young person's age, understanding, culture and level of maturity. Without this children and young people cannot fully participate in decision-making processes. Skills are needed in the professionals to be able to encourage children to present their views and to demonstrate to them that their views are being taken seriously. This, amongst other things, involves making sure that there is uninterrupted interview time with the young person. The use of pro formas containing all the areas to be covered can be helpful, if they are not overbearing and oppressive to the worker and young person, becoming mechanistic and alienating. They can help focus the interview, as emerged in the research on the use of pro formas in the development of the Looking After Children materials in Scotland (Hill and Wheelagan 1998).

- Professionals should have access to support services, such as skilled supervision, consultation, personal counselling, and peer support networks, in order to identify and address their own difficulties, counter-transference and anxieties.

- Put strategies in place to ensure full and independent support for the child throughout and after any proceedings. This may be from another social worker, counsellor, other professional or advocate, as appropriate. Provide independent advocacy services to listen to the young person and help represent their views in the decision-making meetings where necessary. Given the best will in the world, some-times the professional/client power relationships can be difficult for young people to work with. It is important that children and young people are told immediately after a decision-making process exactly what has happened, and who said what. They can then be thinking through the implications of the next set of actions which might take place. Written information on the decisions should be gone through in debriefing sessions with the young person.

- Liaise with other agencies involved in court and child protection procedures, such as health workers, police, education staff, local magistrates, judges and court workers and clerks in order to help overcome barriers to children's participation.

- Provide local training for single and multi-professional groups. Take into account issues of empowerment and the potential abuse of power and control in order to develop good practice.

- Develop forums within which young people who have been through the system can discuss problems and help to work out ethical policies and procedures to overcome them in the future. The young people need to be given feedback on what changes might be implemented in policies and procedures as a result of these discussions and recommendations made by them. Team meetings and policy-making groups can be made aware of the issues involved in young people's participation. As far as possible, enable young people themselves to be part of such discussions.

- Incorporate a model such as Schofield and Thoburn's (1996), to develop a means by which to measure practice and policies on children's and young people's participation, with full participation at the top of the list, and the poorest level at the bottom:

> **involvement in service design**   *(Best level of participation)*
> **delegated power**
> **partnership**
> **participation**
> **involvement**
> **consultation**
> **keeping fully informed**
> **placation**
> **manipulation**   *(Poorest level of participation)*

There are movements for change. The Children's Rights Office, the Children's Legal Centre, the Voice for the Child In Care, and the National Youth Advocacy Service are developing ideas and in some cases services which further children's rights in relation to social work and social care with young people, which are beginning to challenge and change the concept of social responsibility. The NSPCC provide support services for young people giving evidence concerning abuse in court proceedings. The Voice for the Child In Care provides advocacy for young people looked after by local authorities, for example in complaints procedures. The National Youth Advocacy Service is also developing an advocacy service for children who are involved with local authority social services departments. These approaches are, however, far from being embedded within all agencies and procedures. This may be helped by the government's announcement in its launch of its Social Services White Paper in November 1998 that Children's Rights Officers would be established in each new Commission for Care Standards region in England and Wales (*Professional Social Work*, 1998).

Conclusion

I examined earlier in this chapter how the child protection field is now required to be closely regulated and monitored by central government. This affects agency procedures and practice to a considerable extent. It may be that such regulation is the best – and maybe the only – means at present to ensure that effective procedures are put into place to ensure children's right to participation within current paradigms of social responsibility. This is not ideal. However, the current paradigm of social responsibility can be employed to increase participation, if the paradigm itself cannot be changed in the short term. This being the case, local authorities and individual social workers need to be accountable through regulation and guidance, to ensure that young people are respected and have their voices heard in proceedings. This would ameliorate some of the secondary abuse and disempowering effects, as there would be a requirement to demonstrate the active pursuit of the young person's participation in child protection processes, and how this is being achieved within agency policy and procedures, as well as with individual young people. All child protection agencies, and the family and criminal courts, should be required by government regulation and guidance to demonstrate how they have taken into account the knowledge there is of children's rights, vulnerabilities, concerns and fears in child protection and court procedures, and how:

1. They are achieving active participation.

2. They applied active participation policies to individual children's situations.

3. The child's views have been taken into account within the Convention's framework.

Court personnel, social work agencies and the police should operate under government guidance and regulation with a checklist to demonstrate through their recording how they have to put these procedures into practice. The records should demonstrate how their procedures have engaged with the child/young person in a sensitive manner and in a way which can allow the young person to make fully informed decisions concerning with whom they talk and when, and how they would like to proceed in relation to any forthcoming decision-making meetings with knowledge of both the outcomes and processes involved.

The long-standing issues of power and control invariably involved when any form of abuse – physical, sexual, emotional, or neglect – is being challenged greatly unsettles everyone, including the social workers. These professionals can often feel oppressed by the current regulations, particularly in relation to child protection. The culture of regulation could be used to meet the vision and letter of the Convention and the Children Act 1989, by detailing not just how such participation could take place, but moreover how it can be monitored, by whom, in order to examine and enhance its effectiveness and the accountability of all who work in this field.

References

Abdullah, Z. (1998) 'Listen to Me'. *Community Care Inside.* 26 March.

Audit Commission (1994) *Seen But Not Heard: Co-ordinating Child Health and Social Services for Children in Need.* London: HMSO.

Bainham, A. (1998) *Children: The Modern Law.* Bristol: Family Law.

Barford, R. and Wattam, C. (1991) 'Children's participation in decision making'. *Practice 5*, 2, 93–102.

Bridge Child Care Development Service (1998) *Listening to Children?* Report of a Debate held on 17 November 1997. London: Bridge Child Care Development Service.

Brock, E. (1995) 'On becoming a tight rope walker'. In H. Owen and J. Pritchard (eds) *Good Practice in Child Protection.* London: Jessica Kingsley Publishers.

Butler-Sloss, Lord Justice (1988) *Report of the Enquiry into Child Abuse in Cleveland 1987.* London: HMSO.

Carson, D. (1996) 'Risking legal repercussions'. In H. Kemshall and J. Pritchard (eds) *Risk Assessment and Risk Management.* London: Jessica Kingsley Publishers.

Cooper, K. (1998) 'Law Commission ruling could open the doors to claims in child abuse'. *Community Care,* 1 June, 6–7.

Department of Health (1988) *Protecting Children: A Guide for Social Workers Undertaking a Comprehensive Assessment.* London: HMSO.

Department of Health (1991) *Child Abuse Deaths: A Study of Inquiry Reports.* London: HMSO.

Department of Health Local Authority Circular (1995) *Children's Services Plans.* London: Department of Health.

Department of Health (1995) *Child Health in the Community: A Guide to Good Practice.* London: Department of Health.

Department of Health (1998) *Modernising Social Services.* London: Department of Health.

Doyle, C. (1990) *Working with Abused Children.* Basingstoke: BASW/Macmillan.

Franklin, B. (1995) *The Handbook of Children's Rights: Comparative Policy and Practice.* London: Routledge.

Fox Harding, L. (1996) 'Recent developments in "children's rights": Liberation for who?' *Child and Family Social Work 1*, 141–150.

Gillick v West Norfolk and Wisbech Area Health Authority (1986) AC 112.

Guardian (1998) 'Social workers face new care rules'. 19 September, 1.

Guthrie, T. (1998) 'Legal liability for child care decisions'. *British Journal of Social Work 28*, 403–421.

Hallett, C. (1995) 'From investigation to help'. In D. Batty and D. Cullen (eds) *Child Protection: The Therapeutic Option.* London: British Agencies for Fostering and Adoption.

Hill, M. and Wheelagan, S. (1998) *Looking After Children Materials.* Paper presented to Child Welfare Policy and Practice: Issues Emerging From Current Research. University of Glasgow/Queens University Belfast, September 3–4.

Home Office (1989) *Report of the Advisory Group on Video Evidence* (Chairman Judge Thomas Pigot QC). London: Home Office.

Home Office Department of Health (1992) *Memorandum of Good Practice.* London: HMSO.

Inman, K. (1998) 'Social work opened to challenge'. *Community Care* 29 April, 8–9

Iwaniec, D. (1995) 'Supervision and support of workers involved in child protection cases'. In H. Owen and J. Pritchard (eds) *Good Practice in Child Protection.* London: Jessica Kingsley Publishers. 202–215.

Joseph, Y. (1995) 'Child protection rights: Can an international declaration be an effective instrument for protecting children?' In C. Cloke and M. Davies (eds) *Protection and Empowerment in Child Protection.* London: Pitman Publishing.

Kennedy, M. (1995) 'Rights for children who are disabled'. In B. Franklin (ed) *The Handbook of Children's Rights: Comparative Policy and Practice.* London: Routledge.

Lansdown, G. (1995) *Taking Part: Children's Participation in Decision Making.* London: Institute of Public Policy Research.

Morris, J. (1998) *Still Missing? Volume 1: The Report of the Review of the Safeguards for Children Living Away from their Families* and *Still Missing? Volume 2: Disabled Children and the Children Act.* London: Who Cares Trust.

Newell, P. (1991) *The UN Convention and Children's Rights in the UK*. London: National Children's Bureau.

Parton, N. (1998) 'Risk, advanced liberalism and child welfare: The need to rediscover uncertainty and ambiguity'. *British Journal of Social Work 28*, 1, 5–28.

Professional Social Work (1998) 'New officers will safeguard child rights'. *Professional Social Work*, December, 1–3

Schofield, G. and Thoburn, J. (1996) *Child Protection: The Child in Decision Making*. London: Institute for Public Policy Research.

Shemmings, D. (1996) *Involving Children in Child Protection Conferences*. Norwich: Social Work Monographs/University of East Anglia.

Social Services Inspectorate (1998) *Social Services: Facing the Future*. London: Department of Health.

Spencer, J.R. and Flyn, R. (1993) *The Evidence of Children: The Law and the Psychology*. London: Blackstone Press.

Spicer, D. (1995) 'An injudicious approach to child protection'. In D. Batty and D. Cullen (eds) *Child Protection: The Therapeutic Option*. London: British Agencies for Fostering and Adoption.

Trowell, J. (1995) 'Understanding the child: The importance of thinking about the child's feelings'. In D. Batty and D. Cullen (eds) *Child Protection: The Therapeutic Option*. London: British Agencies for Fostering and Adoption.

United Nations (1990) *Convention on the Rights of the Child*. Geneva: United Nations.

United Nations (1994) *Human Rights and Social Work: A Manual for Schools of Social Work and Social Work Professions*. Geneva: Centre for Human Rights, United Nations.

CHAPTER 4

The Need for Ethical Practice in the Family Legal System
Theatres of Justice

Lee Heal

Introduction

The following was too painful for me to write in the first person so I have decided to write in the third person as a way of distancing myself from the material. The first part of the chapter tells the story, including a perspective from my daughter. In the second part I am taking up a broader position in my professional capacity as well. Finally I offer some recommendations for change. The story may sound unbalanced at times, suggesting that the whole family court system is seen to be abusive. Rational thought may lead some to question this perception. However, it cannot be the case that this story of two severe court experiences is coincidentally the only rotten apple in the barrel of justice.

It is feared that these experiences are not isolated cases: hence the need to voice these examples. It is thought these are a microcosm of the wider field. What is expressed in the story is not necessarily tarring all court welfare officers (CWOs)/guardians ad litem (GALs)/judges and social workers with the same brush. However the writer has only encountered these particular representatives. Human nature being what it is, there are bound to be benign professionals in the system who do not succumb to the brutalisation of the primitive, blunt, reactionary instrument of court operations.

It is acknowledged that all have a role to play in the system, including the writer (for which she forgives herself). However, no one human being should be forced to carry the negativity for everyone else involved. As a consequence they may lose all positive, trusting feelings towards any one in the system. This is clearly a tragic loss as we all need to believe in our justice system having the ability to sort out complex entanglements. The experience has inflicted damage on, and shaped the mother's view of and trust in, both the social and legal services. This loss saddens her.

The legal proceedings were public and both a guardian ad litem and a court welfare officer were involved. Private proceedings for increased contact and parental responsibility were under way prior to an assessment by social services for a supervision order. The private trial never took place since the public one overtook it. The mother had asked social services for help and they thought the conflict between the parents would significantly harm Julie. They sought to prove the mother was the one responsible for all the conflict despite evidence father was angry with mother. Mother agreed to all contact as demanded by father or recommended by the CWO. From the private proceedings a second CWO report was 'mislaid' by the court. It was about a year later when it was finally forwarded to the mother after repeated requests. It was surprisingly supportive of her views.

One mother's story

It was a dull, drizzly afternoon, the last in a long court 'battle' in which a mother, grandmother, headteacher, godmother, psychotherapist, family friend and mother's partner all fought to help the child remain with her mother.

From then on the special days between mother and daughter were gone forever. The collections from school followed by an activity or snacks and cuddles, chats about their respective days, playing together in the lounge, the routines for bedtime and rising in the mornings were amongst the regular special times Julie would now miss with her mother. She would also miss the physical and emotional daily, supportive, holding contact so necessary for a child's development of self-confidence and security. Mother had always been there for her when she had worries. Now Julie needed a security blanket instead (until she saw her mother again that is).

The child has tried to discuss her situation with her father but he refused to listen. She now feels unable to discuss anything intimate or important with him. She has isolated herself in her room with a TV and Nintendo player. Father was not, and never had been, in a position to offer Julie 'holding' and 'understanding' on a consistent basis; theirs was a loving but entirely different relationship from the mother–daughter relationship. Julie herself is able to articulate this difference from her perspective.

Unfortunately Julie is now a sad, depressed little girl who feels held in the opposite kind of way, held against her will. She feels stigmatised and different. She has exhibited sleep problems, psychosomatic symptoms such as stomach aches, appears unusually needy when with mother, angry and lonely. She also appears to blame herself for her situation and is self-denigrating.

The child, Julie, a little girl of six, was forced against her strong wishes to leave her mother by her father who, with the support of the most powerful authority in the land – the law – applied for a residence order and won. At first father was supported by social workers in the roles of GAL, assessor, the child's social worker, a child and family clinic social worker, CWO, and an unqualified nursing assistant sent in to the mother's home to babysit Julie for two hours when mother had a solicitor's appointment. Later in the second trial, and after considerable contact with the father, this very same social services department supported Julie's return to her mother following the advice of their well-known child psychiatrist as the acknowledged expert.

Unfortunately the all-powerful GAL (who insisted on her view prevailing despite more than eight witnesses against her) won the case and Julie was again legally kidnapped from being with her mother. To the author's knowledge there is no research documented which demonstrates that one home is more desirable for a child than two or more homes. It is security a child needs, and this can be met in a number of ways. Yet the contact order for Julie with mother does little to help Julie feel she has two homes, notably alternate weekends and one week of the holidays. Julie has had her mother excluded from her life – a deprivation which is indefensible.

The GAL also persuaded the registrar to legally 'handcuff' the mother (with a section 91 order) preventing her from ever turning to the courts to rectify the decision. This despite the mother only once making any applic-ation, that is for residence based on the psychiatrist's recommendation, hardly amounting to malicious, repeated court applications, which is the usual reason for imposing a section 91. The father had been making frequent applications (for residence and more contact), beginning these only three months after leaving the family home. He made these despite mother requesting mediation and consistently agreeing to all contact dates insisted upon by father or recommended. These multiple applications felt like harassment which the mother had to defend. Currently father relies on the fact mother cannot use the legal system when, for example, he breaks the ordered contact. Mother has to struggle endlessly to ensure her daughter is provided with the minimum ordered contact with her mother.

The father was driven to attack the mother, to humiliate her in public not just once but twice. His calculated battle to win the child for himself appeared to be generated by his feeling of powerlessness and need for revenge in relation to the mother. No professional could see this because of their lack of understanding of family dynamics. It was by taking the child from the mother (a wish he had stated only two months after leaving the home since he applied for legal aid for that very reason at that time) that he achieved this end.

The court personnel's wrongly held opinion that children have no preference for either parent is not based on any research to date. In fact common sense and research shows the opposite is the case. There is a belief that girl children feel closer to their mothers, particularly singletons in a single-mother household. In relevant studies younger children described parents' roles as being gender specific, clearly diffentiated according to gender. Older girls in particular described mothers as very important to them, particularly to talk with; boys were less likely to describe this need (Joseph Rowntree Foundation 1998). It appears to have been a politically correct view that a father can be exchanged for a mother rather than a view based on findings from rigorous research. Findings stress it is crucial to acknowledge the child's perception as to whom they feel closest. Studies concerning the child's needs for attachment with mother are profuse and require close attention by court professionals.

Social services' and GALs' practice of repeatedly exchanging one primary carer for another who has often been less involved with that child since her birth is unforgivable. The recent case publicised in the press (McGowan 1999) of social services insisting on removing young foster children, for no good reason and on the recommendation of one worker, from the fourth set of parents who were willing to adopt them is another example.

Everyone knows how desperately a child needs a mother. Adults in times of stress/trauma will often call out for their mother. A child also, as we know, needs a father, albeit in a different way. However, this child's father chose to leave her when she was only three years of age. He said he was thinking about his needs, and only his, at that time. This child has now been through considerable distress upon the separation from her mother, deprived of the day-to-day contact with a loving mother and that particular, irreplaceable continuity of care by the actions of her father. He had assumed that his poor relationship with the mother was the same for the child. He defended his actions by way of taking on the role of 'rescuer'.

The torment and trauma of the court hearings was intensified when mother realised that her child was being poisoned against her. She has been undermined as a mother by the court personnel and by the father. No one should have to find themselves in the position of having to defend their mothering. A roving spotlight on anyone will illuminate something to be criticised. No one is perfect, nor has to be.

The father would say to Julie that she had to stay with him because her mother was not safe and loved her too much and it was not good for her to spend much time with her. He also told Julie that her mother found having her around was 'inconvenient' to her. There was no evidence for any of this. This was very painful for mother to hear from Julie. No explanation was given to the child for why she had to live with father. He claimed to be concerned for Julie yet left her without a regular father when he had chosen to leave her mother and move for his work over 70 miles away. She had been born in a village and attended the village school. All her friends and family were local. She was uprooted with the intention of replanting her in an experiment based on the speculation that mother would make future contact with father difficult due to her anger with him for leaving her. It was not mentioned she had considered leaving him the year before. Neither was it acknowledged that the court applications and procedures themselves aroused strong emotions (naturally) for mother which were misinterpreted. Any criticism by her of any professional resulted in them becoming intensely angry and using her comments as further evidence against her. They could not accept they were wrong.

Instead of bridging the divide, the social service and court interference created a massive chasm. The two proceedings polarised the parents to a far greater extent than the mere separation and resulting conflict.

However, the experiment failed dismally. The child never settled and depression overwhelmed her. She developed a very strong false self for coping with life without daily access to her mother, to whom she was far closer than father who had been away from 6.00 am to 8.00 pm (Monday to Friday) and numerous weekends all her life. Childminders came and went as she suffered her fate living with father. Julie bravely tolerated the two-week periods between weekends when she had contact with mother and the long three-week gap in the summer. In between she secretly called her to leave tearful messages about how much she missed her. Both mother and child are stigmatised in the village now, and the child stigmatised at school (she told her classmates her mother lived in Canada and that was why she did not see her much now).

It is ironic that a child whose mother has been convicted of a criminal offence and sentenced to several years in prison is often enabled to visit her mother more frequently, sometimes every weekend. Mother may even have permission for 'staying contact' with the child regularly. Julie has been denied the availability of her mother to her to an even greater extent than the child of a prisoner. In this case it is Julie who is the prisoner.

Mother was determined to walk through the minefield she found herself in without violating the law (the court order) and she did. She supported the child's need to be with her more whilst not undermining the residence order. A very brave and difficult if not impossible way of being. She had to learn to be comfortable in her own discomfort, knowing how much her child suffered and felt unheard. The swords of criticism and lashes to her self-esteem were a trial more than any criminal's lot and more stressful than the split itself.

Mother had to stay self-confident if she was to be any use to her daughter at all. She had to withstand two trials of four days each in which she was brutally criticised by up to ten people. The second trial had an expert witness recommending the child's return to mother which offered a reparative symbol to mother. However, the opinion was ignored, as were the social services and mother's. Apparently the assistant registrar, who admitted she had had an early separation from her own mother and her own children, thought she knew more about a child's psyche than a trained, experienced child psychiatrist and psychotherapist or social workers who knew the child and father much more than before and now were of the opinion Julie should return to her mother. One interpretation which might be made is that the judge was unaware of her deeply repressed feelings of loss from her own mother at an early age and from her own children and was therefore unable to empathise with Julie.

Presumably the group members (all women) who were attacking mother had difficulties with expressing their own anger as women/mothers. It is highly likely that in this case the mother, although understandably expressing anger at the threat of her child being removed, was in fact the scapegoat for the rest of the group's anger. Women and particularly mothers are not allowed to express anger in our society even when there is the threat to their self-esteem or their child being legally kidnapped. The fact that one of the social workers disclosed she had panic attacks every time she saw the same name as the mother's anywhere illustrates how much of her was personally involved. Another example of this unconscious entanglement is when another worker shouted 'yes' and punched the air with her fist when coming out of the court room. The worker appeared full of defiance and on a high at winning the case.

Julie's story

When Julie found out this story was being written she wanted to tell of her experience. What follows is Julie's unedited, factional (fact and fiction interwoven) version of events:

> I am four years old. Dad comes from work, he is cross and upset. Mum is worried. Dad wants to go to a cafe to settle down. Mum takes me to a dinosaur museum. We come home and Dad comes back saying 'I'm leaving'. Mum insists he stay. Dad does not agree grabs me by the hand and drags me to his car. I push and shove and shout but it's no use. Mummy comes out secretly and takes the keys from his car and undoes my seatbelt. Mum takes me back inside. I am very upset. Mum and I cuddle.

> I am now older, it is two years later. Dad comes back and grabs me by the hand I am taken for visits to his house. I feel cross with myself and very upset. I am cross with myself 'cos I have not saved myself from going with him. A few months later a court case starts.

> The solicitor who has been trying to help me thinks going to my Dad's is the best thing to do so she tells the judge this and the judge starts to make comments and my mum says I'd be happier with her. The judge decides and I have to go to my father. All the family disagree. The judge says 'I have spoken!' I go and live with my father. I am very upset because I wanted my mum.

> On my seventh birthday I miss my Mum, I do not enjoy my birthday at all because my Mum was not there. I could not even open my presents 'cos my Mum was not there to help me work it out!

> I hated school because I had no friends. Later I made some. The teachers helped me, especially one, by listening to what I had to say. I told my teachers sadly that I wanted to be with my Mum. I am not a Christian yet have to go to that type of school. My Mum phones and write letters to me. I

keep telling my Mum I want to be with her. I draw pictures for her to show her how I feel and what my Dad is doing to me.

I am now eight years old and determined to get back to my Mum. I feel a bit wimpish but still got a lot of courage to get back. I shout at my Dad 'I'll never forgive you for this!' At one point I was almost getting back because there was another court case. I felt pleased with myself for getting this far but my dad was too strong. My feelings got sadder as I move towards nine years old.

I was in year 5 at the school and got good reports but I felt I was not doing well. My best friend moved away from my village which made everything even harder for me. I began to feel stronger in my feelings, words and actions. I felt angry and said 'I wanna go home!' to my teacher and my Dad. Now I am 10 years old and can speak stronger and get back to my Mumma by doing what I feel is right.

Coercion and threats from the father followed the hearings, for example he said to Julie that if she continued to make a fuss every time he collected her he would ask the judge to stop her seeing her mother at all. He refuses to discuss further contact with Julie despite her efforts. Mother also tries to act on Julie's behalf but there are no agreements – in fact he manages to effectively reduce contact by using anomalies in the court order on a frequent basis. (Will judges ever be able to write orders in a clear manner which do not aggravate or confuse further the situation?) He is obstructive and is seemingly unaware of the emotional trauma the child is experiencing. It is imperative to him to be the parent with all the power and he acts without consultation with the mother and without sensitivity or consideration towards his daughter. This situation was created for him by professionals, namely the GAL who preferred his personality to the mother's thus rendering her more partial to his case. The child's welfare did not appear to be the first concern, otherwise they would have listened to her. There were no welfare needs identified with supporting evidence.

It has taken years for mother to be able to articulate the humiliating experiences in writing like this. The pain felt when remembering the abuse is excruciating. For example, when a letter concerning the case drops on the doormat she has a strong allergic reaction with flashbacks marring her life for days following. Any reference to court on the TV and the sweating and shaking sets in. She is saddened that trust in professionals has become so damaged that she no longer looks to them to help vulnerable people in our society. She is far more compassionate towards her clients who have been abusers now as she understands the framework in which they operate and the way their own childhood experiences have brutalised them.

Themes emerging from the story

Crucial threads can be drawn out from this case study. There are some themes such as the ethics of the court; the issue of war versus peace; confidentiality; neutrality; children's views and accountability which may be of interest to those considering changes to policies and practice in this field.

Ethics

Ethical practice means having the welfare of those who depend on us in mind in all our actions. It can be a code or a set of moral principles. Who in the legal system is responsible for drawing up a code of ethical practice and ensuring that those running the system adhere to it? Is there a code? If there is, it was not made available to the author nor was it apparently influential.

Whether or not there is such a code is immaterial to this chapter, which tells of a system which abuses and harms – this chapter tells of a genuine experience.

Without such a code it is difficult to identify emotional abuse in this context. However, we can say that such abuse is concerned with making use of a position of power to take advantage of someone's vulnerabilities. In family proceedings it is mainly due to the 'against' relationships which have to be set up for a court to operate. From this user's experience there can be aggression and maligning, together with scathing, slanderous and libellous words. It can be a humiliating, brutal, cruel and destructive forum injuring people who fall victim to vitriolic performances by court personnel. For example, in one trial reported in this story a barrister stood up and asked rhetorically, 'How can we crush this woman?' – a very useful attack for his case as it turned out. Research findings (Hunt *et al.* 1999) support the view above that representation (in care cases) should be restricted to accredited family lawyers.

The very term 'trial' is so inappropriate for family hearings. It is indeed a trial for the so-called defendant, however. The adversarial system which was set up for administering justice to those charged with criminal offences whereby there is 'guilty', 'not guilty' or even 'innocent' is totally indefensible as a system for managing families in distress. The legal system and literature even uses the term 'family justice' as if justice is handed out by the judge.

Children and families associate courts with such meanings and court personnel and the atmosphere perpetuate these ideas. Is it conducive to the welfare of chidren to be involved, albeit by implication, in such persecutary settings? CWOs work in a set of buildings run by the 'probation' service and often were in the probation services. Probation officers appear to monitor criminals on their release from prison or those people on probation – not an appropriate training nor environment for managing family discord and very confusing for children and parents alike.

Court rooms (and buildings) are not user-friendly and are austere at best and intimidating at the very least, particularly to those adults and children who have never been in a court setting before. These experiences are verified in research by King and Piper (1995). Mother was required to stand up while barristers/judge alike fired questions antagonistically for three hours at a time without even the offer of a drink or a seat. It was only her robustness which carried her calmly through the ordeal.

The court personnel dress up as if in a theatrical play, which intimidates users even further. The judge sits on a throne behind a huge bench presenting as if a queen or king. They frequently dispense rude comments to solicitors and users, behave irritably and appear to be under huge time pressures. They are aloof and unapproachable, seemingly so removed from normal life as to be almost inhuman.

Far from being part of the solution the court becomes part of the problem (iatrogenic), aggravating an already volatile and acrimonious family dynamic. For the court process to become enacted there has to be an aggressor (the applicant) and a defender. The assailant attacks in a hostile, hurtful manner all facets of the defender's case, including personality, to 'win' the case. Is winning a construct which is helpful to families in need or breaking up? They are unable to communicate and are adversarial anyway or they would not be splitting up. Why does the 'justice' system feed this dynamic? There is research demonstrating that these formal procedures of law increase and even creates hostility between separating parents (Edwards et al. 1998). A study on parental conflict (Smart and Neale 1999) found structured formal legal arrangements and lack of flexibility due to this division of labour created conflict. In addition it illustrated how parental views of their own childhood influences their parenting and these in turn influence the management of the separation transition – for example the belief a child needs its mother more frequently than its father and so on.

This offensive attitude is often shored up by the legal system in which roles are not ones of mediator and peace-maker but those of agitator and assumed 'rescuer'. The system seeks to 'put right' a situation, in the 'best interests of the child', in the context of a perceived wronged victim. Court personnel, such as CWOs and GALs, 'siding' with one of the two opposing parties is thus not uncommon. Often this depends on the personality of one of the parties as perceived by the GAL, due to her counter-transference.

The predetermined oppositional stance whereby two opposing parties have to 'fight it out' hardly benefits parents who are vulnerable enough – as illustrated by the fact that they have reached a court in the first place. The communication problems inherent in families which fall apart can thus be exacerbated by a legal system. Research has demonstrated that the courts fail to support the most vulnerable – the children – and neither encourage bridge building between persons nor understand the complexities of family life, dynamics and lifestyle values (King and Trowell 1992).

In public care proceedings there are normally four parties (the mother, the father, the child's social worker and the GAL whose duty it is to represent the 'interests of the child' – which is subjective in itself). Two parties may side with either mother or father, making it three versus one. The rationale for being 'right' which is commonly used by 'professionals' is expressed by phrases like 'well the sheer numbers on our side prove your case is useless'. However, if there are more people on the opposing 'side' to the GAL then she does not appear to apply the same rule. It can happen that the GAL opposes the social services who also have a duty to act in the best interests of the child. This is very confusing.

In this case when professionals are split and it becomes two versus two, the final recommendation appears to be based on the GAL's view as apparently the most neutral. It is based on their view of which parent is most at fault rather than assessing the child's own feelings on the matter. However, the GAL, like a CWO, is a court official and therefore they cannot be impartial as it is claimed. In addition, judges appear to feel they have to trust the GAL's opinion as being the right one for the child as they are their right-hand 'men'. In private trials two parties (one of which comprises a parent and CWO) aim to 'squash' the other party.

From this case it all appears to be concerned with who can put the best arguments the most powerfully, even if that means reporting inaccuracies, embroidering the facts and physically gesturing dramatically to enhance a point being made. Much goes on court performance. Social workers/

CWOs/GALs together with expert witnesses have training in court craft and are experienced at court performances – often knowing just 'how to tell it' to any particular judge as they are known to each other well. Parents and their witnesses do not have the benefit of such experiences, contacts nor training in court craft. The whole idea is to convince the almighty, omnipotent judge they have the best case.

In this case there were none of the issues normally associated with the removal of a child. For example, the mother had no psychiatric history, no history of substance misuse, no criminal convictions, nor was she suffering from depression. She did not have a handicapping condition nor incapacitating illness, she was not in poverty nor was she homeless. There was no hint of child neglect/abuse by the mother. She had encouraged regular contact, albeit building slowly from one day to fortnightly weekends and two weeks in the holidays. But then the child was only 3½ years old when the father left the home. Therefore the case rested on court performance and minor details to try to build a convincing picture that she was incapable of mothering full time.

The GAL told the author the judge would rightly place most weight on her view of what was in Julie's best interests since she claimed to have such a great deal of experience and knowledge about what was best for children; 'after all,' she said, 'you do not have a duty to place Julie's interests first as I do!'

Children's views

Much more notice needs to be paid to children's views on their own welfare. Research demonstrates that children frequently find their own way of managing parental conflict, for example by suggesting flexible solutions. They are able, at quite young ages, to weigh up a range of factors in arriving at their view about their own well-being (Smart 1998). In Germany, children of seven years of age are seen as mature enough to know with which parent they wish to spend most time (Layelle 1997). Professionals (and parents) need to take account of the children's perspective when separating. A common complaint of parents to the Children's Legal Centre (1998) is that welfare officers often have preconceived views as to the desirable outcome of the case, do not spend sufficient time listening to children and fail to consider their wishes, needs and feelings. In a study reported on TV entitled 'Children of Divorce' a large percentage of children stated that contact with the non-resident parent was inadequate. A similar finding was true for the non-resident parent, ie contact was insufficient.

In fact no cognisance whatsoever appears to be taken of the child's wishes and feelings, however strongly they are expressed or no matter how good an understanding she may have of her situation and the implications. It can be said that the GAL/CWO are aware of the child's preferences and even go so far as to state them and say that even a child of seven can be fully aware and understand her situation. In this story these comments were made to the grandparents by the GAL. But this fact concerning the child's perceived maturity and level of understanding was then selectively omitted by the professional in the trial as it did not suit their 'case'.

Head (1998) claims that children need consulting on matters concerning their future and when they have acquired sufficient understanding that they should be empowered to make decisions about things that are important to them. This is reflected in the 1986 Gillick Judgement and in the 1990 United Nations Convention on the Rights of the Child.

Mediators now consult children directly and find their proposals very practical. Children are seen by the justice system as capable of acting as witnesses to abuse in a court hearing from as young as six years. They are seen as capable of moral reasoning and to know unacceptable actions from acceptable ones (see the Bulger case) from as young as ten years of age. They are also seen as capable of caring for a parent and this is acknowledged by a society which gives financial allowances under such circumstances. If children are expected to hold responsible positions such as carers and witnesses and to be responsible for their actions then the same rules need to be applied in other situations. Otherwise we could have a situation whereby a child of nine years is responsible for the day-to-day care of her disabled, single mother yet denied the information to make an informed decision about how much time she would like to spend at her other home. She is capable of understanding the implications of staying with father every weekend and all the holidays just as she understands the implications of breaking the law. There is no 'competence' test demanded of children in these situations.

War versus peace

Each year 150,000 couples divorce affecting 175,000 children (OPCS 1995) and 250,000 children are affected by unmarried parents separating. By the year 2000 it is expected that 3.7 million children will have experienced at least one parental separation; each year approximately 30,000 children go through divorce with their parents a second or third time. Instead of trying to forge alliances within the family, the system and its operators (since we cannot speak of one without the other) force the members even further apart. Rather than acting as agents for diplomacy, the court personnel can be ambitious, avid and purposeful in their intentions to win and have their recommendations taken up (this despite no evidence of significant harm to the child). The professionals appear determined not to lose face, which is understandable in one sense since their assessment and professional judgement is being tested. Ammunition used may include (as in this case) annihilation of personality, alleging 'madness'; shooting at lifestyles; shelling untruths about events wrongly seen as pertinent to being a good enough mother or father. The normal criminal rules for evidence, such as the right to silence, are not followed nor is there any attempt to employ 'objections' when a witness is being led by a question.

Despite the 'pantomime farce' flavour which operates overall there is a sense in which it is conducted like a war (albeit of words). Contrary to the old adage, words can and do significantly harm persons, particularly when they are about their personal lives.

This is an abuse of power by court personnel and professionals who do not appear to have the awareness to recognise the social ranking and power they hold. In one trial a barrister for the father gave an extremely dramatic performance to mimic an event which had been thought to have taken place between mother and child. He shouted expletives and shook himself to put his point across, waving his arms as though attempting to shake a poor little child. This, despite the mother having made it quite clear some time previously to a social worker that the actual event was nothing like that reported. Unfortunately for the mother there were no witnesses to support her recall of the event except her daughter, who was not asked. The 'professional' reporting it had been clearly trying to make some sort of case against the mother where there was no evidence for one.

Autocracy informs the actions of the legal system; this is a belief that there is right and wrong, black and white. This absolutism in the hands of authorities can lead to complex situations being reduced to the 'baddie' and 'goodie' roles. These in turn activate the archetypes in the collective unconscious of both those persons in authority and the other parties to the proceedings. The acting-out is automatic.

Within the system, populated by the educated, middle classes there is an underlying failure to respect those people disabused of their power and to abuse their rights to dignity and respect. In this country's family court system, there is a distinct lack of respect for the individual's thoughts, feelings and physical needs. Dignity is completely annihilated. There is also complete disregard for the awful legacy visited on the children caught up in this 'professional theatre'. Far from facilitating a 'participatory' approach, courts and the individuals operating in them dispense the antithesis of such a philosophy.

Confidentiality

Part of the harm experienced in the story referred to in this chapter concerned confidentiality. At no time did the social workers/GALs/CWOs inform the mother, nor others they spoke to either on the phone or face-to-face, that the information discussed would not be confidential. In fact it was sometimes explicitly said the discussion would be confidential and then later they relied on their recall of the conversation in court. Neither did they make it clear how the information which would be disclosed would be used. It would have been easy to have given the interviewee details of, for example:

- the aims of the interview
- the identity and role of the social worker
- the nature of the court system
- why they were selected
- precisely what involvement would entail
- how access to reports could be gained
- whether amendments to reports could be made (to include what had been omitted)
- whether mistakes in the report could be corrected prior to any court hearing (or tape recordings made of the interview)
- the right to ask questions and make notes
- the right to opt out silence without penalty or being deemed non- cooperative
- the fact that nothing is confidential nor anonymous.

If it is a child who is unable to give informed consent to the interview then this consent must be sought from a parent.

The cynic would appreciate that the relationship-building process undertaken by these workers with 'clients' or other interviewees is a ploy to increase their access to information which could be used against the client later in court. It is deception to fail to inform someone that what they are saying will be taken down and may be used in court or passed on to another professional. It is also highly manipulative of the process.

Consent from interviewees for the use of their information should be sought before a report is written. All reports should be shown to the person providing the information for their approval and amendments made when requested by them. All visits to interviewees should be prefaced with a statement revealing the way information might be used. It can be significantly harmful for a person to have their privacy invaded by strangers through observation and interpretation, interviews, or obtaining information from a third party.

Coercion of the interviewee was evident – for example, intimidating interviewees to such an extent that they would say anything to have the worker leave their house. The practice of coercing 'co-operation' from someone by threatening they will be termed unco-operative or non-compliant in court is emotional blackmail when there is no legal obligation to comply. In any event adverse labelling is unhelpful to someone who already blames herself or has low self-esteem.

The fact that a professional disallows the disclosure of contents of all reports and all statements by parties to any other than the judge makes it impossible to uncover the cover-ups. It says on court statements that one could be imprisoned for revealing any part of a report to an 'outsider'. This effectively prevents the use of the contents to gain contradictory evidence, such as showing that third party their quotations which may then be deemed inaccurate or misleading.

The myth of neutrality

Objectivity exists when the observer/investigator is value-free, and has no impact on the situation of those observed. It is simply not possible to state that judges and other professionals involved in family court hearings are entirely objective. The fact is, different basic beliefs lead to different claims and different criteria. For example, the disparaging body language and denigrating tone of voice of barristers and judges meant to humiliate the mother in this story reveals personal over-involvement. It would take a great deal of personal work on their inner worlds before they could claim to be aware of all their beliefs, prejudices, biases, etc and acknowledge the influence these might have on interpretation and judgements.

The judge, GAL and others are powerful, active co-creators of any meaning evolving from the hearing. Transactions in a courtroom, like anywhere else, are a manifestation of the real world and are both subjective and objective. They may state they are not intentionally biased or prejudiced but it is their unintentional and subjective processes that are the most damaging and concerning. For example, at the first 'trial' the judge, who apparently was a Moslem, commented on the first day that she had already decided the child would live with her father and even if the mother 'brought the whole village to the court room' it would not change her mind. A religious belief that fathers 'own and control' their children may have been partly influential on this early decision. Although in western society there is some evidence for this also. Even today children normally take the father's name. In America seventy per cent of cases where fathers seek residence it is granted. Mothers in such cases were seen to be judged by far more demanding standards than the fathers (Chesler 1985).

In a court the meaning of events or actions is changed by replacing the words used to describe them and the posing of alternative explanations. For example, the father's barrister said that the mother as she presented in court and by the way she gave evidence was not a typical representation of her at all. This implied to the judge that the mother was a totally different person normally and one should not believe what one was hearing and seeing – in other words mother was acting!

The GAL in the story was over-identified with her position, caught up in her view of the situation. Unlike mother, she was not open to bracketing off her view nor to non-attachment to it in order to consider another perspective. She did not allow the situation to breathe freely because she emotionally invested in her view as the right one. Other options, even the expert's view, were disallowed by her. Her neutrality was compromised, her bias was unintentionally present and she changed facts and meaning to suit it. By and large we do not remember well what we do not pay heed to or value. She had unconsciously (or consciously) hidden from the judge what she did not think was important. Her report was extremely unbalanced as a consequence.

The social and physical sciences demonstrate unequivocably that findings of the observer are shaped by the observer in interaction with the phenomenon, so there can be no independence or neutrality. It is impossible in family law to have observers (CWOs, GALs, etc) who neither disturb nor are disturbed by those being observed. In this case the mother was disturbing those assessors as she became more and more concerned for the future of her child. The assumption appears to be there is one reality that can be objectified, rather than multiple realities. Findings and interpretations are constructions and must be credible. This is achieved by carrying out the investigation in such a way that the constructions are adequately represented and approved by the constructors of the multiple realities being investigated. Just saying one is neutral does not mean that bias, prejudice and so on are not present.

One judge presented herein admitted the case was an 'anxious one', revealing something about how her own feelings had been provoked. Emotions play an important part in any proceeding where children are involved. If they are denied or ignored they will be projected into the case itself, distorting both the process and the outcome. (See Chapter 6 by Judith Trowell and Lois Colling in this book – *Editor's note.*)

Unless court personnel learn to confront their own distress by using a variety of experiential and psychoanalytic psychotherapies to deal with their defensive mechanisms, old hurts and bias/prejudice that their business stirs up, their so-called statements of fact will not be so. They make statements formulated within a pre-existing set of theoretical assumptions which are value-laden with their own preferred values, all unconscious. It is crucial that this issue is addressed as a matter of urgency.

Accountability

Those in positions of power have a responsibility to provide procedures whereby they can be called into account for their actions. Social workers, for example, do not appear to be bound to any code of ethical practice. Neither are they obliged to become a registered practitioner with their professional association, nor even become a member of it. How then can complaints be independently handled? As with our police or education service an independent body is crucial to the monitoring of professional standards and evaluation of the system by users. It is interesting to note in a Department of Health, Home Office, Lord Chancellor's Department and Welsh Office consultation paper (1998) on family proceedings reorganisation it was stated that:

> ... there are a number of persons and agencies who play a central role in, or who are affected by, court welfare services. These include children and families who are involved in family proceedings or have contact with linked services before or after such proceedings. (15, 1.29)

This document omits views of the users of the services in both its analysis and action plan. Astonishingly the document was not disseminated to users of the services under discussion yet it is acknowledged in the document itself that the user has a central role to play in (or was affected by) the service. Only social services directors, major childcare voluntary agencies with interest in guardian ad litem services and their panels were consulted. It appears there is no place for users to give evaluations of the GAL or court welfare services in any formal way, yet it is they who are seen as the major players. It is these court personnel who by admission influence decisions made by judges.

These services employ people who are in positions of power. There is no jury in a family court which adds to the intersubjectivity and allegation that it is not similar people to the parents who are making the judgement. The media are normally excluded. There is no public accountability; however, the services have to be morally accountable for their actions. These so-called professionals such as judges, GALs, CWOs, solicitors, barristers and social workers are apparently trustworthy, respectable people. They are in positions of privilege – an awareness clearly unacknowledged by them – in relation to those being judged by them in their interpretations. To be responsible in their roles is to make a decision or judgement and to remain accountable for that judgement at any future date. It is not possible to challenge a decision since no other judge would counteract a colleague's decision. They do not see the suffering inflicted as a result. They sleep at night. Criticism is seen as the need for retribution for having 'lost' so there is never a justifiable complaint in their view. Judges have no code of ethics nor are they accountable to either the parties or the child for any unbalanced decisions which result in actions which serve to further significantly harm our children. Of course they make mistakes, we all do, but their mistakes, unlike those who do not have their authority and power, may affect someone's whole life. This is the reason why they must be accountable.

The phrase 'in the best interests of the child' is often a cloak behind which a myriad ill-informed decisions about children are rationalised and justified. It can be defined to mean anything which the 'professional' decides it will mean in that particular context, and to further the professional's desired conclusion facts and statements are misrepresented, omitted or exaggerated. However, because of the inaccurate, easily manipulated system of evidence gathering there is no way to disprove these. In a recent discussion with the official solicitor's office the term 'best interests of the child' was a phrase which was seen by them 'to stink!' Alice Miller's book (1983) *For Your Own*

Good demonstrated how adults who oppress and abuse children trot out this phrase (also see Miller 1985).

'Power tends to corrupt, and absolute power corrupts absolutely'. This is the perfect construct to lay at the door of CWOs/GALs. They appear to be unaccountable to any one but the judge who is advised by them, and who in turn is not accountable to anyone, apparently. Who judges the judges? There are no evaluative systems in place and no reviews of decisions which affect children's whole lives. We have no evidence of any investigation into GALs'/CWOs' reports where it has been proved that incorrect decisions have been made by a judge. A complaints procedure for GALs is in place but it appears only drunkenness and physical/sexual abuse is considered.

Finally, the procedure of swearing to tell the truth is laughable. In this case the mother witnessed a number of incidents of misleading pieces of evidence given by professionals and others at the trial. Deceit and duplicity appears to be the norm, particularly when it is a child who refutes something; the professional adult is normally believed. There is no accountability for fabrication and no procedure to call those responsible to task either, it appears. To say they are accountable to the 'court' (which is to the judge presumably) is a nonsense in a collusive system.

Recommendations

In view of these experiences the following recommendations have been drawn up for social work and legal personnel in the family proceedings system if the courts continue to be used. It is highly questionable whether the 'justice' system is an appropriate one to manage family issues at all. In the meantime it is a hope that these recommendations will be considered when working towards a less brutal and more ethical, participative and inter-disciplinary practice (Walsh 1998). Perhaps some of these procedures are already in place, but it was not apparent from the mother's experiences.

First, it appears to be essential that there are independent evaluations systematically collected from service users at every point of contact with the professional institution. For example, the establishment of an independent GAL and CWO feedback channel for service users to provide comments and make complaints. Coupled with these an independent complaints system for feedback and comments is required about the court procedures offered in family disputes. Finally there needs to be access to an independent advocate for parents in family court procedures, in addition to solicitors.

It is recommended that where families are breaking up the best possible form of support for families should be little or no formal intervention, or at most a Family Assistance Order. Social services often form part of the problem rather than the solution. It is far better to provide the resources for families to gain independent support where the legal system does not inform the objectives and outcomes of families and social services working together.

An awareness of the need for full user participation and 'no blame' attitudes in social services, legal services and private and public hearings is required. For example, parents cannot be expected to be able to spend the amount of time preparing a case as a CWO/GAL or social work department. The balance is weighted in favour of CWOs/GALs because of this. A fair trial means an equal distribution of resources to all parties, which clearly is not the case at present [see Chapter 5 by Sue Williscroft in this book – *Editor's note*]. The provision of parent advocacy, not court related, is one way to achieve this balance.

The whole family justice approach should exclude the possibility of a 'trial'. Court rooms should be user-friendly and terms reframed accordingly. The use of costumes such as gowns and legalese jargon needs to be eradicated. Instead of encouraging adversity, a participatory and collaborative system should be set up. For example, solicitors could send the 'facts' or intentions to the other parent before issuing court proceedings and invite her/him to mediation as a very first step. Then at least ten days' written notice should be given of any application for court proceedings so the other party could respond first. The writer is aware of some recent research by the Joseph Rowntree Foundation (1998) which thankfully recommends to the government 'information meetings' in relation to divorce proceedings to facilitate agreements on arrangements for children and finance.

Children need to be respected and their views listened to, and particularly to be given more authority in deciding their own futures when it comes to with whom they are to live and have contact (Smith 1999). Currently they lack the power and opportunity to voice their concerns as the situation affects them. Adults around them have a motive to conceal children's' views if they do not agree with their own (parents' and professionals'). It could be a requirement for mediators to inform children of the relevant factors and request children's views. All children need to be informed of their rights in general with a citizenship programme in schools. In particular, all children need to know it is their right to have access to independent advocacy when adults oppress/abuse them or decisions about their lives are being made by others.

Court welfare officers, guardians ad litem and social workers

It is essential that there is an immediate investigation of social services at all levels. All social workers need to be encouraged to disclose their own abuse as children. They should then be carefully assessed and if working with children attend therapy and monitored regularly. Vulnerable children are not only those subjected to physical and sexual assault. Action is needed to promote user-friendly accountability where complaints are not open to being vindictively used by social services against the user in the guise of non-co-operation.

Social workers could be trained in family and group dynamics and, through personal therapy, learn to recognise the power of their own unconscious processes which may be acted out on families (Russel *et al.* 1989).

It is strongly recommended that a mandatory register as part of a professional body for all social workers (including CWOs and GALs) practitioners be set up. Members would agree to abide by a code of ethics and practice. A complaints procedure as part of the professional association should be developed with a mandate to deregister members in breach of the code of ethics. There could be a policy that no member may be employed as a social worker, CWO or GAL without registration which would need to be maintained annually and reviewed, say, every five years.

It should be made clear to all service users that social worker's and GP's notes are not confidential and are not the property of the individual (contrary to popular belief). It should be made quite clear to all NHS patients when they register with a GP that the GP/health visitor may discuss their personality and provide personal views of a non-medical nature to CWOs/GALs on the telephone or in an interview. This should also be the case for headteachers/teachers who are called to give personal views on those caught up in the system. Parents should know once their child is in full-time education that this is the procedure.

All interviews should be conducted in the manner of criminal court hearings, for example audiotaped and/or signed as a true record of what was said. This would ensure an accurate record is made to be copied to the interviewee in their presence. All child interviews should be videotaped and ownership given to the child (if too young to have the original in their possession it should be kept on file until a request for it is made).

Judges

If judges are to continue, unsuitable as they are, to preside over family matters, it is recommended that training for judges include psychoanalytical thought, infant, child, adolescent and adult developmental needs, the emotional needs of children (such as attachment, mothering/fathering issues), familiarity with research from relevant disciplines, an awareness of group dynamics, a basic understanding of the nature and purpose of counselling, family therapy and psychotherapy and an understanding of their motivation for entry to the field. A full assessment of their knowledge and understanding should be mandatory prior to their practising as judges. These inclusions would not be so essential if judges were seen to rely on expert witnesses such as psychiatrists' and psychotherapists' opinion.

In developing a code of ethical practice for family law judges, together with a system of accountability, more assessment of performance would be possible. Part of this should be the setting up of a registration system for all family law judges with an independent complaints procedure which should be made accessible to all users of the court system (this would be different from an appeal). A regular 3–5 yearly review of judges' performance would monitor their practice.

Judges of a different culture or religious belief may need to be limited to cases of that culture. Otherwise their in-built doctrine could result in faulty decisions and lead to a miscarriage of justice. As a general recommendation psychoanalytic psychotherapy (minimum of 40 sessions) should be mandatory for all family law judges, social workers, GALs and CWOs during training.

Barristers and solicitors

It is strongly recommended that solicitors/barristers in family law have regular and mandatory supervision with a group analyst whilst conducting family law cases. In addition, solicitors should have had a thorough training in system abuse issues, child development, the emotional development of infants, children, adolescents and adults, life stages, loss and attachment theory, family dynamics and group dynamics at postgraduate level before specialising in family law. The recommendation of law practitioners being fully accredited family lawyers is one the author would agree with (Hunt 1998; Hunt et al. 1999).

It is hoped that these recommendations make a contribution to discussions on how to democratise our family justice system and social services. The major reason for writing was to help others, particularly children, avoid the pitfalls, suffering and disruption involved in court procedures.

For professionals it is hoped the story goes some way towards illuminating to them the power that their destructive criticism has to significantly damage parents' self-esteem. The comment by the GAL that 'the judge does not wish to hear anything positive about you' serves to show just how all-encompassing the 'trial' is intended to be. To criticise everything about a person (particularly their identity as a parent) often results in that person beginning to believe in that perception of them. Vulnerable mothers without a network of support may easily find themselves so undermined by the whole process as to be driven to psychiatric illness, medication, addiction, self-harm or even suicide. There is a constant reminder of the harm this kind of criticism can do when the child has visitation contact, which may be too painful for the parent, resulting in the parent initiating restricted contact, or no contact which would be detrimental to the child.

Family problems do not require a 'justice system' but a conflict resolution process. No court can ever provide this, however much it is modified. As long as a parent sees the legal system as the only way to gain power that is what it will be used for. Punitive and adversarial measures are endemic in the family justice system. It will never be open to change and is totally inappropriate in forcing a solution whether there is agreement or not. The whole system is outdated and in the long term needs dismantling, not modifying, to be replaced with a system operating on a different philosophical basis such as that found in Scotland. In particular the systematic psychological violence which results from users' involvement in the family court system must therefore be addressed as a matter of urgency. Rigorous research and public investigation would be ways forward in gaining a greater understanding in this field.

Acknowledgements

Many thanks for the support and all the thoughtful, helpful comments on the chapter from friends, family, colleagues and the editors of this book. Without these people the writing of these experiences would have been impossible.

References

Chesler, P. (1985) *Mothers on Trial: The Battle for Children and Custody.* New York: Harcourt Brace Jovanovich.

Children's Legal Centre (1998) 'Support services in family proceedings'. *Childright 150*, October, 18–19.

Department of Health, Home Office, Lord Chancellor's Department and the Welsh Office (1998) *Support Services in Family Proceedings: Future Organisation of Court Welfare Services.* Consultation Paper.

Edwards, R., Gillies, V. and Ribbens, J. (1998) *Biological Parents and Social Families.* Oxford: Oxford Brooks University Press.

Head, A. (1998) 'The child's voice in child and family social work decision making: The perspective of a guardian ad litem'. *Child and Family Social Work 3,* 189–196.

Hunt, J., McLeod, A., Freeman, P. and Thomas, P. (1999) *The Last Resort: Child Protection, the Courts and the 1989 Children Act.* London: Stationery Office, in press.

Hunt, J. (1998) 'Child protection, the courts and the Children Act.' *National Council for Family Proceedings 13,* 3–6.

Joseph Rowntree Foundation (1998) *Understanding Families: Children's Perspectives.* London: National Children's Bureau.

King, M. and Trowell, J. (1992) *Children's Welfare and the Courts.* London: Sage

King, M. and Piper, C. (1995) *How the Law Thinks About Children.* London: Sage.

Layelle, G. (1997) *Two Children Behind a Wall: The True Story of a Family Torn Apart.* (Publisher not Known)

McGowan, B. (1999) 'We want the girls' voices to be heard' (letter from the Bramleys). *Express* 13th January.

Miller, A. (1983) *For Your Own Good: Hidden Cruelty in Child-Rearing and the Roots of Violence* (trans. Hildegarde and Hunter Hannum). New York: Pluto Press.

Miller, A. (1985) *Thou Shalt Not Be Aware: Society's Betrayal of the Child.* London: Pluto Press.

Russel, R., Gill, P., Coyne, A. and Woody, J. (1989) 'Dysfunction in the family of origin in graduate social workers'. London: Pain.

Smart, C. (1998) 'Children's views on life after divorce and children managing parental conflict. Leeds University Centre for Research on Family, Kinship and Childhood'. Paper presented at National Family Mediation Conference, November. London.

Smart, C. and Neale, B. (1999) *Family Fragments.* Cambridge: Cambridge University Press.

Smith, H. (1999) *Children, Feelings and Divorce: Finding the Best Outcome.* London: Free Association Books.

Walsh, E. (1998) *Working in the Family Justice System.* Bristol: Family Law.

CHAPTER 5

Representing Parents

Does the Legal System Prevent Them From Playing a Real Part?

Sue Williscroft

Introduction

In this chapter I explain how the experiences of parents in proceedings brought by the state to remove/help/care for their children show that the system fails to allow such parents and their families to play a real part and diminishes the contribution they have to make. Such parents are often vulnerable, increasingly with learning difficulties, mental health problems and addictions. This process is effected by courts, lawyers and social workers setting down all the parameters for decision making, and social workers dominating the language and concepts of child rearing to exclude such parents from proper participation in the legal process. My experience of this is as a solicitor for parents, and sometimes for children observing parents' participation in the court process.

The failure to enable real participation comes about through a variety of means:

- Failure to use language and procedures that are understandable, including failure to record important things in writing to the parents and families.

- An assessment process which is a test of parenting rather than informed by how best to support parents.

- The courts' process revolving around the convenience of 'the courts', primarily the lawyers and social work professionals (in which I will include guardians *ad litems* (GALs)) who dictate the agenda, language and timescales.

- The parents being seen as isolated individuals rather than members of complex family networks and communities whose support and understanding is frequently ignored or diminished through concentration on the legal process.

- Failing to see that parents are properly represented through skilled and independent legal and other advocacy – something which the state has prevented happening in respect of children's participation in these proceedings through the creation of a specialist child care panel of lawyers together with the use of experienced GALs to pursue children's interests working in a useful tandem model. The social network of the children's lawyers, GALs, social workers and their lawyers may in fact act to exclude parents and their representatives, meaning that concentration on the child's best interest by lawyers in the absence of a professional or advocate arguing 'for' the parents may result in an imbalance of power.

- A concentration on what is perceived to be the needs of the child in a paternalistic way, where they can, and are, seen entirely in isolation from the needs of parents and indeed siblings and other family members.

To answer these concerns I would argue that many parents and families need to have available some form of professional advocacy service, separate from the social services, which should support them through the litigation process to ensure they know exactly what is going on. Such social advocacy is intended to empower the less powerful to enable them to make informed decisions and participate meaningfully in our court process. In particular, it enables challenges to be made against the inappropriate standards against which some parents are judged.

What service do parents get and need?

In any form of interaction with authority – social services in care proceedings – parents are entitled to the same service they would get, say from their legal advisors. For example, they should be informed in writing as time goes by of exactly what is happening and why, the timescales and what the roles of key people and themselves is to be. As with their lawyers, parents should know who is in charge and who to complain to if necessary.

My experience is that the language and ethos of the Children Act 1989 changed practice and approach in a positive manner but that parents are excluded from actively sharing parental responsibility with social workers who exercise their power and authority in subtle ways (perhaps because it feels uncomfortable or is unclear to most of them). Social workers who are straightforward about their power and authority seem most likely to be clear with parents.

Case conferences are examples of what is intended to be participative decision making involving parents. Yet only the parents are invited (not grandmother, aunts, etc.) and they are only able to take a supporter *or* a lawyer and the lawyer's function is severely curtailed. Indeed, it may be that nationally practice is a great deal more varied than this. It is only within the last two years, where I practise locally, that decision making has taken place in the presence of parents. I have spent many boring hours in waiting rooms at the end of difficult meetings waiting for decisions. Having participated or observed such 'secret' discussions on other occasions I have felt uncomfortable that 'gossip' or rumour can end up as fact when parents are not there to challenge it. But is due weight given to the challenges they do make? Parents can be seen as people with vested interests, unlike the other participants, preventing them from being listened to fairly.

Parents often see the reports a day or two before the meeting but do not have the time, nor are they given the reports, to review with their lawyers. Nor is there an opportunity, for example, to put their own views in writing beforehand. Commonly the document will be handed out 10 minutes before the start of the case conference or meeting. Well-meaning conference chairs try to explain the purpose and meaning of the meeting, which in reality usually does more than simply decide if the children's names are registered – it also sets the agenda of primary concerns, usually in a language which social workers and GALs share.

Chairs are poor, in my experience, at ensuring that all the contributions are properly addressed or are in plain enough language for parents to understand. This is combined with the difficulty of professionals sometimes being reluctant to be clear, in front of the parents, about their real views. Such meetings, I feel, should be both formal to enable all to say what they want, and informal, to enable discussion to really take place. Parents need to respond to concerns bit by bit rather than simply getting the offer of a 'closing statement'. When parents interrupt or get upset I feel responses to that demonstrate how uncomfortable the whole experience is for all concerned. If it is 'participative' both anger and distress are acceptable. These feelings would be accepted in a serious family meeting at home. We would not discuss a decision about, say, a brainy 18-year-old choosing not to go to university, or having dubious friends home, without a bit of ranting and interruptions.

My local experience is that I frequently meet with parents whose children ought to be registered, or be the subject of care proceedings, but are not because of social workers' reluctance to be clear – due perhaps to their misguided concepts of 'working in partnership'. I may later be asked to represent children who have been frequently accommodated and who have been harmed by repeated delay. Injustice to parents happens in those cases, as longstanding problems are often more difficult to address, especially when they didn't seem serious enough to merit earlier proceedings before. Nationally this experience is not unusual.

In my view social workers inappropriately use their power and responsibility in every accommodation agreement where they tell a parent, 'If you don't agree, your children will go into care.' This is especially the case where the level of family support that could prevent care proceedings taking place has not been ascertained or when 'resources' mean that fostering allowances through different budgets can be paid but there is no nursery place or family support worker to help the family to manage. It is a case of fitting the 'problem' into the current system and budget rather than vice versa. It is also remarkable in my experience how rarely the wider family network is explored. One of the ways the GALs provide such a useful service is in spending time to track the extended family down and listening to them.

Claire Norris (1998) states:

> The reality they (parents) live in every day is interpreted in the Court by tests they hardly recognise, in a double layer of unfamiliar language. In that forum as the months progress that inferred world gains a life of its own. Incidents that may have seemed to them insignificant have great significance placed on them, are loaded to become 'facts in dispute' and 'issues in the case'. The identification and agreement of what are to be the issues is constrained by the available law and can be influenced by the scope of the remedy available. Decisions are needed to fit the remedies available, so that the essential points from the legal perspective may not correspond with the essential points previously established with the social work professionals and may well differ greatly from the family's own perceptions of important points in their own life. They grow, recede and shift in family

proceedings in a way which simply does not happen in other forms of litigation. Drug abuse and sexual differences are frequent examples of topics where established views of the protagonists pull the case very unpredictably. (Norris 1998, p.35)

The Grandparents Supporters Project, a research study by the University of East Anglia (Tunnard and Thoburn 1997), provided grandparents with a professional and independent supporter to see how 'partnership' was working.

Conflict with social workers was also a common theme. Many people seemed to expect trouble, seeing the social workers as unhelpful right from the start. Family members 'got into a corner' and the resulting conflict with the professionals could jeopardise the outcome of the case. Social workers saw grandparents as difficult or challenging rather than as a resource to their grandchildren. Those seeking advice from the Federation often came too late to alter the difficult situations. (Tunnard and Thoburn 1997, p.4)

Tunnard and Thoburn, for the Supporters Project, set out examples of practice:

Delays and lack of response or information were viewed by grandparents as – at best – lack of common courtesy, and – at worst – a deliberate attempt to exclude them from children's lives. Grandparents found it intolerable that workers would ignore letters, not return phone calls, and fail to visit at agreed times. Supporters were much more successful at getting responses, but in three cases they commented that their attempts to speak to workers were ignored repeatedly. In one other case, the social worker would tell neither the grandparents nor the supporter what the plans for the child were. Several grandparents found it difficult to gain permission to attend reviews and other planning meetings, even when their adult children had welcomed their participation. (Tunnard and Thoburn 1997, p.23)

They continue:

In relation to attitudes, grandparents were dejected by the way social services seemed to have set their minds against them so intransigently. They felt judged badly for not acting sooner, for not contacting the department earlier to offer support, for worrying about how they would manage on a family income... Several commented on the lack of professional approach in workers who made false assumptions about them, failed to discuss worries openly, and worked on misinterpretations or misunderstandings rather than checking out facts. (Tunnard and Thoburn 1997, p.23)

If you look at how parents who are struggling with children in education with development problems in early years are assisted by schemes such as 'portage' nationwide there is a completely different approach to 'partnership'. In these cases partnership is based on enhancing skills of parents by offering practical examples that will each improve the child functioning through parent and child interaction, the whole being achieved entirely by positive reinforcement. The non-judgemental approach is highly effective, but of course time-consuming. It is primarily offered on a voluntary basis and is not part of the coercive state system. The important point here is that there is no blame attached to the parents in these schemes.

Tim and Wendy Booth (1994) were concerned in their research into the experiences of parents with learning difficulties, and as I am in practice, by the way in which parents involved with statutory agencies are judged or assessed against inappropriate standards of care. They state:

> For example, several study families reported having been warned against smacking their children. Ever fearful of losing them, they did as they were told. However, generally lacking powers of verbal reasoning, they were left with no effective method of discipline and began to encounter problems of control. These problems were then cited by social workers as evidence of parenting deficits. Or again, many parents were expected to maintain standards of household tidiness and cleanliness that were foreign to their neighbourhoods, family and friends, and unnecessary in terms of the health or well being of their children. As Ms Burnley complained: 'They want me to get my house perfect but I cannot get it perfect. I'm not like other people, them posh people. It's just like other houses round here. With Tessa you've to wipe your feet when you come out.' (Booth and Booth 1994, p.51)

I agree with social workers who through their national association have long argued that their training is not long enough nor of a high enough standard. In addition they are not given sufficient continuing education to enable comparative techniques to be explored from other social/educational fields.

Tim and Wendy Booth explore how the agendas set by social workers ignored and devalued the parenting skills of the group of parents with learning disabilities whose experiences they recorded. They felt that for this particularly vulnerable group, 'parenting competence is not just a matter of possessing adequate skills. It is also an attributed status that owed as much to the decisions of professionals and the courts as to the behaviour of parents'. They recommended that social workers:

- work together and with parents to explore the meaning of adequate parenting
- ensure the standards against which parents are assessed are made explicit to them
- avoid making value laden judgements about the adequacy of parenting on the basis of unfair comparisons with middle-class standards
- pay equal regard to people's parenting skills as well as their deficits
- watch out for self-fulfilling prophecies of parenting failure based on single-minded concern only with parental inadequacies. (Booth and Booth 1994, pp.145–149)

They point out, too, that parents they met suffer many obstacles to parenting: housing, poverty, lack of transport, poor upbringing from which to learn, little support, lack of good legal representation, 'negative perceptions of parental competence within the service system', discrimination, abuse, as well as real limitations in parenting skills. They also state that: 'Their (parents) problems need to be located, as it is possible for each of these factors to provide obstacles which can then be seen as proving their incompetence.' Examples are given of parents struggling in the most daunting experiences whose struggles are seen as wholly related to parenting failures, yet ought to be seen as our failure as a society to adequately support them and their children. Our society chose to pay social workers to exercise that function on our behalf. That responsibility is a hard one, but is misused when implemented so negatively.

They felt there was a lack of research looking at how parents with such difficulties coped well – as some clearly do – and the use of that knowledge to better support parents. In their own experience a very basic support, such as the authors being available to chat and listen to parents, provided immense assistance. For example, those parents felt they had someone who valued them for who they were, would listen to their concerns about being patronised by service workers, and would talk over how they might be able to disagree with workers – without losing their children. The authors' views were that lack of systematic training in parenting skills before things had reached a crisis point together with a lack of inadequate representation for parents meant that negative assumptions had made actions against this group of parents more likely. From their experiences, key elements of abusive social workers' practices seemed to be concerned with a lack of respect of parents as people, and a blinkered approach to support, with a 'pass my test' approach to gateway support in the future.

As a solicitor I represent both parents and children in childcare cases and am a longstanding member of the Children Panel, from before there were GALs or the Children Act. It would be wrong of me not to make clear that there have been huge and impressive changes in the way courts are able to deal with intervention in family life in that time – for example advance disclosure of written evidence, proper representation of children and the interventionist role of the GAL.

There is, however, now a childcare law industry – journals, associations and, despite the aims of the new Children Act in 1989 meant to provide a codified and simple legal regimen, increasingly complex law. Interestingly it appears there are nationwide local groups of solicitors who regularly represent children appointed by GALs, who are commonly seen as cliques (See Chapter 6 by Judith Trowell and Lois Colling in this book – *Editor's note*.) and can certainly present a rather self-satisfied air about the skills and care they spend on their hard jobs. These social groups spend most of their weeks together sharing a common language, social status and authority. They are often very dismissive of the representation of parents by non-childcare panel lawyers.

There has been some concern that the relationship between the GAL and child's solicitor can have an unhealthy effect on occasion. They would feel they were advocating for children but, as Claire Norris (1998) says of the child's solicitor.

> ... is it surprising then that where the relationship is so easy and accustomed, the approaches and beliefs shared and tested, the foundation patronage and mutual regard, that some of these marriages develop into holy or unholy alliances? In the small world of public law family proceedings ... large characters occupy the stage. Some pairings of solicitors and guardians loom large. You know when you see them there's always a good chance of rumble [she means a good argument in court]. (Norris 1998, p.33)

She continues:

> At its worst, this close relationship can become a parody of itself at its best. You can begin to see an adversarial style, with stances on issues taken early

leaving no 'safe zone' for discussion of planning and options. Some of these solicitors show their independence in point scoring in court and correspondence. Perhaps the most doubtful area, because it often strays so far from the agenda of the child and the family, is where the protagonists become absorbed in a point of pure law or in winning and losing. Norris 1996, p.33) (See Chapter 4 by Lee Heal in this book – *Editor's note*.)

In 1986 the Law Commission in their annual report said, 'In disputes about family matters the emotions of everyone in the Court (including the tribunal) are likely to be more deeply engaged than in most other forms of litigation' (Law Commission 1986). In his book, *The Family Justice System*, Murch (1997) comments, 'Family proceedings invade the most personal areas of our lives and makes us live through painful events in public. The emotional pressure in the family proceedings court may cause the advocates and the protagonists to become close to each other, become inappropriately hilarious, personally over-involved, in the case.'

Representation of parents is considerably harder, I would argue, than representing children. It requires social skills with parents and professionals, a high level of negotiation skills and a similar knowledge of law, ethics and the practice of state intervention in family life.

Claire Norris (1998) states that:

> The court is looking at that family, who have their own reality with their own rules, hierarchies and language. When cases come to court and enter the legal domain the family must learn the concepts and belief systems of that domain also. To some extent their success in the proceedings may be determined by the ability to make these adaptations. Cases can be decided by the ability of the family to establish rapport with significant figures in the process ...

> Before they come before the court the family will already have been worked with by social work professionals, and 'share social workers' and 'plans' and had been 'offered services'. Being 'able to demonstrate ability to change' is quite significant there too. In setting up the current system, the legal world has tried to learn the language of the social work world and appointed guardians chief interpreters. Families in care cases have generally a traineeship in one and then get a crash course in the other new language.

The reality they live in every day is interpreted in the Court by tests they hardly recognise, in a double layer of unfamiliar language. (Norris 1998, p.34)

Guardians, of course, are almost exclusively former social workers and share that language and ethos whilst having little accountability in reality (See Lee Heal Chapter 4 – *Editor's note*). As they will point out, they report to the court; however, the court does not employ them.

Communication skills with children are an essential asset of the child's lawyer. Though many of us may have some experience of this with our own or other's children we are unlikely to have among our social circle the educationally disadvantaged, emotionally manipulative and volatile, sometimes stunted, group that many parents comprise, or be very familiar with the serious effects on attention and social skills of major addiction and mental health problems. We are likely to drive everywhere, carry pens and diaries, to write reminders and have credit cards for emergencies. We will all have at least one phone where we can be contacted. We do not live on estates where drugs are openly for sale, or home safety is more of an issue than in what I regard as my local burglar's paradise.

I often notice that solicitors have little concept of how important it is to communicate with clients in their first or only language. Our firm gets frequent referrals from clients who have had to take children or others to solicitors to make themselves understood since we have trained interpreters and some lawyers able to speak their first language. On such a basic level, then, proper communication – the sharing of understanding – is not seen as a priority and the courts or the Legal Aid Board who deal with our bills are often quite punitive on the many hours we spend communicating with our clients to ensure they understand the process. The new fixed fees regime for family work will not reward firms that employ properly trained interpreters in-house. Those whose clients have learning difficulties will get paid the same fee as those with articulate clients even though of necessity more time is spent with them. Spending time in teaching your clients the language of social workers is unlikely to be financially remunerative, but probably makes a lot of difference.

It is common for parents involved in this system not to use solicitors on the Childcare Panel. The Grandparents Federation research conducted by Tunnard and Thoburn in 1997 was clear that particular experience in childcare work, not just family work, appeared necessary. Parents and grandparents tend to use solicitors they have known or been recommended who have little experience in the area of childcare law and practice at all, and even if they do, if they do not have 'clout' they may still be at a disadvantage. 'Clout' means that other workers would recognise that the lawyer knew what they were talking about and would take active steps to promote their client's interests and challenge plans. The following comment of one of the federation's grandparents supporters captures the view of several: 'It is crazy that solicitors without specialist skills can take such cases willy nilly, just because grandparents go to them because of the help they've been given in divorce and other family disputes.'

Similar points have been made by the Thomas Coram Research Unit. In a recent study (Brophy and Bates 1997) of the legal representation available to parents in care proceedings it states:

> Parents are not required to choose solicitors from the Child Care panel to represent them … and for many reasons they may select a solicitor who has no real expertise in the field. The result, when this occurs, can be not merely a divergence of approach and philosophy but consequential delay and lengthening of hearings due to the unfamiliarity of non-accredited solicitors with non-adversarial practice and procedure.

Good solicitors can have a large impact for this particular client group, doing so by using communication and social skills to persuade clients to co-operate to their advantage, for example advocating more useful forms of assessment to social services departments, GALs or the courts; involving, on behalf of their clients, appropriate experts who may be able to look at things afresh; and, importantly, keeping their clients going through what is usually a prolonged experience for clients of feeling depressed, humiliated and isolated.

Where solicitors for parents fail to ensure parents are assessed appropriately it may be very difficult for other participants to feel able to support this at a later stage, since delay may prevent possible rehabilitation because of the child's timescales. A small baby may be unable to cope with a further four months of assessment before settling into a permanent home, for example. It is frightening how often lawyers ask at a late stage for further reports or assessments because they hadn't really put their minds to what the issues were for the court and their clients were earlier. Inadequate representation of parents in very difficult cases also creates great difficulties for the child's lawyer who might perhaps advocate some form of order that would support the parents' plans but needs to ensure this is presented with the proper independence that reflects the GAL's special role for the court and that independence would seem to be compromised if leaning too heavily in favour of one party.

It takes a great deal of advocacy to move the juggernaut of social services assessment down a different road. I recall how I was able to get a psychologist, at some public expense, to advise social workers how to restart and retry an assessment of parenting skills of a vulnerable parent with learning difficulties. She simply could not take in what she was told or what was in a book but could learn through repetition of tasks and constant reinforcement. She did get (but lost on other grounds) another chance of 'proving' herself but still struggled throughout very long proceedings without any worker for herself to help her budget, manage shopping or just to be there for her. It seems odd to me that she might have a volunteer to read her books and take her out if she was blind but not because of learning difficulties. The Grandparents Federation research quoted above found progress hindered by the overwhelming distress of grandparents, delays, social services attitudes, lack of cash and communication problems. The kinds of practical support the parents that the Booths met found most valuable was provided by workers who liked and respected them, and were available for a long time.

Chopping and changing of key people is a major problem for some of my clients. Our local system of 'intake' social workers who hand over complex cases a few weeks later in itself I feel tells parents (and children) that social workers do not value their relationships. Parents do not get to know and trust anyone because they will shortly move on – the opposite message, I think, from that which they should get. Support needs to be directed to teach and reinforce the parent's own skills, recognise parents' needs and include independent advice or advocacy where one worker could not represent the interests of parent and child. The parents the Booths met experienced many difficult and hostile experiences from those meant to help them, for example being treated as children, having their authority undermined or removed, and failing to be involved in decisions.

In Charlton, Crank and Kansara (1998), which concerned birth parents compulsorily separated from their children, the experiences of running an advocacy and support service for parents is described. Funded as trial short-term projects by charitable foundations, two separate projects in different parts of the country spent some time working directly with and for birth parents. Their projects were as a response to concerns about the availability of post-adoption counselling but they covered all aspects of the court process. Contested adoptions now form 57 per cent of adoptions, are a key part of childcare planning, and are quite commonly linked with care proceedings at the final stage. The Adoption Law review, now in a form of legal limbo, suggested that local authorities should have a statutory duty to provide advice and counselling by a social worker who is not involved in the birth plan if the birth parent so wishes. There are pitfalls to this suggestion, for example it would be a hard task to 'counsel' someone whose child your own department has just taken away. Social workers should be able to fund private counselling to parents in this situation, perhaps in conjunction with the referral and funding health authority. One questions how ethical it is to provide counselling themselves and what parameters of confidentiality apply. It is odd that now social workers have clear duties to provide counselling when mothers at birth wish to give up babies but not to parents whom they take to court to enforce adoption or separation. In para. 28.5 of the review a suggestion of a role for independent advice and counselling was given. I would suggest from the evidence they collected, together with my own experience, that such a confidential service should be provided by an independent agency for all parents involved in the public care process, including child protection investigations:

> Interestingly the workers for this project, who had been social workers for children at times in previous professional lives, found they were able to listen to clients' stories with a different understanding and response since they then didn't have the duty to put the child's interests first; 'this... highlights how one's perception of a situation is formed by preconceived ideas, assumptions, expectations and the role we are playing. (Charlton *et al.* 1998, p.28)

> Social work assessments are often carried out on what is immediately observable and measurable ... the quest of social workers to find observable methods of assessing risk ... serves to alienate parents and families from their support systems ... this is a dehumanising approach which discourages respect for the individual, discounts the psychological effects of loss and trauma, promotes inequality and disadvantage, and results in humiliation and stigmatisation. (Charlton *et al.* 1998, p.29)

They described how parents had found the court process reminded them very painfully of the original traumatic events, they found it hard to participate and found final hearings humiliating and distressing. (See Chapter 4 by Lee Heal in this book – *Editor's note.*) Those who had been in care themselves found descriptions of their childhood in care used to prove they would be poor parents or inadequate for what they felt was no good reason (particularly since it was social services who had put them in care) and of course it raises the question of the benefits of care given that they were perceived to have received only negative effects from it. They were upset that friends and family could not be in court with them. Going to court was a traumatic event in their lives which other participants in the court process did not appear to appreciate.

Solicitors were often not seen as supportive. When other solicitors from the same office or a barrister had to go to court for them instead it was seen as being 'dumped'. There seems to be no good reason to me why solicitors representing parents should not have to sign the same personal undertaking as solicitors who represent children, that is that they will conduct the case themselves except in limited circumstances or when another advocate is requested. Solicitors were seen by parents as participants in the court arena rather than personal advocates. Many solicitors would disagree with me but it seems to me the professional job of an advocate, with an overriding duty to the court not to mislead the court etc. is to represent one's client to the best of one's ability but within that to support the understanding and experience of a justice system which aims to listen to all and be accessible to all. This means being the parents' 'translator' or 'gladiator', perhaps being there as a resource for them. In panic, it was reported by the parents, many tried to change solicitors just before important final hearings. The parents had no idea how to choose a good solicitor and most did not choose the best.

It is concerning to read in Charlton *et al.* (1998) that the legal representation these parents had received had not only not helped them to understand the adoption process, but also that even different stages of the care order legal process were unclear to these parents, leaving them feeling humiliated and powerless. I am often surprised by how solicitors so often fail to convey legal advice to their clients in letters. They appear to assume they will understand all the legal words in common currency for us, but as ancient Greek to our clients. Obviously information given at times of huge emotional distress can be hard to absorb but it needs to be repeated clearly until it is understood. In the study, it appeared few parents had something simple in writing to help them understand what was happening to them and their children.

It is very common for the social worker's solicitors and the child's to sit together at court and outside of it. (See Chapter 6 by Judith Trowell and Lois

Colling in this book – *Editor's note*.) I have to confess to being guilty of this on occasion. The GAL will be there but not the parent(s). During such apparently social meetings evidential matters and concerns will inevitably be discussed that may not be known at all to the parents. GALs of course have access to all the social work files, however inaccurately recorded or full of prejudicial hearsay they may be. Indeed, because our local care centre is some distance away, and this is nationally the case, it is uncommon for parents to go to directions hearings in the county court. The GAL can copy the files and give/discuss them with their legal representative. Why do parents and their solicitors not have that same right, without application to the court? It is possible with editing, conscious or otherwise, for a version of events to be presented which supports one's own opinion.

There are court rules and authoritative cases meant to ensure that anything that does not support the local authority case must be disclosed. In reality the 'life' of a 'case' is more important – in other words, how decisions are made while the investigation and court process is ongoing, leading, in the end, to decisions that can mean care orders being sought to remove children permanently. It is an abuse of power for all evidence not to be fully disclosed by social workers and GALs and, in fact, a breach of a local authority's and GALs' duty to the court if there is a failure to disclose. In such a subjective field clearly this does happen: witness cases still reported in which judges have tried to keep secret some parts of GALs' reports or what children have directly said to them in a meeting.

Here is an example of a case in which I became involved afterwards. At the final hearing, feelings on the side of the natural parents and the proposed adopters ran high. The natural parents and other parties were represented by skilled advocates. Advocates for all parties were invited to see the judge, without their clients, and did so more than once. The judge made his views clear: he was going to support the adoption. A 'hearing' took place where no evidence was given but the natural parents' case 'at its highest' was put and all advocates made submissions. Inevitably an adoption order was made. The natural parents were unsuccessful in appealing because it was decided the course of action taken by their advocate had their 'consent' and effectively a form of collusion between the court and advocates resulted in a denial of justice to those parents.

How could these natural parents give proper consent to what I would argue was a travesty of the legal system? What real choices did they have, excluded from the judge's private discussion? Whose interests were involved here? Parents often say, 'I couldn't sign them over, what would they think if they knew I'd done that?' In a system of family justice where children's 'rights' to be brought up in their own families can be removed, I feel children are entitled to feel their natural parents' views, even if 'wrong', are represented forcefully so that the judge can powerfully hear what they think and later the children can know what they said.

This 'coffee/courtroom collusion' is not an isolated example of court-room practice. It is common for advocates and GALs to attend private discussions with the judge about children's cases before they start. Maybe the judge wants to know what the issues are, how long the case will really take and so on, but why have this done in private without the parents there? One answer might be that it makes the hearing process less painful for parents who are inevitably going to lose their children, but this reason should have been discussed in the parents' presence. Not doing so demeans the participation of parents in the judicial process, which could be seen as an abuse of power.

Why has the GAL been traditionally allowed to be present at such discussions? Locally while Taylor HHJ was Family Liaison judge he rightly said this practice must cease and also that GALs, like other clients, should sit behind their lawyers not on the front row with them. Unfortunately that pronouncement has not been universally acted upon.

It seems to me that the judge's management of cases can be an important element in the understanding and involvement of parents. Some local authorities now have informal meetings at an early stage to put in writing what exactly the social workers are saying they intend to prove has gone wrong or is at risk of going wrong; then parents can be clear. Such procedures seem to me highly beneficial to parents. Judges taking an interventionist role can direct that this procedure be undertaken nationally.

Lessons for social workers in speaking and writing in plain English would be helpful. I frequently have to 'translate' documents into plain English so my clients can understand them. It is small wonder that those same clients can be poor at picking up exactly what they have to do to get their children back. Recently I struggled to translate a psychological report which told the court my client had serious learning difficulties and capabilities. I came to the conclusion it was almost impossible to translate it without hours of thought and preparation. It was bizarre to me that an 'expert in communication' (a psychologist) had so poorly communicated to the one essential person, my client. I shall now insist on résumés being prepared at a level of language that my clients can understand. I also think some forms of assessment mis-communicate. How many parents feel they have to prove each single aspect of the parenting tasks, as a test, rather than showing they can achieve the important one for their children e.g. 'managing for a few months without letting another man you barely know move in' or 'not being too drunk to look after your children', etc.

It is a dilemma for all involved in children's work that the evidence of experts now seems so essential for the courts to make decisions; and how, bizarrely, a GAL who is sometimes an employed social worker for one authority, and never allowed to profess 'expertise' has such a definitive and authoritative role as a GAL in other proceedings.

I would suggest that the experience of assessment is in many ways more damaging to parents than anything else in the process. An 'Orange Book Assessment', named after the orange book in which guidance to social workers on conducting community assessments was first spelt out (Department of Health, 1988), is prepared in most social work cases that go to court, unless there has been some form of comprehensive assessment work already done with the family before such proceedings. The guidance sets out parameters for proper and full assessments to be carried out, giving headings for areas of work and issues that need to be addressed in reports. This work, perhaps conducted by unqualified and untrained family centre workers, presents outcomes that can, in practice, only be challenged by expert evidence unless the GAL too disagrees. What happens when the GAL disagrees with an expert? Surprisingly often the inexpert view of the GAL prevails in court, which can then too be an abuse of power. (See Lee Heal Chapter 4 – Editor's note.)

I feel there is a real danger of the now commonly seen parade of experts, just joining in a well-meaning but mistaken 'trashing' of parents who are clearly hopeless. In the same way that children ought to be protected from wrongheaded and intrusive medical and other investigations by GALs and court case management, this protection ought to be considered by the courts for parents as well. For example, reports that prove the glaringly obvious are all too often commissioned by parents' solicitors or GALs on behalf of children. What would children make of such evidence looking back on it as young adults? It is surely not helpful to their self-esteem, let alone their parents', to have reports saying how bad/hopeless their parents were. After all, they come from the same material. And I'm afraid I have done it myself – but should I have been allowed to? My clients do not have the language to explain what it must feel like to be branded hopeless by someone with a lot of letters behind their name. It is abusive for us all to be participants in a process that allows this to happen to people.

In the best interests of the child

In court the expert evidence for parents is often discounted unless its total premise is what 'is best for the child'. If an expert dares say that was not central to their thinking it allows the court to discount their evidence. Indeed the same game happens to any fool who says they have not read the Cleveland report, although I question how much can be learnt from it. I am sometimes concerned that this emphasis on, 'the best interests of the child', a mantra which many hopeless and, in private law, bitter parents seem able to repeat, ignores the centrality for children of their parents. How often do we all, magistrates, solicitors, GALs, repeat this mantra to ensure our opinion wins out?

Murray Ryburn, a respected adoption social sciences researcher, at the Association for Lawyers for Children conference in 1997 held in Plymouth, described how he had on a number of occasions given evidence in children's cases that his research demonstrated continued contact was in the interests of many children post-adoption. His only success had been (on a rare occasion) in persuading the listening prospective adopters to change their views about this. Unfortunately it had no impact on the thinking of judges and he received quite a hostile response from the judiciary at the conference. His research outcomes are unchallenged. I suspect that because he was called 'on behalf' of parents, his evidence was discounted. The decisions of adopters, seen as 'good' people, about children they wish to parent are always taken as unchallengeable as against what natural, 'bad', parents might wish for their own children.

Advocacy

If parents are particularly disadvantaged by mental health difficulties and unable to instruct solicitors directly under rule 9.5 of the Family Proceedings Rules 1989, like children, the court can appoint a 'next friend' or guardian ad litem to undertake litigation on their behalf. Though the rules stress the official solicitor should first be asked if parents have no one willing to act on their behalf, it has become common practice for GALs to be appointed to undertake this task. One has to leave aside concerns about their funding, the blurring of their entirely different role, to ask the participants in this social experiment of expert advocacy how useful they have felt this to be. One could see all family law proceedings as a form of social experiment and perhaps it is worth remembering the days, when I was in practice, when local authorities could acquire parental rights over children by administrative action only. Think, too, of those in psychiatric hospital because their social and sexual behaviour was outside the, then, norms to remind ourselves why proper process is so important. Locally this has happened where parents have had major learning difficulties too. I have some problems with the concept since I feel quite comfortable taking instructions and have rarely felt unable to understand what my clients have wanted to instruct me about their children, nor been unable to explain to them the concerns that have led to proceedings being issued. But, that being said, there was a high degree of satisfaction by solicitors and GALs about their joint role enabling the solicitor to concentrate on legal issues and the GAL to provide a very different advocacy service. My own experience was very positive when a professional worker was able to 'translate' the experiences and feelings of a client with some particular physical communication difficulties, very vividly and helpfully for me.

Other advocacy schemes for parents are run by different agencies, such as Parents against Injustice and the Family Rights Group, but they are inevitably limited in scope. The Grandparents Federation supporter service (provided on a temporary basis for research) felt their impact had been helpful. For example, they were able to provide information about social services policies and legal duties, about research on best outcomes for children, practical and emotional support for grandparents. One grandparent said:

> She gave me advice on how to handle social services, she listened to me when I needed to talk to someone, and she was always able to suggest the next course of action.

> I am normally described as a very strong person but the events that overtook my life were very hard to understand. Others in my own or similar positions need all the help they can get, if only so they come to understand that they are not alone. I felt there was someone there for me, someone I could talk to about absolutely anything. I never felt that she did not want to talk to me, she always gave an honest opinion, and she was ever persistent in pursuing the social services. (Tunnard and Thoburn 1998, p.31)

Parents, too, need a service like this.

Locally our Community Health Council (CHC) has employed advocates for people with learning disabilities, and disadvantaged members of the Asian community, both funded by the community care budget, and of course hugely overstretched [see Chapter 11 by Mary Neville in this book on the usefulness and pitfalls of the CHC in this role – *Editor's note*].

The parents' need for social work is often not met in the care proceedings process. The social worker allocated to the family is the 'child's' social worker, not able to support or encourage a parent. In many cases I have felt it has been absolutely clear that parents have major needs of their own which will need addressing whether this child comes home or not. There is a simple need sometimes for someone to talk to, who will listen and whose job is not to be part of a team 'examining' or assessing them for legal purposes. I cannot think of an occasion in cases I have been involved with when that need has been met and where any help has been provided – even, for example, an unpaid social work volunteer who may offer help with budgeting [see Chapter 10 by Sue Amphlett in this book for discussion of this – *Editor's note*]. Far better to have someone with a clear role who can, if needed, support parents through the end of proceedings, particularly if the outcome is bleak, when everyone else then disappears from the scene. It is essential that these people are not part of, nor do they feed back to, the social work team and provide further evidence for the social work case.

If those who exercise power in this system could begin to understand how their 'helping' is seen by those they attempt to help this may improve understanding, communication and provide real support and advocacy for parents. Parents need to be properly encouraged to participate within the legal and social work system as it could otherwise result in children being separated from their families of origin because the language and agenda of the helpers has not been adequate.

Recommendations

My suggestions for improving ethical practice are:

- Parents should have the use of solicitors from the child care panel to represent them as mandatory.

- Social workers, lawyers and other professionals working with children should have better training in communication skills at a very basic level. Social workers should, as a matter of practice, record all advice and actions in writing to parents at every occasion; even if hand-written.

- Courts should ensure that at an early stage appropriate procedures ensure parents are aware of the exact issues the court will be concerned with and outline how the parents will need to address social work concerns through the court process.

- Advocacy schemes should be set up on a professional nationwide basis, funded by joint health and social services funds with an aim to assist vulnerable parents through complex child protection investigations, court processes and the aftermath.

- Social workers in their care plans to the court need to address their plans to support parents whose children may be removed and, for example, have funds available for the provision of independent and confidential counselling.

References

Booth, T. and Booth, W. (1994) *Parenting Under Pressure.* Oxford: Oxford University Press.

Brophy, J. and Bates, P. (1997) 'The position of parents using experts: A failure of partnership'.

Charlton, L., Crank, M. and Kansara, K. (1998) *Still Screaming. Birth Parents Compulsorily Separated From Their Children.* London: After Adoption.

Department of Health (1988) *Protecting Children: A Guide for Social Workers Undertaking Comprehensive Assessment.* London: HMSO.

Law Commission (1986) Annual Report. Cambridge: HMSO.

Murch, M. (1992) *The Family Justice System.* London: Jordan and Sons.

Norris, C. (1998) 'Horse or carriage?' *Seen and Heard 8,* 32–37 (National Association of Guardians Ad Litem (NALGRO) Journal.)

Tunnard, J. and Thoburn, J. (1997) *The Grandparents Supporters Project, A Research Study.* Norwich: University of East Anglia.

CHAPTER 6

A Child Psychiatric Perspective on the Use of the Courts and Child Welfare

Judith Trowell and Lois Colling

Introduction

The Children Act 1989 (DOH) was introduced in October 1991. Prior to this Act, public and private law in relation to children was much less focused on children. The Children Act changed the emphasis with its opening statement: 'The child's welfare shall be the Court's paramount consideration' (1.1) and (1.3). A court shall have regard in particular to:

- the ascertainable wishes and feelings of the child concerned (considered in the light of his age and understanding)
- his physical, emotional and educational needs
- the likely effect on him of any change in his circumstances
- his age, sex, background and any characteristics of his, which the court considers relevant
- any harm which he has suffered or is at the risk of suffering.

Harm is defined (31(9)) as ill-treatment or the impairment of health or development: 'development' means physical, intellectual, emotional, social or behavioural development; 'health' means physical or mental health; and 'ill-treatment' includes sexual abuse and forms of ill-treatment which are not physical.

How has this Act worked in practice and what has been the impact on both child and adolescent psychiatry and the family division of our legal system, on social services, on guardians ad litem and on the Official Solicitor? But, perhaps most importantly, is it possible to understand the process psychodynamically; to think about the impact, for good or ill, it has had on the children the system is meant to serve? Then, in the light of these reflections, are there any thoughts, suggestions and ideas about how the system could be improved? It is these questions that this chapter discusses.

Literature

The document *Child Protection: Messages from Research* (DOH 1995) had a striking message about the 11 million children in England. There were, roughly, 160,000 child protection referrals per year, 120,000 family visits leading to 40,000 child protection case conferences with 24,500 children placed on the register, about 3000 children voluntarily accommodated and about 3000 entering the care system. The suggestion arising from this, raised by the DOH, is that the vast amount of resources invested in child protection investigation, both visits and video interviews, and the very small number of children entering the care system, and the even smaller number of successful criminal prosecutions despite many police investigations and video interviews (Plotnikoff and Wolfson 1995; DOH 1994), could more usefully be used to help support children and their families. However, it is not clear from the document what 'family support' means and what will be the threshold that children and families in need will have to cross to access these services; or if, in reality, a reduction in child protection work will be used to justify a reduction in resources.

Hence, questioning the value of the child protection industry and the legal system that decides and implements the wishes of society for the extreme cases is less straightforward than it would appear on the surface. In spite of these reservations, the problems that have emerged are of such concern that discussion is required. Research by King and Trowell (1992), demonstrated in their book *Children's Welfare and the Law*, show the deleterious effects for children (in many cases) of using the legal system as the only or the main forum for protecting children and promoting their welfare. Cooper *et al.* (1995), and Hetherington *et al.* (1997) show that child protection in the UK and USA places much more emphasis on the legal rights of parents and children compared with other European countries, the emphasis on rights rather than on child welfare within the context of the family unit leading to a 'win or lose' approach rather than a problem-solving approach (see Chapter 4 by Heal in this book). Schofield and Thoburn

(1996) conclude: 'it is not a question of choosing between balancing children's rights and the rights of other parties, or weighing in the balance the welfare of the children against their wishes and feelings'. What appears to be needed is an integrated approach to developing the child protection system, and in linking child protection to family support practice.

This is in contrast to Jean La Fontaine (1990) who, in her book *Child Sexual Abuse*, sees 'an irreconcilable conflict' between the authority of the state and the independence of the family. If children are to be protected, she argues, the agency protecting them on behalf of society must have the power to intervene against any threat. She states that if the possibility of children being damaged by the people normally responsible for them, their parents, is admitted by those parents the protection of children and the complete autonomy of the family are incompatible.

This is, of course, self-evident but, in our view, it is this 'irreconcilable conflict' that is at the root of the problem for society. Any system can only be wrong, at fault, because society would like to believe all adults, all families, want and do the best for their children the majority of the time. That there is rage, hate, violence, envy and destructiveness within human beings, and that vulnerable children are both the recipients of these from those around them and also feel those emotions themselves, is what prevents a perfect family and child-rearing system. Suffering children, difficult, frightening children, arouse guilt and outrage and any system is dealing as much with these responses as it is trying to promote the best interests and welfare of these children. Since the feelings and the impact of them on the system are frequently unconscious, it is perhaps hardly surprising that the system we have developed to manage these situations is heavily procedural, dominated by ritual, and, all too frequently, prone to irrational, puzzling and contradictory outcomes.

Professionals, particularly social services departments, have retreated into defensive practice. The justice system appears to have responded by trying to gain more control. The hearing has heard all the evidence and made agreements or orders and a care plan has been written. Judges then feel concerned if they think after the proceedings these plans will not be implemented and try/want to ensure decisions will be implemented. Child and adolescent psychiatrists cease to be child mental health professionals with a clinical focus and become 'experts' who fight for their 'client' *now* rather than maintaining the longer term case management therapeutic perspective for the child and family.

King (1997) suggested that a large part of the problem is the continuous search for a perfect system that could provide for all possibilities. Of course, such a model does not and cannot exist. Whilst agreeing and supporting his view that we should not waste time searching for the ideal, we do believe that the current system is unacceptably flawed and that it is possible to make some improvements. These improvements are required not only in practice in the external world but are also needed in professionals' understanding of the emotional impact at an unconscious level. The dangerousness of violence, the life and death threat and fear, the coldness of hatred, the brutality of sexual exploitation, leave no one immune, however senior, however experienced, and these feelings have to be managed and processed by the individuals and the system day after day. For further reflections on this issue, see *Rooted Sorrows* (Wall 1998).

The Children Act

This was an enlightened piece of legislation that seemed set to transform Matrimonial and Child Care Law which involved children and their families. It was also a consolidating Act, although it did not include Adoption Law. It was innovative in its understanding of children and their needs, and mental health was seen as significant alongside physical health. However, since its implementation in October 1991, considerable problems have emerged. For example, social services departments, education authorities and the National Health Service have all been subject to major reorganisations. The Family Court proceedings system is also under review at the time of writing. Also, courts and judges have been confronted with cases where poor practice and very limited resources have seriously limited what could be offered. Judges have responded by attempting to intervene more actively. This can be understood, but the increasing involvement of judges in decisions about the use of experts has caused problems. The implementation of care plans – or lack of it – also causes problems, for the judiciary and for child and family mental health professionals.

Seriously overworked social services departments urgently need to consider rethinking their use of resources. Frequently, experts from child and family mental health are brought in at the time of a court hearing whereas the use of this expertise earlier in the case might be a more effective intervention and might be less damaging for the children and families. Thinking about the issues before legal intervention or very early on in cases where there are children in need or in need of protection would be more helpful to the family.

Working Together under the Children Act 1989 (DOH 1991) is currently being revised but it did give a clear framework to encourage interagency planning and work when concerns about a child or family arose. Police and Social Services (Children and Families) have trained and then worked together to conduct investigative interviews with the possibility of criminal prosecution, but other aspects of the suggested interagency working have been more patchy.

Social services have tended to have something of a siege mentality. There has been shock and dismay to discover many cases were unallocated, ie had no social worker; while those that did often had a social worker who had the expectation that they would undertake an initial assessment and, if at all possible, would then withdraw and close the case. It may well be that there have been longstanding concerns about the child or family within the health system from the general practitioner, the health visitor or perhaps a hospital department (paediatrics, adult mental health) or within education from the class teacher, the educational social worker or the special needs co-ordinator; or perhaps within an organisation in the voluntary sector. But none of these may be brought together to gather a full picture of the child and family. Or if they are, the worries and concerns of non-social services agencies can be seen as not sufficient to cross the threshold of concern for social services.

There are particular problems that have been recently recognised where this is extremely important and where good interagency communication and assessment early on can be enormously helpful. Mental health problems in adults is one such area that is particularly fraught. The recognition of depression in many mothers by children's and families' social workers does seem to be low; and similarly is recognition of the problem of personality disorder. These adults do present all the services with dilemmas because there are, so far, no specific interventions. However, sharing the concerns, and planning how the agencies will both assess the possibility for change and how to proceed if change is or is not possible early on, can prevent agencies becoming drawn into disagreements or fights which reflect and mirror the conflicts and splits in the family. The needs, wishes and best interest of the children and the needs and wishes of the parents in these families can take over the professionals if they become caught up in the family dynamics. Other problems that greatly benefit from close interagency collaboration are domestic violence and alcohol and drug abuse where similar powerful dynamics can trap the professionals.

Because of the uncertainty of the outcome of the court hearing, particularly where social services have a view and then health, education, the guardian ad litem and any experts may have differing views, for example on whether children are to be removed or not, there has often been no planning until after the court hearing. Children are, therefore, frequently placed in several bridging placements until permanence can be arranged. The quality of foster care is a serious cause for concern.

Another problem that has emerged is that the Children Act stressed the need to listen to the child's wishes and feelings. Now there seems to be a displacement of difficult decisions on to the child whose views are taken 'too' seriously. Due weight must be given to the child's statements, but often the situation is complex and the longer term view and the responsibility for any decisions must be the task of the adults. All too easily, a legal system keen to push through as many cases as possible can only take a snapshot view; decisions are made on the evidence on the day. Often, it is almost impossible to retain a view of each family as unique and to really explore all aspects of the child(ren), the parents and the family, to arrive at an integrated and digested view. If it were so, the view of the child(ren) could be considered thoughtfully, these views could be set in a context and more decisions be made that made sense to the child and family even when the outcome was not what they wanted. There was, with the Children Act, the expectation that the move would be towards Family Courts with an inquisitorial approach where this type of hearing would occur. In reality, the division has become increasingly more adversarial (see Chapter 4), partly due to the migration of criminal barristers into the family division and partly due to the lack of respect and trust for social services. Parents immediately expect to be accused of being 'bad', rather than seeing that there is a problem so that they can work in partnership with social services. Social services are driven to 'prove' to justify their view that the children need intervention. Ironically, the legal process is so expensive that after a court hearing there is often little to pay for the treatment, support and placements recommended and required.

A number of reasons for these failures can be found, but the fundamental reason seems to be the need to give increasing emphasis to 'facts' and 'evidence', and yet the major problems to be dealt with are the intense emotional relationships in families and the emotional vulnerability and neediness of children. Inevitably, these dynamics become projected and evoke responses in all those involved in the case. Until these processes can be recognised and managed, fundamental changes are unlikely.

Some methods of intervention that can contain and process these conscious and unconscious emotions so that more thoughtful, reflective and less destructive solutions can be found are discussed below.

What actually takes place in a court room?

The excitement of the Children Act encouraged the professionals to think that now there is a legal system which would be (somehow) different for children. The paramountcy principle seemed to suggest that children's interests would now be at the heart of decision making.

Alongside this was the opinion that the process in court was to be inquisitorial, rather than adversarial. Hopes for this were high. Clearly, the rules had changed, but the subject matter of the cases coming to court had not. So many family cases contain emotionally overwhelming material often involving not just one generation of harrowing events but several. Each individual (whether professional or not) involved in such cases has emotional reactions to the material. How this is dealt with influences, and is potentially an area of, abuse. All involved have been a child; some will be parents as well. All will have had their own unique experience of being parented and, possibly, their own experiences of abuse. This impinges both consciously and unconsciously on how the material is understood by each individual. It is hoped that those working with children and families have the mechanisms and self-reflexive capacity for considering their objectivity alongside their own potential unconscious processes. But do they? Many professionals, during training or early on in practice, seek personal therapy, counselling or consultation as they see the need to work on their own emotional issues. But it is also extremely important that all the professionals involved in this work have good case supervision. This is not management supervision (which is of course important) but a forum to help the individual explore and understand the emotional dynamics in the case that they may well find are influencing them unduly. They can also, during this period of reflection, recognise when their own emotional issues are biasing their judgements. This may be particularly pertinent in cases involving race, gender and culture.

Of course, race, gender and culture are extremely important: they have the capacity (by dint of the powerful reactions they invoke in individuals) to obscure the child's needs as the adults use the case to flag up their own issues. Most recently, I saw this in a case of two African boys who had been fostered by a white woman for a considerable period of time. This had always been on the vague assumption that the real mother would, at some point, want the children back. It became a long drawn out process when attachments were being considered alongside racial issues. The case had black psychiatrists, white psychiatrists, and black and white social workers. The professionals became split off from each other with different professionals identified with a particular party in the case. Splitting means that strong feelings are held and the total picture can become obscured. The children became lost in this process, and the case went on for a considerable time until someone was able to look at the case as a whole, both systemically and analytically, with the children's needs at the top of the hierarchy. Culture, race and gender are clearly extremely important, but the emotional needs of children can so easily get lost. Each individual involved in a case needs to be thoughtful and have in mind his/her own agenda in relation to issues such as these.

How each deals with their own agenda, stress and trauma of the case will very much be related to their own earlier experiences. If one has developed a secure internal world (Bowlby 1988) with primarily supportive internalised relationships, then this can provide the internal capacity to explicitly reflect and digest both the experience and the emotional impact which can sustain them and help them make sense of their experiences. As has been explained earlier, this may have been with external help or with good clinical supervision. Clearly, the reverse is true. Those with insecure internal worlds will, at times, with certain material, find it unmanageable and unprocessable. The ways of avoiding emotional pain which are then used affect the objectivity of the individual which, in turn, can affect the already value-laden decisions being made. For example, if a person is made anxious and upset, it is easier to revert to clichés or stereotypes, such as patriarchal values or personal prejudices, on which to base thinking (King and Trowell 1992).

In one case recently, whilst giving evidence as an expert, one of the authors explained to the magistrates the reasons why the young boy in question would not be best placed in a boarding school at this time. The boy too had expressed a wish not to go to this type of school. The judge wholeheartedly agreed and told us how awful his own experience had been. At this point his evoked memories were such that it spilled over into the courtroom. It seems so hard for children in need to be heard. On this occasion, the judge agreed with the expert's view expressed, but it could have been an opposing view had he had a different experience of boarding school himself which may well have also influenced the final decision.

For the 'expert witness', the court experience itself can be daunting, as recalled by one of the authors. Attending my first court case, approaching the

Royal Courts of Justice, I can remember feeling anxiety paralleled in intensity only by medical finals. The entrance to the imposing building was obscured by cameras, crews and reporters crammed thirty deep on the pavement. Having negotiated this and the X-raying of bags, I found myself disorientated momentarily by the grandiosity and size of the building. Not knowing where to go, I wondered how this would have felt for a family travelling up from a different part of the country, perhaps never having been to London before, let alone to a court. I stood in a queue of lawyers with trolleys; then, having got to the front I asked where my case was to be heard. The clerk replied 'It's not on my list,' and looked away. I asked her to look again and this time I spotted it. She looked irritated, as did the queue behind me.

I was looking for Court 44, and then I realised that I had no idea how to locate it and had to requeue to ask for directions. Having located the court after several wrong turns and going up and down in several lifts, I realised I was extremely early and went for a coffee. Having got my tray, I then had to decide where to sit, by a notice that said 'advocates' or 'non-advocates' as a seating arrangement. One room was a sea of black suits, the other virtually empty, I was put in mind of apartheid notices seen on benches in South Africa. With no clues except my own emotions, I sat with the advocates, as I was nervous that I might otherwise have to sit with a family with whom I might be involved. It became clear from the people's looks from this part of the coffee bar that I was in the wrong 'camp'. Outside the courtroom, the different parties were sitting separately. They started to form their own little 'camps' which externally created the immediate impression of sides at war, different teams waiting to enter the fray. It became very clear in which camp one was allowed to sit. Those in attendance from outside the legal system did not interact at this point according to some unspoken rule. (The whole process began to feel like a game.) However, in each camp, the number varying with each case, there is at least one special dark-suited member who seems at ease moving from one camp to the other. Sometimes this is with whispered messages concerning the case, and at other times we are allowed to hear their exchanges of pleasantries to each other. I am reminded that outside this arena, some members of the camps have knowledge of each other in a context which is not about 'sides', their ease making it hard for them to understand the unease of the awaiting participants, who like myself, must be feeling very different from them. I am reminded further of how hard it is to understand the process of being a patient until in that situation oneself.

Often, for the expert witness, having taken up cases where a neutrality was thought to exist (by being instructed by all the parties), the experience outside the courtroom starts the process of one's understanding that the neutrality was only in relation to thinking about the needs of the child. The external result (the recommendations of the expert's report), places one in a 'side' position by the fact of what has been written. Neutrality does not really exist for the parents if one is writing about their child or their parenting capacity or for the individual as the expert. Outside the courtroom, the parents' emotions can be palpably felt. It is uncomfortable to be seated in a particular camp at this point. The visible formation of the sides now becomes a more recognisable format, those for the child(ren), those for parents, mother and father separately, and those for the local authority.

This persists in the adversarial state of the seating arrangements within the courtroom. The family or families, fathers or mothers – whatever sides exist in the case – sit separately. The row of lawyers seem more like a homogeneous group, often side by side. Each barrister or lawyer who will be acting in the case has, behind them, their solicitor. Then, behind them, perhaps, a junior, then their party, that is, mother, father, grandparent, local authority and guardian ad litem. The expert particularly, if instructed by several or all of the parties, slides into a seat but then realises they are in the 'wrong' place. There is an assumption by those familiar with the justice system that the expert knows what to do. The trouble is that we don't know what we don't know until it is happening!

The judge comes in and all have to rise at the clerk's command. The expert is called to the witness stand in the front and the oath is taken. Then, sometimes, one is asked whether one would like to sit or stand. This is presented as though once one course of action has been embarked upon, the other is no longer available as an option. I assumed that I could not change once I had indicated I wished to stand, silenced by the enormity of the oath, by the sensation of all eyes looking in my direction, by the intimidation of the stenographer, letting me know that every word is serious. The sudden understanding, hitherto not fully appreciated, is that this is a real court – albeit a family court. This instantly presents to everyone connected to it the concept of a trial in which the outcome, therefore, is a party who wins and a party who loses (Chapter 4). For a moment, one can feel on trial oneself (see Chapter 7 by Pozzi in this book), and there is a longing to escape or a determination to defend one's innocence, 'I've done nothing wrong'. Only with a deep breath does one recall, 'I am here as an expert, I am not on trial'.

However, although it is not a criminal court, parents often do have the feeling of being found 'guilty' if the court finds their parenting inadequate. This is not conducive for the child, who, whether she/he lives with her/his parents or not, still needs them in her/his life as the biological parents. Hopefully, they will not be alienated by the process to such an extent that they feel unable to comply with the level of contact that the child needs.

I am reminded of a recent lecture given to child psychiatrists entitled 'Giving Evidence in Court'. As the extremely eminent expert witness spoke, I became aware that what was being prepared for was an experience akin to a battle which had to be defended against. I became fascinated by the manner in which the child and her/his family became lost. I had been expecting, given the context in which I work, a lecture on the psychodynamic processes occurring in court; which would increase my capacity to think and keep the child in mind, whilst other professionals and families became inextricably wrapped in different positions. I was also hoping for ways to increase my capacity as an expert to understand the justice system as a whole.

However, the opening line was 'You must dress in a dark suit, not necessarily black' followed by the reminder that 'to stand is far more powerful than to sit'. Once dressed and standing correctly, we were advised that the opposing lawyer's opening gambit would be to discredit our authority. Strategies as to how they did this were then discussed, as were strategies on how we could deal with it. (It is not surprising that the court hearing rapidly ceases to be an inquisitorial process.) There then followed detailed descriptions on how to listen to barristers' questions and turn to speak to the judge when asked a question by a barrister. In practice, this latter suggestion is hard to do. It is against all known instincts and communication skills to direct an answer to a third party when the questioner is still maintaining eye contact with the respondent. The only comparable experience is when using an interpreter, with all the awkwardness that entails. It is compounded by the fact that during the response, the judge is often writing with her/his head down. While attending to this aspect of etiquette, we were reminded in the lecture to avoid eye contact with any of the relatives in attendance. 'Ask to consult your papers if you need time to think about your reply to the questions.' I remember thinking, what sort of system involved in trying to help understand what will affect a child's future could possibly not allow for saying 'I need time to think about it.' What sort of process is going on that thinking people are stopped from doing so?

Surely, this was what we should have been discussing, not the colour of suits and the tactics.

Consequently, the lecture did not help me much, except when the opening questions about qualifications started; there I was on familiar ground, qualifications over, the barrister asks the expert to look at the 'bundle' in front of her/him. I remember thinking that was an affectionate term for a small baby wrapped in blankets to such an extent that all that can be seen is the bundle; the baby hidden but implied within. For me, it was a metaphor for the lost child inside all the paperwork. The lawyers seem particularly attached to 'bundles' rather than documents. Perhaps it is easier to be in touch with a 'bundle' than with its occupant. The questions, at times, can feel like an assault course. It can make one feel one is not being seen or heard as one would wish, and, hence, not as helpful to the examination and discussion of the case as one might be. Similarly, a family entering a court might wonder how they could possibly be seen and heard.

On one occasion, having arrived early for a court case (which involved a considerable delay due to a heating breakdown), I was able to watch a case prior to becoming a witness. Two half-siblings, whose mother was in prison, were being fought for by their grandparents. One of the fathers had already been deemed unsuitable to care for both and the other was uninterested. There had been a substantial amount of work done by family therapists to assess the grandparents. Sitting in court, I observed one of the lawyers cross-examining a family therapist. It was a brutal interrogation. The barrister's aim seemed not to hear the concerns she had about the grandparents nor the positive qualities they had in their parenting capacity. Rather, the aim seemed to be to discredit any personal ability she may have had and her methods. Knowing the case, as he must well have done, it seemed a very unhelpful line of questioning and was pursued relentlessly for over an hour. As I arrived in the middle of this interrogation, the judge acknowledged my presence and said that he hoped I wouldn't 'get cold'. He had already informed the court in an irritable manner that he was not going to pursue the case in court if the heating continued to fail.

In the middle of this interview, the judge had to leave for a paper directions hearing which needed his signature. Upon his return, he displayed his irritability, saying the case would not continue until the heating was repaired.

As I entered the witness box I felt prepared, having seen this particular barrister's style, and was able to respond to his questioning by apologising for my inability to convey my meaning clearly and, perhaps, I could try to find another way of explaining it. I turned it around and suggested that he was not understanding due to the inadequacies of my answers. I was eventually given the space to explain my thinking to help the process. The emotional abuse of the children seemed to fill the courtroom so that hostility and blame attributed to each witness take over. Each case is such an emotional journey, the involvement starting long before the case begins. One thinks of the family, the child, and the best possible way forward. It is a defeating experience not to be able to inform thinking in this context; much time is lost in the adversarial style of questioning, with no increase in understanding (see Chapter 7).

The effect of the proceedings themselves can readily move from a position of feeling that one is in the position of informing a decision-making body as to the best outcome for the child, into being manoeuvred towards defending one's stance. Thinking seems to cease at times. It has been my experience that multicomplex issues can rapidly diminish to two-sided issues, the either/or position. For example, care order or no care order, contact or no contact. These polarised positions are fought for. It is as though the whole mind-set of the court is stuck on guilty/not guilty, consistent with the feeling of 'camps', 'sides' and 'teams' (see Chapter 4 for the service user's perspective). Inquiring after one case as to what was going on with the questions, the reply from the lawyer was, 'I have got to give the mother a day in court'.

This is not an uncommon statement from lawyers which in some ways illustrates the care dilemma and problem with the present system. Justice demands that the mother has 'her day in court', ie her cause be presented loudly. But this process generally further alienates the mother from those involved with her children; the situation becomes more hostile and acrimonious, so that the relationships after the hearing have been made even more adversarial.

Having done a lot of talking, the lips get dry to the point where the tongue feels it can no longer move. The lips start to stick together and enunciation proves extremely difficult. The new expert drinks water (if it is provided! – *Editor's note*) instead of moistening the lips. On one occasion, during a long stint in the witness box and having consumed too much water, I needed to be excused, but had no idea what the terminology for this was. Nevertheless, I was convinced that, given the nature and the process of the experience I had had thus far, there would definitely be a correct way of extricating oneself.

The presence of the families and the occasional older child affect the professional participants in the court process at both a conscious and unconscious level. Unless some degree of awareness and thought is given to this, the difficulties experienced by the family can be re-enacted within the court itself. (The young person may be present if they have independently instructed their own lawyer.) A recent case involved a 13-year-old boy, whose difficulty was that he was dangerously out of control at home and domineering and controlling in every other arena of his life, to the extent that we were in court about this issue. I felt I needed to ask for him to be excluded from the proceedings because information about the backgrounds of his parents was about to be discussed and he might find this extremely disturbing. With the skill that had brought him to the attention of the social services and, ultimately the court, he was allowed in court to watch the entire proceedings. This might have been the right decision, but his power and the achievement of remaining in the court and the impact the information might have on him was never alluded to. He sat with his lawyer in a black suit, and was indistinguishable from the lawyer; his excitement at being involved as a 'temporary lawyer' was evident. It severely limited what I was able to say about his mother and father, as one of the difficulties in expressing these comments in full would have been in his ability to use the information to further attack and overwhelm his parents with his new-found power. Thus, the way the proceedings were conducted mirrored precisely the family dynamic we were all struggling to resolve.

The expert involved in a case necessarily has an emotional investment in the outcome. The judge in the case conveys the impression that she/he maintains a right and proper neutrality. She/he is attributed with logical and thoughtful arguments. It has been my experience that they do seek clarity on points they feel need more elaboration. For example, a judge may say to the lawyers 'Are you finished with X?' Once the lawyers have agreed they have finished with X, the judge may say to the witness, 'I wish to ask you some questions' and after this then states, 'You are free to go'. It always seems odd that there is no slot for the question, 'Is there anything you would like to add to help us understand?'

The ending of the court proceedings is abrupt, which reminds one of the experience parents may have in 'ending' with their children, for example when the child is taken in care. Experts become involved with other cases and have other avenues on which to displace their emotions. Parents, though, are left with all that they have seen and heard together with the outcome. For them, the 'trial' will always mark their lives. The professionals go home. Presumably, many of the parents are left with overwhelming feelings of anger, which are projected onto agencies such as the social services. This is unhelpful for children, as they are often in the position of needing co-operation between their parents and the social services to implement care plans effectively.

In another case, a mother lost residence of her two sons to their father. She was devoted to her sons, but was unable to parent them adequately. One of her difficulties was her impulsive outbursts of anger when upset. The impact was so enormous on her and her anger so uncontainable towards the social services that she was unable, in the first instance, to hear that what was being proposed was a programme of increased contact which, if it went well, would amount to regular weekend contact. Instead, she focused on the fact that the initial contact sessions were to be supervised by the social services, with whom she was uncontrollably angry. It was only at a later stage, when another agency was able to supervise the contact, and time had lapsed since the end of the court case, that she and her sons were allowed contact. This was a very sad outcome for the boys.

Removing children from their families becomes emotionally harder for an expert to recommend as it has been clearer that the power of the courts to enforce local authority care plans seems absent. The future plan for the child starts after the court hearing and it is this that leaves the expert frustrated and bewildered, since so much time, effort and skill has gone into arriving at the recommendations following the assessment.

The 'end' of the trial is the antithesis of expectations. One's adrenaline in the witness box pounds away in the hopeful position and in the belief that your opinion is both right and acceptable. This excitement is contained in achieving what one feels is as emotionally correct for the child for that situation as possible. However, at the end, and out of the witness box, it rarely feels satisfactory. The local authority may or may not implement the recommendations and the practical problems are also immense, resources are limited and, frequently, a change in social worker means different views are introduced. Even when there is every intention to follow up the recommendations, a good substitute family or a vacancy in the appropriate institution may not be available (Thorpe and Clarke 1998). After a session in the witness box for the expert witness, there is a feeling of being left mentally exhausted, not from presenting one's expert opinion, but from the adversarial nature of the system. The outcome for the barristers appear as though it is another 'win/no win' situation.

Final reflection

But, if we return to our original questions (much as when one is writing a court report one presents the interviews and one's opinion then tries to answer the questions), first, how has the Act worked in practice and what has been its impact on the different professional groups. It would appear that, in many ways, social services departments have become more powerful, have more authority. And yet, their resources have been cut and they have been encouraged to adopt a more managerial style. The social worker organises packages of treatment for their clients and buys in services so that their involvement is less with the children or families. Once a care order is made, social services implement it as they see fit unless there is a return to court. Children and Families social services teams now cover duty, child protection and children looked after; general family case work has all but disappeared.

Child and Family mental health are involved in many more court cases: the Act paid attention to the emotional and psychological development of the child and mental health issues and so, perhaps, this was inevitable and a good thing. But, in addition, the increased involvement of guardians ad litem has been significant. The role of the GAL is both to represent the child and, hence, they often instruct experts, and they are also expected to review and comment on the social work practice. This has meant guardians have occupied very powerful positions both on behalf of children but also in their comments about the relevant social services department. Guardians are independent practitioners and they very frequently employ experts to help them in complex cases. The result has been a considerable growth in legal aid expenditure. Now this has led to questions being asked about the need to have guardians, perhaps they could be restricted or even dispensed with since social services departments are there to protect children and promote their welfare.

The official solicitor and his officers were expected to have less work but, in the event, the use of the official solicitor to act for the children in acrimonious divorce proceedings has led to a very considerable increase in their workload. This has led to a need to recruit more officers and hence considerable expense. There is currently a review of the role and functions of guardians ad litem, the official solicitors' office and court welfare officers, with the aim of reducing legal aid costs. The idea of children's interests being paramount and their voice being heard begins to seem less important, or so it would appear.

The impact on community health workers and general practitioners and the education system has been less, although they have continued to be required to give evidence and there are more complex long hearings.

The impact on the justice system has been considerable. The family division has expanded. Court time is constantly under pressure and the work for lawyers seems ample. The involvement of the justice system, the court, at each step with the introduction of directions hearings, means that the court has to approve every change and decide each small issue during the wait for the full hearing. These frequent brief hearings are expensive in legal fees, court time and professional time, and they repeat an adversarial experience for the family.

Second, how can we understand the process and the impact it has on children? Society has to have a system that can deal with conflict and aspects of our humanity that society would prefer not to know about or have to acknowledge. Social workers were expected to protect children and promote their welfare. They made mistakes, either didn't remove or did remove the child. Social workers lacked training and professional status and were seen to have failed. Perhaps doctors could have taken on the task but doctors, despite their higher status, longer training and research base, also made mistakes and were seen to have failed. The knights in shining armour were to be the legal system, lawyers, judges, the courts. There is intentionally a gender implication: social workers in Children and Families are predominantly female, paediatricians, child and adolescent mental health and health visitors are predominantly female. The legal system is predominantly male. But, now, the Family division is at least half female, and slowly, there are more women judges. Not surprisingly, questions are now being raised, not least by us in this chapter, about whether the legal system can do any better than medicine or social work. If we consider the psychodynamic processes, this makes complete sense. Powerful emotions are aroused by children in the adults around them. The adults also have to manage their own anger, pain and distress, as well as contain the child's feelings. Many adults cannot perform this task: the feelings are projected onto others around one person being seen as good on your side, another as your enemy to be hated and feared. This splitting by the family has an impact on the professionals around. No one discipline, no one person, can be subjected to and process these powerful feelings that are directed at and on to them (this is meant both consciously and unconsciously).

The only way to hold on to objectivity and rationality is to have a range of perspectives and a space to reflect and think about all the powerful emotions that are evoked by the child and the family. Only then can the least detrimental way forward begin to be clarified. Only then can it be recognised that no one discipline, no one person, can know the 'right' answer. The proposed decision or recommendation can only be the best one can do with the information available at that moment. Decisions have to be made. Children cannot wait – they need a settled place to live, good enough carers, education and trusting relationships. In France, the children's judges review their cases every six months so that decisions can be amended and progress monitored. Children are seen as the responsibility of the state, not the property of their families, but there is always the expectation that, except in extreme cases, they will return to or remain in contact with their families.

The impact on children of the system in England and Wales is that the social workers, doctors and, increasingly, the legal system, feel that somehow they are in the wrong, to blame or, at least, that the process is not right for children.

This, sadly, does seem to be correct. Many children still have to wait for long periods before their case comes to court. Once the case has been heard, they wait anything up to two years for the recommendations to be implemented and they have to survive in the middle of a circle of adults who are more angry and distressed than they were at the start of the process. In terms of their mental health, their emotional and psychological development, what occurs does nothing to promote this. Any adult around is likely to be caught up in the conflict and only rarely is there someone who can help the child understand both what has happened to them and the emotional state of their adults.

Finally, what could be done to improve the system? Children will be abused or neglected despite all the preventative work and family support. Parents will fight each other and divorce; children are inevitably caught at the centre of an emotional storm involving passions, love, hate, sexuality, hope, joy, shame, disgust and despair. Decisions about their futures need to be made to promote their welfare and protect them. It would seem that many cases do not need the whole range of professionals and the court system. There is a current vogue for family group conferences, a modification of the New Zealand Maori system, where the extended family and social network come together to devise arrangements for the child. In England and Wales, these family group conferences are being co-ordinated and organised from social services. This inevitably has changed how they are perceived, but many cases can arrive at a solution acceptable to all parties. Mediation is very much in vogue and is an integral part of the Family Law Act that applies to parents divorcing. Specialist mediation is being used in public child care law cases and there are pilot studies (King, Roberts and Trowell 1999). What does seem important in all of these is to involve the child or young person, to hear their views; the adults must decide but the wishes of the child and their understanding of the reasons for the decisions is essential. The child, the parents and the professionals all need to own and accept the decisions.

Perhaps one day, instead of social workers, health workers and the legal system all struggling together, or separately, to be the agency that can manage these cases, there will be multidisciplinary teams with regular group consultation and supervision to assist in grasping and understanding the emotional dynamics in the family and in the professional network. Then, perhaps, the child in her/his family, in her/his social setting, will be understood, the problems and difficulties faced and possible solutions implemented, monitored and reviewed regularly.

However, there is no question that the law is vital and has a crucial part to play in the lives of some children. In some cases, only the authority of the law can make the parents and the local authority undertake the mental and emotional work required to really think about the children. As indicated, this is because this much-needed work becomes skewed and results in a battle to protect or defend oneself and one's actions rather than a working together to consider the child(ren) when the emotions are very intense and the situation complex and dangerous.

The need to prove or disprove facts and gather 'evidence', rather than focusing on the best way forward for the child, consumes time, energy and financial resources. Recently, in a case with several children, the lengthy hearing with the involvement of many parties and experts resulted in the local authority having used up so much of its budget that there was little left to spend on the placement and support the children and parents needed. This does not seem a good use of resources. But, the need to 'prove' who had harmed the children and whether they were harmed or not was important. It appears very difficult for the current system to arrive at a balance between gathering evidence and decision making and agreeing ways forward. This, in turn, leads to the greatest frustration – lengthy and thorough assessments are undertaken. We recognise this will be a slow process but that it is important to work towards as full an understanding as possible. Considering recommendations for the future, we suggest a review system that can look at the assessments and consider how the decisions of the court and the subsequent events have been of benefit to the child or not. In the short term, such a review of a case involving say the expert, the guardian ad litem, or the judge, would make proper use of all the money, thought, expertise and debate that has been invested in the family. This would use the clinical model based on:

- implementing an intervention
- reviewing it
- modifying the intervention in the light of what has occurred.

It follows a feedback loop approach and would be a useful model with growing and developing children (see recommendations in Chapter 4).

A worrying issue that is more difficult to consider is the position of the parents. Very often, if they are troubled with issues in their own past, they seem to be disadvantaged in the court, since the situation is so adversarial as previously indicated. For example, a parent with limited intellectual capacities, past abuse, mental health problems or where there has been alcohol or drug misuse, may often come to court with a history of court attendance or, at the least, problems with 'authority' figures. Very often they have lawyers who have limited child care experience and so the advice they are given and the style of their advocate does not help them to either understand or to communicate. Where they have good legal representatives the situation can be dramatically different. The outcome can be beneficial to the children because the parents have understood the process and, hopefully, can support and accept the outcome. Parents need well-trained lawyers in the childcare field and access to expert advice.

Children need the court system to be in place, not just for the few cases that are heard, but so that they are aware, as with Child Line, that they are taken seriously. As illustrated in the public law arena, we still have a long way to go for the system to be administered both in the child's best interest and with the child's needs as paramount. The French system of children's judges when the child, the parents or a professional can seek an audience and where an informal, inquisitorial style is adopted, could be considered, but the work-load and responsibility for the judges, given their prolonged and very close involvement, may result in problems, particularly if they receive little training in family dynamics and self-reflection. The children's panels in Scotland are another model where the division between adjudication and disposal clarifies the task. The two-tier system of the sheriffs' court and the panel can be very useful. In Flanders, the confidential doctor system, with built-in mediation and the judge as the final adjudicator, also has advantages. Families are more willing to seek help, as with the French system, and more cases are dealt with where the court is not involved.

Attempts to produce a better system may well include elements of any or all of these. What seems to be important, though, is the recognition of the need to be constantly reconsidering how best to reduce the secondary abuse of children by the system that is intended to protect them and to promote their welfare within the community so that prevention and early intervention can be as effective as possible.

Acknowledgements

Grateful thanks are due to Roshan Mewawalla for her patient secretarial support.

References

Bowlby, J. (1988) *A Secure Base: Clinical Applications of Attachment Theory.* London: Routledge.

Cooper, A., Hetherington, R., Bairstow, K., Pitts, J. and Sprigg, A. (1995) *Positive Child Protection: A View from Abroad.* Russell House Publishing.

Department of Health (1991) *The Children Act 1989.* London: HMSO.

Department of Health (1991) *Working Together Under the Children Act 1989.* London: HMSO.

Department of Health, Social Services Inspectorate (1994) *The Child, the Court and the Video.* London: HMSO.

Department of Health (1995) *Child Protection; Messages from Research* London: HMSO.

Hetherington, R., Cooper, A., Smith P. and Wilford, G. (1997) *Protecting Children: Messages from Europe.* Lyme Regis, Russell House Publishing.

King, M. (1997) *A Better World for Children.* London and New York: Routledge.

King, M. and Trowell, J. (1992) *Children's Welfare and the Law – The Limits of Legal Intervention.* London: Sage

King, M., Roberts, M. and Trowell, J. (1999) *Alternative Dispute Resolution Report – Specialist Child Care Mediation.* ADR report. London: DOH.

La Fontaine, J. (1990) *Child Sexual Abuse.* London: Polity Press.

Plotnikoff, J. and Wolfson, R. (1995) *Prosecuting Child Abuse.* London: Blackstone Press Ltd.

Schofield and Thoburn (1996) *Child Protection: The Voice of the Child in Decision Making.* IPPR.

Thorpe, M. and Clarke, E. (eds) (1998) *Divided Duties – Care Planning for Children within the Family Justice System.* Bristol: Family Law Jordans Publishing.

Wall, N. (1997) *Rooted Sorrows.* Bristol: Family Law Jordans Publishing.

CHAPTER 7

The Experience of a Professional Witness in Court
Wading with a Child Against the Tide

Maria Pozzi

Introduction

In this chapter I share with the reader my experience as a professional witness in court. I had agreed to go to court to support a 7-year-old boy's residence with his mother, against the father's application to have his son move in with him. As a child psychotherapist I had seen the mother and child together for three years in a Child and Family Consultation Clinic in the north of England, following parental separation. My opinion was that — at the time of the court hearing — mother and child had a good and healthy enough relationship, party due to the therapeutic work they had done. Here I am going to suggest that Leslie and his mother had been the unfortunate victims of the judicial system.

Background

The names and facts have been carefully disguised to preserve confidentiality. At the time of writing this piece, Leslie, as I shall call this 7-year-old boy, had to give up living with his mother and move to live with his father following the outcome of court proceedings. All his life he had lived with his mother and his older brother, who had recently married, and for the past three years he had seen his father at weekends and during holidays. He was a lively, sturdy, competent, sociable, intellectually bright and emotionally well-adjusted little boy, but despite this evidence the court had decided to accept his father's view that Leslie's mother was a damaging figure. But what had gone wrong?

In my capacity as a child psychotherapist, specialising in psychoanalytic psychotherapy with parents and children under five, I began to see Leslie and his mother three years before this court hearing and following Leslie's father leaving their home. Before the father left, his mother had given up a number of activities she had enjoyed, to ease the financial pressure on their family life. Needless to say, when father left, both mother and child were in a state of shock. Leslie was no longer the happy child he had been, his mother recounted. He had turned to play-acting fictitious characters of either Superman or the tough guy, omnipotently believing that the world was in his power. Alternatively he acted as if he was the daddy. In this way he had managed to protect himself from the rage, bewilderment, abandonment and sadness about his father's sudden disappearance from home. Mother, on her part, was very distraught, fluctuating between depression, despair and rage, accusing her ex-husband and other people in authority of not understanding or supporting her enough. In the following three years, the situation had improved in all areas of their life, due – amongst many factors – to their capacity to use counselling, to the child's strong character and to mother's insight and acceptance of parental guidance. Mother was also determined to re-emerge from the depth of despair and from the early dead-end path she had taken. Nevertheless, the accusation that she was a damaging mother, who was jeopardising her son's future development by her own strong and angry personality, remained unchanged for many of the professionals involved. When the father applied for a Residence Order to have his child live with him, his request was granted by the court.

Many of 'the factors to which the court must particularly have regard when considering whether to make an order' (Children Act 1989) – in this case a Residence Order in favour of the father – were not properly considered here, in my opinion. For example, the first one is the 'ascertainable wishes and feelings of the child concerned' considered in the light of his age and understanding. Leslie was a bright, articulate and intellectually advanced 7-year-old who was able to have a genuine and critical idea of what he wished for himself. In the course of a few individual sessions with myself he pleaded openly to go on living with his mother and to continue seeing his father at weekends. He wanted to see a lot of his mother, he said repeatedly. This was a completely unprompted declaration which struck and deeply moved me. However, when evidence of this plea was given in court with the child's consent, no notice was taken of it. The guardian ad litem (GAL), who supposedly has to 'represent the child's interest in the court', unfortunately responded to Leslie's request to live with his mother by maintaining that Leslie had been excessively influenced by his mother's feelings and by loyalty to her. In my view Leslie was very able to express anger and disagreement with his mother without being taken over by a fear of losing or hurting her. Therefore he was not dominated by a loyalty conflict but knew his mind clearly.

The 'checklist' in the Children Act (1989) continues, to cover 'the physical, emotional and educational needs' of the child, 'the likely effect' on the child 'of any change in his circumstances', any harm which he has suffered or is at the risk of suffering, and the capacity of his parents to meet the child's needs. Leslie had to be uprooted from the very safe home and village environment where he was born. He was well known there and loved not only by his mother and grandparents but also by the people in the community. He was popular and successful in his friendships and at school, where he was doing well academically and socially. All this seemed to be the effect of good parenting and satisfactory maternal care. Was it really for the good of the child to wrench him away from all these and to plunge him into an unknown and new set of experiences, even though in the company of his beloved father?

It seemed to me that the child was thoroughly caught in the bitter, adversarial relationship between the parents which – unfortunately – was not resolved by either the social or legal agencies involved. In my view, the agencies found themselves acting out a split-off aspect of the controversy between the parents: good and bad parenting were the two major aspects at stake. Those two agencies thought that Leslie's mother was a bad mother, while the mother thought that she was 'good enough'. Sadly, in the months and years following the removal of the child from the maternal home, Leslie appeared more torn and pulled between the parents than ever. He also developed skin problems and other symptoms of a growing psychological discomfort. He continued to plead to go back to live with his mother when he was with her or his grandmother and even at school.

Court experience

I had been asked by the guardian ad litem to meet him to express my view of Leslie and his care. I agreed to this and expected to find a person with whom to share views honestly and openly. However, I found someone who already had a very precise and, in my view, rigid opinion about the situation and who tried to find proof to confirm his opinion. It was at this point that I decided to go to court, at the formal request of the mother's solicitor, and I withdrew my statement to the guardian ad litem. However, he continued to quote from it inaccurately in his document presented to the judge.

At that time I was not at all familiar with the adversarial system in use in the UK, nor with the courtroom's 'games' which, at times, do not seem to be in the service of the child's welfare. My preparation for the court hearing was based on consultations with both a senior child psychotherapist colleague and with my client's solicitor, in the short available time before the hearing. However, I had not imagined the sort of cold war I was to enter as I stood in the witness box, nor the impact of the cross-examination and relentless attempts to put me down.

My experience in court was gruelling and hair-raising, though I know that other child psychotherapists have had different experiences. They were heard in court and felt that the child's best interests were safeguarded (Baylis 1993, p.11). I had chosen to go to court as I felt I had to speak up on behalf of this boy and to support the good-enough mothering that he had been and was receiving. Since it was my first experience as a professional witness in court, I was aware of my anxieties, lack of experience and of how difficult it would have been to think there and then. In discussion with a senior colleague, who had longstanding court experience, I was helped to highlight some strong points in favour of the child's welfare, to reduce my fear and to support the evidence that Leslie had received good enough care from his mother. I was also aware that, as I had never met the father, I was more likely to have a partisan view. Hence I took advice and strived to be as objective as possible. This case was particularly complicated because two professional witnesses, who had known the mother and child thoroughly through the years, were strongly opposed by social services, the guardian ad litem and the court psychiatrist who had all reacted without understanding the mother's anxieties about the possibility of losing her child. Prior to the court hearing I had become aware both of the clashes of personalities between the mother and some of the above-mentioned professionals and of the unconscious group dynamic of the whole network. The network reflected and was caught up in the parental split between good and bad parenting and lost a professional stance. As I had strived to be in a neutral position, to rise above both parties and to speak on behalf of the child's best interests, I had become the recipient of the confidence of some professionals involved in the dispute.

I was told of the disturbing effect of this case on some highly skilled professionals who literally had nightmares about it.

My evidence was given in court in the afternoon of the third day of a four-day-long hearing. Before entering the hearing-room, the mother's barrister told me in a resigned and hopeless tone that nothing would change things: the judge had already made up his mind to remove the child from the mother. A sense of tiredness and futility was floating around the room. It was hard for me to keep a sense of purpose in that atmosphere and when defeat seemed unavoidable. I had also been told that the counsel for the father and the judge wanted to prove that: (a) Leslie had been taken to too many therapists and specialists unnecessarily; and (b) mother had done so in order to get some help for herself, thus damaging her son. This was their belief and proof was being searched for as they began to question me.

Reder, Lucey and Fellow-Smith (1993) write:

> The court's philosophy is not inquisitorial but adversarial: one version of events is proposed and then opened to critical counter-proposal, presenting a thesis and antithesis, using the witnesses as the vehicle through which they are presented to the judge. It is for the judge to construct a balanced meaning in making the final judgement. Thus meanings are not co-constructed and the witness is not an equal in negotiating the process of the communication. (Reder *et al.* 1993, p.3)

I soon realised that the content of my opinions was challenged by the father's barrister who tried to discredit me as a professional, as the above authors put it so clearly. They also write:

> Any phenomenon can be understood differently when described from a contrasting perspective: a mother who puts her child into care might either be seen as abandoning that child or ensuring that s/he receives adequate parenting, albeit from someone else. In court overall meaning can be transformed by the selections of different words, or by posing alternative explanations for events. (Reder *et al.* 1993, p.8)

My opinion was that the mother had acted very sensibly in asking for help at a time of severe stress for the family and her child. However, a contrary psychiatric view of a greater expert than me was quoted. This said that if a child is labelled as having a problem and taken to therapy, that child will behave accordingly and be stigmatised. What did I think about that? How could I disagree? But indeed this seemed to me to be off the point and only intended to discredit me and to score points for the father's counsel. The reality was that the child was not being labelled but was really behaving anxiously and showing signs of disturbance, after he was suddenly abandoned by his father leaving home, and this was my reply to the father's barrister.

I learnt, in a painful way, that in court they use this well-known and accepted strategy to discredit the professional witness to the point of obliterating the child's welfare. King and Trowell describe this as a common tactic among lawyers – to 'discredit the witness's recommendation versus the learned professor's writings and opinions' (King and Trowell 1992, pp.94–95). Little of this had to do with my clinical judgement about the child's welfare and needs, which was based on years of work and understanding of Leslie and his mother. What mattered was to give a super performance in the legal arena, which I was not able to do.

I was also asked if I was treating the mother or her child. In my written statement to the court, I had explained clearly the sort of parent–child counselling I had been doing. This, in my view, had been very necessary and helpful to both mother and child. However no one seemed to be interested or curious to find out about this sort of work, nor could I mobilise their interest. Their agenda had already been set up a long time beforehand. While I was giving evidence, it seemed as if I were not 'I' but an incompetent dummy, who was there to be punched down because I had provided mother and child with counselling. To think, to wade through the confusion, to hold onto my sense of purpose, professional integrity, belief, and to speak some sense, was hard in that atmosphere.

King and Trowell highlight an impossible dilemma for parents. They risk losing their children in the adversarial contest if they admit problems in court. But if they deny or minimise these difficulties 'they risk falling into the clinical trap of being branded as parents who refuse to admit the existence of problems' (King and Trowell 1992, p.51). From my standpoint as a clinician I experienced a similar dilemma. I realised that the GAL's point of view was diametrically opposed to mine and the mother's. The fact that she had asked for help and guidance at a difficult time was but an indication of both her sense of responsibility towards her child and of her humbleness and realism. However, it was interpreted by the court as an admission of failure.

Moreover, I was aware that I had not said anything about Leslie and how he was managing his present life, his learning at school, and his relationships with his separated parents, his peers and his teachers. I had sent a very detailed and explanatory report to the mother's solicitor prior to the court hearing. However, in court no one had asked me anything about this child. Finally, my feeble 'protest' addressed to the judge came out: 'Your Honour, I have not been given a single chance to speak about the child, to express my view on Leslie's behalf and on what seems to me to be in his best interest.' Then and only then the judge granted me an opportunity to air my view about the child, which I did – but to no avail. Also the mother's barrister stood up at last, as if he, too, was regaining some potency. That was the only moment when I felt I was not there alone. I left the court feeling like a lame dog, a repeatedly battered child, a complete failure.

More traps in the system

In my view, neither the social services, the father, nor the GAL had been able to really focus on Leslie, nor to see the evidence provided by this well-balanced boy. A child psychiatrist who was employed by the GAL had also expressed her view about Leslie in a telephone conversation with me. In her report to the judge she suggested that Leslie was a well-adjusted and healthy child at present but at risk of becoming a rebellious adolescent. The counsel for the father tried to demonstrate the dangers of the maternal involvement with Leslie when he would enter adolescence. They could not see that, despite some not uncommon difficulties in the mother's personality, she had achieved good enough results with Leslie.

Some of the people the mother had approached at moments of distress – in social services and health services – had not been able to deal with her requests, needs and difficulties as she did not present herself as one of their typical clients. Unfortunately, the mother fell in between two stools as on one hand she was a knowledgeable woman, a professional herself, a verbally articulate, challenging, intellectual and psychologically minded person. She was seen as a threat to other professionals involved, who became antagonistic to her. On another hand she, herself, had turned to social services and the local child guidance for help because she did not have the financial resources to get private help for her son and for herself. She entered, without being one, into the usual group of poor clients of the social services department who are more likely to be placed on the child protection register or find themselves having to defend their parental rights in court. It is well known that – as King and Trowell write – it is very rare for courts, police or social services to be involved with wealthy families. These tend to 'take evasive or defensive measures … at the slight hint of some unwelcome intervention' (King and Trowell 1992, p.24). We could say that Leslie's mother fell between these two groups of clients and the social services and legal agencies, too, got caught up in an unusual situation. They did not understand the mother's predicament, or contain her projections, but colluded with her and overreacted to her. They eventually managed to disempower her by taking her child away. They were hoping to silence and defeat her, as she was also perceived as a threat.

King and Trowell write:

> Our complaint is rather that in this difficult area lawyers and the judiciary tend to apply simple models of mental illness which lead either to their minimising the effects on children, because there is no evidence of physical harm or neglect or to their exaggerating the immediate danger to the child.
>
> The complexities, the subtle individual and family differences, tend to be flattened in the legal process.
>
> In court there is a proneness for judges and magistrates to be swayed by immediate impressions and to discount or underplay the importance of lengthy written reports. (King and Trowell 1992, pp.49–53)

In my opinion the unconscious wish to destroy what was perceived as 'the bad mother' had taken over the professionals' capacity to think clearly, to integrate observable facts and to act accordingly. Sadly, Leslie had been suffering and still is as he continues to pine to be with his mother and to show signs of distress at a psychosomatic level since he is only superficially settled with his father and in his new school.

Conclusion

In this chapter I have highlighted some aspects of how the court functions, based upon both my experience as a professional witness and on my reading. I have questioned whether the present adversarial judicial system fosters the welfare of children and the affirmation of the truth and have concluded that there can be an abuse of power in social responsibility when we look at the outcome of many court cases involving children.

In court we are faced with a different version of the truth. King and Trowell write that the legal and historical truth searched for by the court is concerned mainly with managing parental conflicts and with conveying moral messages to the outside world about both parental behaviour towards the children and the intrinsic fairness of the legal process (King and Trowell 1992, pp.130–131). The clinic's version of the truth is rich with complexities, ambiguities and, as in the case presented here, based on a deep knowledge of mother and child taken individually, in relationship to each other and to their external world. This version of the truth has the child at the centre, not the parental conflicts nor the court prestige.

However, it seems to me that in the fragmentation of the concept of truth in its different versions, an ethical value is also at stake. The truth, ie the welfare of the child in his relationship with himself, with his family and wider social world, is lost because it has been subjected to interests of legal, economic and power-driven nature.

I have argued that Leslie was a healthy child while living with his mother and that he has suffered and continues to suffer from a miscarriage of justice. King and Trowell write that courts 'need to attribute blame' and find it hard 'to promote fairness and justice for the innocent'. The emphasis is placed on winning or losing the child, not on an open discussion and decision made in the best interests of the child. This is due to the nature of the legal training and on the fact that English and American laws 'allow for sudden disqualification of parents through the removal of all rights' (King and Trowell 1992, p.53).

Solicitors' firms are well aware that highly professional people are called to be witnesses, only to leave the witness box having been denigrated and crushed, bewildered by aggressive barristers and frustrated that no one seemed interested in their expertise (Langdon-Down 1997). Some companies have now started to run training courses for would-be witnesses to learn the ropes of court games, to become confident, be able to get the information across and thus to help the court and also their clients (Solon 1997).

More recently, in September 1995, Lord Justice Matthew Thorpe organised a multidisciplinary conference at Dartington Hall, where different professionals – psychoanalytic practitioners and child psychotherapists, judges and lawyers, directors of social services, guardians ad litem, researchers and senior civil servants – were brought together to promote debate and discussion (Wall 1997). It was a successful and collaborative venture, Kenrick writes, as the President of the Family Division's interdisciplinary committee and the committee itself 'showed both a real interest and concern for the welfare of the children, who enter the legal processes of the Family Division courts' (Kenrick 1997, pp.14–17) and a willingness to work together with the mental health professionals (Kenrick 1997).

Initiatives of co-operation with child psychotherapists, who are skilled and trained in understanding the deep layers of children's minds, seem to be spreading. We need a wider awareness, a knowledge of the court system and an understanding of unconscious individual and group dynamics at play as well as psychoanalytic psychotherapy to become a necessary requirement in training psychiatrists, judges, guardians ad litem, social workers, etc. Only then we can hope for the interest and welfare of children to become truly central in court procedures and to reduce the abuse of power when we have social responsibilities.

Acknowledgements

I would like to thank my child psychotherapist colleagues Lisa Miller and Jenny Kenrick, Judge Alex Layton and the editors for their ideas and support before, during and after going to court as well as with writing this chapter.

References

Baylis, M. (1993) 'Being an expert witness'. *Bulletin of the Association of Child Psychotherapists,* September 10–11.

Kenrick, J. (1997) 'The president of the family division's interdisciplinary committee and Highgate House conference', September 1997. *Bulletin of the Association of Child Psychotherapists 73,* 14–17.

King, M. and Trowell, J. (1992) *Children's Welfare and the Law.* London: Sage Publications.

Langdon-Down, G. (1997) 'Sharpening up the expert witness'. *Financial Times,* 15 March.

Reder, P., Lucey, C. and Fellow-Smith, E. (1993) 'Surviving cross-examination in court'. Unpublished manuscript, available for consultation, c/o the editors.

Solon, M. (1997) *The Expert Witness in Court. A Practical Guide.* London: Shaw and Sons.

The Children Act (1989) The Introductory Guide for NHS. Department of Health.

Wall, N. (1997) *Rooted Sorrows: Psychoanalytical Perspectives on Child Protection, Assessment, Therapy and Treatment.* Bristol: Family Laws Jordan Publishing.

CHAPTER 8

The Betrayed Truth

Maggie Lane

Why *shouldn't* children and young people in the care system be abused by it?

This might appear a preposterous question, especially coming from myself as I am an ex-service user and a survivor of childhood sexual, physical and emotional abuse. But why is it such a preposterous question?

After all, is it not possible that these victims of abuse are not really affected by their traumatic experiences? Is it not also quite possible that they can carry on into adulthood with very few problems which are associated with their past? If the outcome doesn't turn out right it is because they were already troubled children and there is only so much the profession can do for them.

Now, I hope you can see that I am talking nonsense and that I do not agree with the above statement at all – and I am sure that if I did there would be many good and truly dedicated social workers who would argue that point with me. In fact I am quite sure that there would be some professionals who would be prepared to lynch me for the statement that I have just made.

Well, why is this?

There is more than one answer here. One is that there are many good social work professionals out there, but another one is that it is much easier to challenge one (so-called) self-opinionated young person than it is to tackle a massively corrupt industry such as the care system.

If only we could all stand together and demand that children and young people who are in the care system get the same rights as children and young people who do not live away from home, then surely we can and will make a change for the better.

You may feel that my argument has no basis. However, then why, after many local and several national inquiries between 1985 and 1992 such as *Children in the Public Care* and *Choosing with Care* (see Utting 1997), has there just had to be in 1997 another safeguards review conducted by Sir William Utting, *People Like Us*? And why after so much legislation on children's rights is there still a massive risk of abuse to children and young people in the care system?

One of the most crucial pieces of legislation on children's rights is the Children Act 1989, which was implemented in 1991. This has had a massive impact on looked after young people's lives, though admittedly it does need some revision – for instance, time and time again it is argued that local authority powers should become duties. In my opinion one of the best and the most powerful influences on children's rights is the United Nations Convention on the Rights of the Child, which was formally adopted (subject to some reservations) by the United Kingdom on 16 December 1991. In so doing it undertook to make the Convention widely known to children and adults.

The Convention covers four broad themes:

- protection
- participation
- survival
- development.

Its underlying principles emphasise the importance of the child's welfare; the child's right to communicate their views; and the child's right to be allowed freedom of expression, thought and association. Also emphasised are the child's rights to be free from discrimination, inhumane treatment, unlawful restrictions of liberty and all forms of sexual, physical and mental violence; the right to information, education and health care; and the right to have these rights made widely known, to themselves and others.

At the end of the day, though, they are only great pieces of legislation and until the plight which faces young people in care, such as the constant threat of abuse, discrimination, lack of education and unlawful restrictions is addressed, this is all that they will remain. If these pieces of legislation were adhered to and implemented properly then it would be much harder to get away with treating children in such ways.

I would like to refer back to my first question: 'Why shouldn't children and young people in the care system be abused by it?' Let me now apologise for asking this question and explain why I asked it. The reason is that as a care-experienced person, especially one who has lived in institutional settings, children's homes, residential schools, etc., I find that this appears to be the general attitude that comes across to us from a lot of quarters, including teachers, social workers and the general public. I do not know exactly where the national in-care magazine got its name, but I can tell you confidently that at some time in a looked after young person's life, whether they are fostered, in children's homes, in residential schools or in family placements, whether they are accommodated on full care orders or in respite care, they have all thought, '*Who Cares?*'

Here are a few quotes from other care-experienced young people:

You feel that nobody wants you …

… Passed around like a package. You feel very isolated and lonely, and don't get enough support.

Social workers and team managers right up to directors cover up mistakes and it is hard to get them to admit. It is so wrong they are supposed to care.

You complain about your parents being cruel but when you're not living with them you'd often prefer the cruel things to being fostered.

At first it was OK – I was just pleased not to be beaten and used in bed. But then these things happened while I was in care also.

The question should of course be: 'Why *should* children and young people in the care system be abused?' Could the answer be one of the following?

- All children and young people who are in care are criminals.
- Nearly all children in care have already been abused.
- Most of the children that go into care are there because they have been in some sort of trouble.
- Children are in care because their parents do not want them.
- They are troubled and troublesome youngsters.
- Hooligans, that's what they are.

Is it possible that one or all of these statements answer the question?

No, because none of them are answers. They are all excuses, and no excuse can ever justify the abuse of power which constantly occurs in the care system. I can sincerely tell you that I have heard every one of these excuses over the years of working with young people in care and also whilst I was in care.

You might think that these statements have come from ignorant and uneducated people, but I assure you this would be a wrong assumption. These statements come from people in responsible positions, such as heads of education departments, teachers, police chief inspectors, social workers, directors of charities and last, but definitely not least, reporters.

If these people ever tried to back up their excuses with evidence they would find themselves in an unwinnable situation as none of these statements are derived from fact. They are negative comments inspired by negative attitudes and are aimed at an easy target – isolated children and young people. Society's indifference to the abuse of power over such vulnerable young people makes these ignorant people believe they are right. In a so-called civilised society the abuses should never happen in the first place, let alone continue.

Well, unfortunately, it is time for more questions. They are questions which have been asked time and time again yet never seem to get answered. Nor does anyone ever answer for the crimes committed against children and young people in care other than a small minority of abusers such as Frank Beck and Tony Latham, whose crimes against children were so appalling that there was no other option than for them to be made accountable. I cannot remember any local authorities being charged with negligence, or the police criticised for not investigating complaints against staff properly. In the case of Beck, for example, it was assumed that the young people who were making allegations of neglect and abuse were unmanageable children who Beck was doing a good job of controlling. The truth is that the agencies appear not to have cared what Beck was doing with his so-called regression therapy as long as it worked, or seemed to be working.

There are essentially two key questions which I, and I believe a great many others, yourselves probably included, want answering:

1. When is abuse in the care system going to stop?

2. What do we have to do to stop it?

As no one else seems to be coming forward with the answers to these questions, then I will give you my views.

In answer to the first question: it is unlikely that abuse in the care system will ever stop of its own accord, and even if there were radical changes it would take a very long time.

As for the second question, I am very pleased to say that the government appears to have taken the Utting safeguards review seriously in its response, *Ending a Legacy of Abuse* (Department of Health 1998). It is a very radical response, and could finally lead to a long-term solution to a long-term problem. Obviously the measures that the government will be enforcing will need time to work and we will not see the results just yet, but it is a start.

There are twenty principal recommendations, and over one hundred and thirty other recommendations. One of the most important ones, I feel, for the prevention of abuse in the care system is the establishment of a new criminal records system to improve and widen access to police checks on people intending to work with children and other vulnerable groups, as a first step towards a 'one-stop shop' sharing of the lists held by the Department of Health and the Department for Education.

The government must also remember Sir William Utting's (1997) criticism of the criminal justice system:

> Criminal justice is not working in a way which protects children from abuse. Convictions are few in relation to the cases that are investigated ... Notification of people unfit to work with children which depends heavily on convictions for criminal offences, loses much of its effectiveness. (Utting 1997, p.3).

So what can we do now?

I cannot answer this question fully but I can make a few suggestions to challenge the system. One of the ways (and possibly the best way) of doing this would be for us all to recognise the practice of 'careism' and abolish it, and promote a non-careist ethos in our workplaces. Mike Lyndsay came up with the term 'careism', which he defined as a prejudice placed upon looked after young people simply on the grounds of their care status.

Lyndsay believes, and I am in full agreement with him on this matter, that:

> If any decision or action could not be justified in respect of any young person then it often represents an example of careism to insist that it is acceptable in respect of young people in care. (Lindsay 1996, p.1)

A prime example of this is the use of control and restraint. In relation to my earlier point, the UK adopted the UN Convention in 1991 which states clearly in article 37: 'Children have a right not to be punished cruelly or in a way that would belittle them ...' Yet it still continues in the system which sought to rescue them from just such experiences.

Obviously there is no one way of safeguarding children and young people in care; we need to be making improvements all the time. Another suggestion of mine would be for us to insist that local authorities do not just listen to the criticisms that young people in their charges are making, but that they actually take on board these criticisms and take some action in order to halt their failures.

Childline (1996) defines emotional abuse as: 'when children are not given love, approval or acceptance.' In my experience this happens more often than not in the care system, and young people suffer this probably every day of their young lives whilst in care, and especially when leaving the care system.

There are improvements constantly going on in the care industry and I believe that after-care services have improved immensely over the last five years. However, the improvements are not good enough. People's lives are being severely damaged by the lack of care and thought which is put into them maintaining independent lives.

A great teacher of mine in this field was, again, Mike Lindsay when we carried out training for First Key. He taught me that most young people who leave their family homes at the average age of 22½ years do not move into independence, as young people leaving care do. They move into inter-dependence, as they still have mum or dad or both, sisters and brothers, aunts, uncles, cousins, friends, neighbours, etc.

Not only is the age difference massively unfair, since the average age of care leavers is 16½ years, but so are the circumstances in which they leave: 99.5 per cent of young people from families who do leave home between the ages of 16 and 19 are living with other people whereas many young care leavers, by contrast, find themselves isolated in bed and breakfast accommodation with no or very little support. Some are lucky (if that's what you can call it) and get flats of their own, though this arrangement has a tendency to break down, and quite a number of young care leavers find themselves homeless within months of leaving care.

Now, to this you might say if they are under 17 years old they can get a residential bed for a few nights. But why would they want to go back to the care system, the one which put them in that predicament in the first place, knowing that the cycle will probably only begin again?

It is now time to act on these matters as I think it is fair to say that many young people (and let us remember that the Children Act defines people under the age of eighteen years old as children) leave the care system more at risk than when they are initially taken into care.

In *Leaving Care* (1986), Stein and Carey advised us that:

> ... a group of young people regarded as being in need of care and control up to the age of sixteen, seventeen or eighteen are catapulted into a position of greater vulnerability than that of other young people their age. (Stein and Carey 1986, p.157)

This was stated some years ago now, yet nothing major has changed. When it comes to leaving care, as with everything else people have advised, recommended suggested and so forth, but there has been very little action. We do not need to reinvent the wheel; it has all been done before. Yet we still face an up-hill battle. If we make sure that all the good suggestions and recommendations are taken on board our task will be a lot easier.

I do not want to leave you on a note of despair; rather I would like to leave you on a ray of hope. But before I do this I ask that you see this writing as more than just a chapter in a book. These are children's, young people's and older people's lives – please let us listen to the changes they want us to make. I know they are called service users, but at the end of the day we are not talking about their consumer rights, we are talking about their basic *human rights!*

My final thought is this. We now have a new government, and after only a short time they seem to have decided to take the plight of children and young people in care seriously. They seem far more interested in these young people than their predecessors appeared to be, as we can see from their response to the Utting review. I was delighted when I read Frank Dobson's speech:

> Too many children taken into care to protect and help them have received neither protection nor help. Instead they have been abused and molested. Many more have been let down, ignored, shifted from place to place, school to school and often simply turned out to fend for themselves when they turned 16. If the whole system has failed these children then the whole system has to be put right. Tinkering with a few aspects is not enough ... (Department of Health 1998, p.1)

I believe that he is sincere and, with a little help and a lot of guidance, plus a fair amount of pushing from us, this government can and will make a difference to the lives of young people in, and leaving, care.

For example, I believe the government gave a grant of £450,000 over a three-year period for the setting up of a national organisation for young people in, and leaving, care. This project has been going since 1996 when First Key was asked to undertake a feasibility study to find out if young people in care wanted a national organisation. The overall majority said they did. So it is being set up, a National Voice by and for care-experienced young people with a little help from First Key (and many other adult advisers) but mainly by the steering group of young care-experienced people. The National Care Leaver Association is also in the making and is a very different organisation for young and older care leavers (18+). It is different because it is, and will continue to be, run solely by care leavers for care leavers. There are also many other projects nationally and regionally, including the National Association for People Abused in Childhood and the All Parliamentary Group on Children and the Utting Task Force.

My final word to you is this: we *can* do it, and now is the best time to act.

References

Childline (1996) *Child Abuse information sheet 2*. London: Childline.

Department of Health (1998) 'Ending the legacy of abuse: Government responds to the Children's Safeguards Review' (Press Release 1998/0494, 5 November). London: Department of Health.

Lindsay, M. (1996) 'Towards a theory of "Careism": Discrimination against young people in care'. International Conference on Residential Child Care: Realities and Dreams. Conference Paper, International In Care Conference.

Stein, M. and Carey, K. (1986) *Leaving Care Policy and Practice*. London: Blackwell.

Utting, W. (1997) *People Like Us*. London: Department of Health/Welsh Office.

CHAPTER 9

Surviving an Abusive System

Anne Wilson and Peter Beresford

This chapter explores the impact of 'social responsibility' upon the lives of psychiatric system survivors. Though the psychiatric system exists ostensibly to benefit those who are deemed to be in need of its 'care' and 'treatment', as well as to protect them and the broader public, we focus on arguments that the system itself is inherently abusive. We examine the processes which come into play when a citizen encounters the power and other structures which shape, control and constitute the 'mental health' system. The notion of social responsibility is an integral part of this discussion because the psychiatric system constitutes one location of broader structures of social responsibility. These structures still seem to be significantly owed to the medicalised modernist system which was established in the nineteenth century and continue to be based on many of its categories, institutions and values. The precursors of today's 'social responsibility' encompassed three overlapping subject groups identified and categorised on the basis of (i) perceived individual impairment, (ii) moral deficit and (iii) poverty. Our focus comes within the first of these, which has been used to include disabled people, people with learning difficulties, older people and 'mental health' service users. We are concerned specifically with the psychiatric system and the service users associated with it. While some of the issues that emerge from this particular context may not be generalisable to overall arrangements for social responsibility, they are nonetheless likely to offer some helpful broader insights into social responsibility in general.

In this discussion, we are not taking 'social responsibility' as a given, but rather as socially constructed. We see it as a concept and set of structures and institutions based on particular values and beliefs. The idea of social responsibility is much less often discussed than other key concepts in social policy, concepts like, for example, 'social justice' or 'equality'. It is an idea which has more often been implicit than explicit. Yet it is no less important than these concepts. It has played a central part in the development and operation of welfare and social care systems. Bearing in mind the increased emphasis on the *responsibilities* as well as the rights of citizenship in political and public debate, we might have expected that there would be more discussion about 'social responsibility', but so far this does not generally seem to have happened. This book is still unusual in addressing the issue.

'Social responsibility' seems to be different in another way from other key ideas associated with the emergence of the welfare state. The idea of social justice, for instance, has generally represented a shift away from highlighting the (defective) morality or capacity of subjects. The same has not been true of 'social responsibility' which appears implicitly at least to continue to be based upon this. Thus the idea of social justice has traditionally been concerned with taking collective action to deal with economic, social and related problems facing individual citizens, while 'social responsibility' has mainly been concerned with taking collective action to regulate individuals and related behaviour judged to be inconsistent with or antithetical to the interests of society.

We wish to be explicit about our affiliations in this discussion as survivors of the psychiatric system, but we would also question any suggestion of the feasibility of 'neutral', 'balanced', 'objective' or 'distanced' analysis of the subject, since it is itself value-laden and ideologically based.

Our analysis of social responsibility focuses upon the purported differences between 'the socially responsible' (mental health professionals, medical social workers, policy makers, academics, researchers, 'carers' and other 'concerned' parties) and psychiatric system survivors who, on the grounds of their presumed pathology, are generally excluded from active participation in many aspects of 'social responsibility'. By considering the situation of psychiatric system survivors, we demonstrate how arrangements for social responsibility serve to maintain the power and dominance of 'the socially responsible' over those they identify and define as 'mentally ill'. Moreover, we argue that the damage-inducing or 'iatrogenic' effects of social responsibility perpetuate the need for:

- 'social responsibility' itself
- those persons deemed to be 'socially responsible'

- the personal distress and madness upon which social responsibility depends (and is practised).

We further argue that existing notions of social responsibility are likely only to be sustained at the (lifetime's) expense of the rights and citizenship of psychiatric system survivors.

Finally, we go on to consider the efforts of psychiatric system survivors to control their own services and supports and to participate in 'social responsibility' itself. We conclude by arguing for an effective campaign for civil rights by psychiatric system survivors. Such a campaign would, of necessity, centre around a re-evaluation of the concept of social responsibility.

'Mental illness' and 'social responsibility'

Before discussing 'social responsibility', it may be helpful briefly to examine the concept of 'mental illness' and how those labelled 'mentally ill' supposedly differ from the so-called 'normal' population.

We should perhaps also add at this point, that we are not suggesting here that people included in the psychiatric system or subject to its processes of labelling and diagnosis may not be experiencing 'madness' or mental and emotional distress. Rather, our argument is that the psychiatric system's general approach and specific diagnostic categories misrepresent and distort people's experience, perceptions and feelings. They tend to present psychiatric service users as 'other' – a separate and distinct group – rather than acknowledging madness and distress as part of a broader continuum of perceptions, understandings and experience which are an inherent part of the human condition and may be socially related.

In his discussion of disability and the disabled body, Lennard Davis argues that 'the "problem" is not the person with disabilities; the problem is the way that *normalcy* is constructed to create the "problem" of the disabled person' (Davis 1997, p.9). Davis' thesis is that the norm, or *average*, has become 'paradoxically a kind of ideal, a position devoutly to be wished' (Davis p.12). He links this idealised concept of the norm with the development of statistical analysis and the bell curve, or normal distribution, where those falling at the extremities of the curve are viewed as deviants. He also points out that 'almost all the early statisticians had one thing in common: they were eugenicists' (Davis 1997, p.14). Though Davis' discussion focuses on the *body*, he does include some discussion of the *mind*.

He argues that much of the work of Freud, and the core principles of psychoanalysis, are founded upon a concept of normalcy and suggests that:

> ... it is instructive to think of the ways in which Freud is producing a eugenics of the mind – creating the concepts of normal sexuality, normal function, and then contrasting them with the perverse, abnormal, pathological and even criminal. (Davis 1997, p.20)

Following through Davis' analysis, the 'problem' is not the person who is 'mentally ill'; the problem is the way that *normalcy of mind* has been constructed to create the problem of 'mental illness'. The key players in this construction of normalcy of mind are, we suggest, those who engage in the apparatus and practice of social responsibility.

Despite any ideological objections we may have to the notion of normalcy of mind, the lived reality of many psychiatric system survivors is that they *are* identified, scrutinised, diagnosed, labelled, defined and recorded as abnormal and pathological. Such notions of abnormality and pathology are undoubtedly founded upon a concept of normalcy. The construct 'normalcy of mind' and its attendant constructs 'abnormality' and 'mental illness' are strongly associated with 'social responsibility': any discussion or consideration of 'mental illness' will almost always entail recourse to a notion of social responsibility as a response to it and 'social responsibility' itself plays a crucial role in the construction of 'normalcy of mind'.

Organisations of psychiatric system survivors such as Survivors Speak Out and Schizophrenia Media Agency are actively involved in challenging stereotypes of 'mental illness' and promoting positive images of people who have been labelled by the psychiatric system. There is also, however, a vast array of other institutions, groups and individuals which vie for 'social responsibility' in the area of 'mental health'. These include:

- 'mental health' professionals – psychiatrists, psychologists, lawyers, social workers, GPs, nurses, counsellors, psychotherapists, occupational therapists and their professional associations

- related professionals (for example, police officers, probation officers, judges)

- organisations *for* mental health service users and 'vulnerable' groups (for example, MIND, Liberty)

- citizen advocacy schemes and organisations

- relatives, 'carers' and their organisations (for example, Schizophrenia A National Emergency and the National Schizophrenia Fellowship)
- psychiatry, psychology, sociology, social policy, social work and nursing academics and their theories and explanations
- politicians and their political parties
- policymakers within the Department of Health and local health authorities and trusts and social services and social work departments
- the Social Services Inspectorate and local authority inspection units
- Community Health Councils
- trade unions and their membership working within 'mental health' services
- the media
- religious organisations and their boards, departments or councils for social responsibility.

The socially responsible efforts of these groups and individuals also contribute to constructions of normalcy of mind and 'mental illness'. By speaking *for* or acting *on behalf of* those deemed mentally ill they ('the socially responsible') also contribute to, and perpetuate, notions of the 'dependency', 'passivity' and 'incompetence' of people with a mental illness diagnosis; *irrespective of whether or not this is their intention.*

In the area of 'mental health', 'social responsibility' is rarely a joint activity; people with a mental illness diagnosis are not generally permitted to participate in the structures of social responsibility. They are viewed as 'mentally incapacitated', 'irresponsible' and 'in need of care and protection' or deemed 'dangerous', 'irrational' and 'in need of control'. Psychiatric system survivors are also effectively prohibited from holding *professional* positions of social responsibility (Sone 1996). The rhetoric of social responsibility places an impasse between such professional positions and people deemed 'mentally ill'. Our own experience (and that of others we know) belies this. The two of us hold professional positions of social responsibility as educators. We are also psychiatric system survivors. However, the boundaries and sanctions of social responsibility are such that we find ourselves in a sometimes uncomfortable position. We are, for example, aware of the dangers of setting on paper our ideas about social responsibility. Whatever we write and however we choose to write it, we too will contribute to constructions of 'mental illness' and psychiatric system survivors. Writing from our dual, sometimes opposing, perspectives creates its own challenges. It is possible that some of the ideas which come from our experience as psychiatric system survivors may be viewed as 'inappropriate' or even 'dangerous' and risk being 'censored' by the system of social responsibility and individuals within it. However, we are familiar with the conventions of social responsibility and only too aware of its sanctions. To what extent do we temper our own perspectives and knowledges in order to conform to, and hence collude with, a social responsibility which labels and defines people as 'mentally ill'? How do we ensure we avoid doing this? How do we take part in such a discussion, without adding to, or legitimating, its damaging potential?

The concept of social responsibility

Unlike concepts such as *social justice*, which incorporate reciprocal responsibilities (Commission on Social Justice 1993, p.iv), 'social responsibility' seems to be based on a *one-way* responsibility. In the context of psychiatric services 'the socially responsible' *assume responsibility for* those defined as 'mentally ill'. A logical consequence of this is that the *personal responsibility* of people with a mental illness diagnosis is disregarded, suspended or removed: their 'problems' are defined, identified, controlled and administered to by 'the socially responsible'. This socially responsible 'concern', 'care' or 'treatment' may also include statutory powers to intervene (sometimes coercively) in the lives of those deemed 'mentally ill'.

It seems that social responsibility itself is viewed by those operating within its structures as both *licence* and *justification* for their supposedly socially responsible action. Such justification usually takes one of the following forms:

- the care, protection or 'best interests' of 'the mentally ill' (for example, Lord Chancellor's Department 1997)
- the protection of relatives or carers (for example, Hogman 1995)
- the protection of society (for example, Bird and Davies 1996, pp.4–13)
- 'professional' duty or responsibility in accordance with their professional ethics or code of practice (for example, Jenkins 1997, p.200; Banks 1998).

When professionals cite 'social responsibility' as justification for their intervention, it seems to us that they are regarding 'social responsibility' as a necessary and self-evident good. Linked to this is the assumption of the unquestionable 'good' of the 'socially responsible' professionals themselves (Wilding 1982, p.99). There is also an implied assumption that 'social responsibility' is ideologically neutral in the sense that it is not seen as being informed by any particular ideological perspective(s) but instead as resting upon notions of *truth* and *justice* and *what is best* for people.

Clearly social responsibility cannot be ideologically neutral. In the area of 'mental health', it is, we suggest, underpinned by ideologies of *personal tragedy* (Oliver 1990), *normalcy of mind, individual psychopathology, paternalism* and *permanency of defect*. None of these are explicitly stated but are masked and bolstered by social responsibility's claim to an ideology of *benevolence*.

The promotion of ideas that psychiatric system survivors in some way have 'flawed minds', 'faulty personalities' or 'damaged selves' *and that these 'defects' are permanent and irreversible* is, for us, the most troubling and pernicious aspect of 'social responsibility'. It also seems to be, as we demonstrate below, a major function and purpose of such 'social responsibility'.

The historical development of social responsibility

The ideological bases, overt and covert, of social responsibility are recurrent themes in historical analyses of 'mental illness'. In his discussion of the rise of capitalism, Mike Oliver describes the construction of 'able-minded' individuals – willing and prepared to 'submit to the new work disciplines imposed by the factory' (Oliver 1990, pp.45–47). Those who failed to live up to these requirements were labelled lunatics and viewed as 'human waste' to be deposited in the asylums (Rogers and Pilgrim 1996, p.26). Even measures such as these to remove and dispose of lunatics may be construed as 'socially responsible'. Anne Rogers and David Pilgrim (1996, p.47) cite Kathleen Jones' (1960, p.149) assertion that the implementation of the 1845 Lunacy Act 'set a new standard of public morality by which the care of the helpless and degraded classes of the community was to be seen as a social responsibility'. The 1890 Lunacy Act, however, focused openly on the protection of *society* and 'prioritised and protected the civil rights of those on the *outside* of the asylum' (Rogers and Pilgrim 1996, p.52). During this period the Commissioners in Lunacy (legal, medical and lay inspectors) were responsible for the legal regulation of the lunatic asylums (Thomson 1998, p.79).

The 1913 Mental Deficiency Act, though concerned primarily with 'mental defectives', also embraced some people who might today be viewed as having 'mental health problems' and indeed some who would be regarded as part of the 'normal' population. 'The motivation of the Act was segregation of undesirable "social inefficients" and, to a large extent, this was achieved' (Race 1995, p.49). The Act provided for the identification, certification and institutionalisation of those considered mentally or morally defective. Local authorities established Mental Deficiency Act Committees and employed an executive officer (known to many of his charges as the 'rat-catcher') 'who was responsible for "ascertaining" potentially certifiable adults and children' and taking care of the administrative arrangements surrounding their certification and removal to the institution (Potts and Fido 1991, pp.20–22).

Segregation from society (and, within the institutions, segregation of the sexes) served the eugenic ideal of the prevention of procreation and 'purification of the race'. Eugenic sterilisation of 'inefficients' was also fiercely advocated by many 'socially responsible' parties during the 1920s and 1930s, though sterilisation legislation was never actually introduced in Britain. Mathew Thomson's (1998, pp.181–205) instructive discussion of 'the sterilisation solution' offers an insight into the role of 'the socially responsible' during this period. The 1913 Act also set up the national Board of Control which took over the legal role previously performed by the Commissioners in Lunacy (Thomson 1998, p.78).

The 1930 Mental Treatment Act made provision for voluntary treatment of those deemed mentally ill. It also incorporated powers to deprive patients of their liberty without a judicial trial. Though the Macmillan Commission (on whose Report the Act was based) 'had wanted information about legal rights for patients and relatives to be posted on hospital wards, this was omitted from the 1930 Act' (Rogers and Pilgrim 1996, pp.60–61):

> The greater medical emphasis of the 1930 Act meant that legal protection was weakened for patients and forced treatment became a mystification of, or rationalisation for, detention without trial. The legislators' trust in a medical-therapeutic ethos in mental health work bolstered professional power at the expense of the rights of patients (Rogers and Pilgrim 1996, p.62).

During the 1940s and 1950s the National Council for Civil Liberties (NCCL) mounted a campaign to free patients who were being detained and exploited in mental deficiency institutions. They also pushed for reform of the mental health system as a whole and submitted 'highly critical' evidence to the 1957 Royal Commission on the Law Relating to Mental Illness and Mental Deficiency. Though the NCCL did eventually achieve their goal of reform, the resulting legislation 'ironically increased medical control and decreased legal safeguards' (Thomson 1998, pp.279–280), which raises questions about the NCCL's own role in the structures of social responsibility.

The 1957 Royal Commission report was predicated upon the following simplistic formula:

1. Cases of mental illness were validly and reliably identified by psychiatrists.

2. The identification of mental illness automatically implied a *need* for treatment.

3. The obligation to treat was so compelling that individual loss of liberty was warranted.

4. Psychiatric treatment was effective.

5. The integrity of medical practitioners was beyond doubt. (Rogers and Pilgrim 1996, p.69)

The 1959 Mental Health Act, which followed the Royal Commission's Report, accepted this formula and increased the power and autonomy of the psychiatric profession (Wilding 1982, pp.44–45; Rogers and Pilgrim 1996, p.70):

> The 1959 Act deliberately set out to free professionals to be professional. In that endeavour the rights of patients were placed in second place. (Wilding 1982, p.105)

It also abolished the Board of Control:

> … with mental health care now simply a medical issue, the Board of Control's legal role was considered redundant and it was completely abolished, leaving mental patients without this governmental watchdog to monitor their rights. (Thomson 1998, p.294)

The abolition of the Board of Control meant that, between 1959 and 1983, no statutory body had responsibility for monitoring the legal detention of psychiatric patients (Curran and Grimshaw 1998). The 1983 Mental Health Act introduced the Mental Health Act Commission (MHAC) as a response to the hospital inquiries of the 1960s and 1970s which had revealed widespread corrupt care practices and patient abuses within the long stay hospitals (Martin 1984). The role of the MHAC is to monitor the application of enforced treatment and detention of patients under the 1983 Act and to investigate complaints relating to individual detained patients. However:

> The first ten years of the MHAC has witnessed a public acknowledgement of its failure to deal with neglect and brutality, whilst, arguably, raising the expectation that civil liberties were now to be protected by such a statutory body. The most pointed example of MHAC failure was offered by the Blom-Cooper team investigating complaints of mistreatment at Ashworth Hospitals ... The Commission had failed where investigative journalists had succeeded in exposing bad practice. Nothing had changed since 1980, when another TV documentary had exposed brutality at Rampton Special Hospital. It seemed that with or without an MHAC, mistreatment was happening in closed isolated hospitals and a watchdog could not even be relied upon to detect such events. (Rogers and Pilgrim 1996, p.89)

The crude formula identified above also underpinned the revised 1983 Mental Health Act which 'did not endeavour to introduce new principles but to alter those of the 1959 Act and to improve administration' (Rogers and Pilgrim 1996, p.88). As a result, the odds are still firmly stacked against the user or recipient of psychiatric services:

> The 1983 Mental Health Act needs to be seen primarily as a threat to patients' rights and only secondarily (if at all) as a means of access to service access or treatment. (Rogers and Pilgrim 1996, p.203)

Historical and contemporary structures and systems of social responsibility have consistently failed the psychiatric service users for whom they are ostensibly intended.

The impact of social responsibility

On the evidence so far, the track record of 'the socially responsible' in ensuring the 'best interests' of those deemed 'mentally ill' does not seem good. We now examine the impact of their action upon the lives of individual psychiatric system survivors. Our examination focuses on the following areas: (a) the 'detection of abnormality'; (b) blame and responsibility; and (c) diminished rights and differential citizenship.

The 'detection' of abnormality

Commonsense ideas about 'mental illness' and 'the mentally ill' are fuelled by both media stereotypes of dangerous, out-of-control individuals and the views and opinions of the 'professional experts' whose columns, phone-ins and associated publications and 'self-help' guides advise upon psychological problems and relationship difficulties (Parker *et al.* 1995, pp.63–69). These ideas reinforce notions of 'us' and 'them': people 'like you and I' who are 'basically normal', but who may experience the occasional psychological difficulties, and those 'suffering from serious mental illness' who are far from 'normal'. In other words, they help construct normalcy of mind and contribute to 'lay' or commonsense identification of 'abnormal' individuals or behaviour. Commonsense ideas also shape ideas and structures of social responsibility to the extent that seeking *professional help* for the relative, lover, friend or neighbour who appears distressed or withdrawn may be viewed, uncritically, as a social responsibility or *duty*; particularly if that individual has a 'previous history' of 'mental problems' or conforms to conventional stereotypes of 'mental illness'.

Most of us may share an understanding that it is better to keep away from 'shrinks' and the 'local bin', yet the individual experiencing distress is expected to believe that the mental health system consists of socially responsible professionals who can do her nothing but good. She is also expected to concur that the socially responsible relatives or neighbours who sought 'professional help' on her behalf, were acting in her 'best interests'. If she fails to see this, or questions the wisdom of the mental health professionals, she may be deemed to *lack insight*. This 'lack of insight' may in turn be viewed as further evidence of her 'mental illness'. She may feel that she *does* have insight into her own situation and the way in which the 'inconvenience' of her distress has been 'dealt with'. However, the 'insight' of people deemed mentally ill, unlike that of other parties, is unlikely to be sanctioned within systems of social responsibility. Indeed, the frequent experience of psychiatric system survivors is that one of the functions of these structures is to limit or suppress patients' own understanding or insight into the oppression they experience both generally and specifically within such structures.

Mental health professionals, like 'lay' people, also employ a common-sense distinction between people who are 'basically normal' and those 'suffering from serious mental illness' (Parker *et al.* 1995, p.65) framed, for example, in terms of 'the worried well' contrasted with 'the mentally ill'. In addition to the formal diagnostic interview, the person 'suspected' of falling into the latter category may find his everyday behaviour and conversation scrutinised by mental health professionals for *evidence* of 'mental illness'. Every (supposedly 'ordinary') conversation may feel like 'a psychiatric checklist of symptoms' (Pembroke 1994a, p.40) and the person on the receiving end of this 'detection' process may end up feeling like 'someone on trial' (Brunner 1996, p.20).

This detection of 'difference' is of crucial importance to the 'socially responsible' professional since:

- without this difference, their power and authority cannot be justified

- the identification and accurate diagnosis of difference ('mental illness') is itself a central function of their role as socially responsible professionals – it is what they are expected, and paid, to do.

As mentioned previously, the rhetoric of social responsibility generally prohibits those deemed 'mentally ill' from holding professional positions of social responsibility (Sone 1996; McNamara 1996, p.200). The perpetuation of a rhetoric of exclusion is crucially important, as if people with a mental illness diagnosis are admitted to professional roles of social responsibility, the 'difference' between socially responsible professionals and those deemed 'mentally ill' becomes blurred; with the 'difference' minimised, the power and authority of socially responsible professionals consequently diminishes. Notwithstanding the rhetoric, the boundary between socially responsible professionals and those deemed 'mentally ill' can be, and is, sometimes crossed, although those who cross it may not find it easy (Rooke-Matthews and Lindow 1998):

> Because I was a mental health worker, the staff couldn't talk down to me quite so much. But the biggest thing it made them do was to treat me differently in one of two ways – either they treated me as a fellow professional who wasn't really having problems, or else they told me that I was not suitable to be a social worker. They had to either negate my feelings or my professionalism. They couldn't actually see me as being both a professional and a user; otherwise it could happen to them. (Fiona, in O'Hagan 1993, p.8)

> The staff in mental health centres are not supposed to talk about their problems, ever. You are in jeopardy of losing your job if you let it be known

that you are receiving mental health services. (Brendan (Clinical Psychologist), in O'Hagan 1993, p.34)

A study by Susan Rooke-Matthews (1993) found that students undertaking professional social work or nursing training usually regretted disclosing past use of mental health services as it resulted in 'increased surveillance and the reframing of their behaviour in a way that emphasised people's vulnerability or difference' (cited by Lindow and Morris 1995, p.81).

Each of these experiences of course, serves to reinforce the rhetoric of exclusion.

Blame and responsibility

The individual identified as 'mentally ill' may have a strong sense of being 'blamed' for his distress and current predicament. He may also feel that he has brought great shame and guilt upon himself and his family by becoming 'mentally ill'. Despite overt protestations by mental health professionals that they do not blame 'their patients', nonetheless, this is how it may often feel to the patient. The individual may feel *personally responsible* for his distress through his own failures or bad management of his life. This self-blame may then be viewed by the professionals as further evidence of 'mental illness'. The individual's feelings of being implicated in his own 'illness' may then be reinforced by the 'treatment' he receives. This may be perceived as punitive or chastising (Pembroke 1994a), a 'violation of ... body and self' (Plumb 1994, p.10), or 'equivalent to rape' (Taylor and Butterfield 1995, p.11).

Though the individual may feel personally responsible for his distress, he may feel unable to take responsibility for other aspects of his life:

> It is common amongst those who have used or been used by the services to feel that they are *not able to be responsible* because they are incompetent and inadequate. Low self-esteem and confidence foster these feelings. If people are treated in a certain way, as an 'inadequate', then invariably they will respond as an 'inadequate' person. (Pembroke 1994a, pp.42–43) [our emphasis].

The mental health service user may end up feeling responsible for *causing* his own distress but unable to take any responsibility for finding a solution to that distress. He may subsequently be identified as 'suffering from serious and enduring mental health problems' and be assigned a diagnosis such as 'schizophrenia'. 'Clinical' diagnosis, intentionally or otherwise, further absolves the individual of responsibility for finding solutions for his own distress. It also 'stops the individual from *owning* the experience and finding his *own* language and interpretation' (Pembroke 1994a, p.42). The 'non-therapeutic' regimen and differential treatment assigned to those with diagnoses such as schizophrenia reinforces this notion of passive 'sufferers' who 'cannot be cured'. For the individual, the refusal of requests for counselling or psychotherapy (see Thomas 1997, pp.66–68) because he is 'unsuitable' (as people with schizophrenia 'don't respond') may be further evidence of his lack of worth and further confirmation of the inevitable hopelessness of his situation.

For those in positions of social responsibility, the mental illness diagnosis may be viewed as licence to *assume responsibility* for the diagnosed. For the disempowered and vulnerable diagnosed individual, this may be a not unwelcome outcome. He may be resigned to loss of responsibility, inferior status and passive future as defined and predicted by 'his' diagnosis. Those with social responsibility may encourage and reward this 'coming to terms' with his diagnosis and may also help ensure its predictions are realised:

> People often submit themselves to the services for a long time because there is little else – it is clung to – even if hated. Eventually you don't recognise the oppression. (Pembroke 1994a, p.43)

Diminished rights and differential citizenship

Anne Rogers and David Pilgrim (1989) provide compelling evidence that the civil and political rights of psychiatric patients, far from being protected, have been diminished and abrogated by mental health legislation and ideas of social responsibility. For many psychiatric patients the right to live in freedom and safe from personal harm has been overridden by compulsory legal detention and legally enforced treatment under the 1983 Mental Health Act:

> The [1983] Act continues to encourage and permit the lawful interference with the bodies of psychiatric patients by professionals without consent. The relevance of this point is that professionals can administer treatments which may be unwanted, cause anguish and distress and may lead to irreversible brain damage. (Rogers and Pilgrim 1989, p.45)

Patients being compulsorily admitted do not come before a civil court. Only 'prosecuting' professionals are involved with no recourse by the patient to those actively advocating their freedom. (Rogers and Pilgrim 1989, p.46)

The right to freedom of thought, conscience and belief likewise may be overridden by intervention and action on the grounds of social responsibility:

> The intervention of psychiatric professionals in the lives of their clients is largely a function of the former seeking to control the deviant conduct associated with idiosyncratic thoughts and beliefs of the latter. Thus it is residual rule breaking which provokes professional social control, albeit usually mediated by lay people. After admission, the mere expression of idiosyncratic 'irrational' thoughts is likely to lead to continuing detention, with the patient having to demonstrate insight as a condition of their release. This also applies to informal patients being discharged from further psychiatric surveillance (Rogers and Pilgrim 1989, p.48).

Since Rogers and Pilgrim were writing, the Mental Health (Patients in the Community) Act has come into force (in April 1996). This further curtails the rights and privacy of those 'patients' in the community who are subject to 'Supervised Discharge' (Curran and Grimshaw 1996).

The validity of psychiatric diagnoses

We have focused attention on the distinction that is drawn, by both mental health professionals and the general public, between people who are 'basically normal' and those 'suffering from a recognised mental illness', but we have not, so far, questioned the validity of the psychiatric diagnoses upon which, for the individual diagnosed, so much can depend. Having been on the receiving end of the diagnostic process ourselves, the two of us seriously question its validity. The latest version of the American Psychiatric Association's Diagnostic and Statistical Manual lists 390 different categories of mental disorder (Bracken and Thomas 1997, p.18):

> Although the manuals would like us to believe that each category is a pure form of pathology, the experience of practitioners is often of ... people whose problems seem ambiguous and messy, not at all scientific. (Parker et al. 1995, p.38)

This coincides with our own experiences of having our distress labelled and categorised, and that of other psychiatric system survivors (for example, Pembroke 1994b, p.19). Consultant psychiatrist Philip Thomas' (1997) book *The Dialectics of Schizophrenia* provides an interesting insight into the diagnostic process. Though he does not dispute the existence of schizophrenia as a disease entity (Thomas 1997, p.102), his thesis does seriously undermine the credibility of both the diagnosis and 'treatment' of schizophrenia. He guides the reader through the diagnostic process: 'positive symptoms are experiences that should not be there, but which are, whereas negative symptoms are features that should be present but which are not' (Thomas 1997, p.18). The positive symptoms are 'auditory hallucinations', 'interference in thinking processes', 'passivity experiences' and 'delusional perceptions'. The negative symptoms ('or strictly speaking ... negative signs because they are things that doctors notice on examination and the people who evince them generally do not complain about them' (Thomas 1997, p.21)) are 'blunting of affect', 'poverty of speech', 'lack of drive', 'lack of pleasure' and 'poor attention'. Thomas questions the usefulness of the 'positive symptoms' as diagnostic indicators and argues that experiences such as hearing voices and 'thought disorder' are present in members of the population who do not use psychiatric services (Thomas 1997, pp.93–101). This means that greater emphasis is placed on the negative symptoms as indicators of schizophrenia – the symptoms that the psychiatrist observes, but which the patient does not usually complain of. As Thomas himself points out, these 'symptoms' are almost identical to the 'side effects' of the neuroleptic medication used in the treatment of schizophrenia (Thomas 1997, pp.112–114). Thomas' assertion that 'we should not throw away the concept of schizophrenia altogether' because of the 'predictive power of the negative symptoms' (Thomas 1997, p.102) is puzzling given his later comments about the strong association between negative symptoms and the 'side effects' of neuroleptic medication.

The negative symptoms also have other explanations as both psychiatric system survivors and interactionist sociologists have highlighted (for example, Chamberlin 1988; Goffman 1961). We have already pointed out that despite popular commonsense ideas to the contrary, the individual experiencing distress is expected to believe that the psychiatric system and those who work within it exist to do her good. If the individual indicates that she does not wish to comply with psychiatric assessment, she may be told that she may have to be 'sectioned' (legally detained under the Mental Health

Act). Fearing, for example, that she may lose her job, she may comply with the assessment, in order to draw as little attention to herself as possible. Having already been pressurised into doing something she didn't want to do, she may feel suspicious of the motives of mental health professionals and feel unable to trust them. As a consequence, she may be very 'guarded' in consultations with psychiatrists. This may then be interpreted as the negative symptom of 'poverty of speech'.

Psychiatrists and nursing staff frequently make their observations or interpretations aloud. This can leave the individual feeling that whatever she says or does is inappropriate or 'wrong'. After a few interpretative comments about her emotional states or responses, she can be left feeling that it is better not to display any emotion during a psychiatric assessment, for fear of adverse comment or interpretation. This may then be viewed as the negative symptom of 'blunting of affect'.

In the absence of any clear diagnostic or laboratory test for schizophrenia (Thomas 1997, p.27), these so-called negative symptoms may be taken as indicators of both the 'disease' schizophrenia and the individual's poor prognosis.

The structures of social responsibility are ostensibly founded upon the accurate diagnosis of 'mental illness'. Yet the validity of these diagnoses is highly questionable, as is their reliability. As Thomas says:

> For a diagnostic system to be useful, it must be reliable and valid. Reliability refers to the extent to which clinicians can agree that a condition is present. Validity refers to its usefulness when judged by other criteria. *The diagnosis of schizophrenia fails on both counts.* It has proved very difficult in the past to get clinicians to agree whether the condition is present in an individual. Although the reliability of the diagnosis has improved with the introduction of diagnostic criteria, the need to do so indicates that the validity of the condition is very low. In other words, the absence of a diagnostic test means that clinicians are forced to use diagnostic criteria to agree that the condition is present. (Thomas 1997, p.102) [our emphasis]

The psychiatric profession cannot agree diagnostic criteria among themselves and even have to vote on some decisions (Parker *et al.* 1995, p.38). Likewise, there is little agreement about legal definitions of mental disorder. The Mental Health Act 1983 does not define 'mental illness' – 'so its existence in law must remain parasitic on the views given by psychiatrists' (Rogers and Pilgrim 1996, p.9). The category 'psychopathic disorder', also included in the 1983 Act, is completely circular: 'People are judged to be psychopathic because of their dangerous and anti-social acts, and they are deemed to be dangerous and anti-social because they are suffering from a psychopathic disorder' (Rogers and Pilgrim 1996). In the absence of any legal definition of mental illness:

> ... judges have sometimes resorted to the lay discourse. In 1974, Judge Lawton said that the words 'mental illness' are 'ordinary words of the English Language. They have no particular medical significance. They have no particular legal significance.' (Pilgrim and Rogers 1993, p.11)

They are, however, all too significant in the lives of individual psychiatric system survivors.

'Dangerousness' and the iatrogenic effects of social responsibility

'Dangerousness' is a concept more usually applied to people on the receiving end of 'social responsibility' than to those who administer the system themselves. It involves estimating or predicting the likelihood of violent or dangerous behaviour (Pilgrim and Rogers 1993, pp.155–158; Stewart 1998). George Stewart (1998, p.5) suggests that:

> Because of the element of subjectivity involved in the use of the term 'dangerousness' and its element of fear, the term, and indeed the concept, can be misused or misapplied by those whose intention it is to over-estimate the risks involved in community care of people with mental health problems.

Sensationalist media coverage of 'violent schizophrenics' has compounded the overcautious approach by those in positions of social responsibility and fuelled a climate of fear (Smith 1997). Despite recent media reports of homicides by 'schizophrenics', there is strong evidence that members of the public are *less* likely to be killed by someone labelled as having schizophrenia than by someone without the diagnosis (Monahan 1993). As police records repeatedly show, the strongest predictors for murder continue to be murder of women by men within the family. George Stewart's (1998) examination of Home Office statistics and the results of the National Confidential Inquiry into Suicide and Homicide by People with Mental Illness found that:

- Out of 238 cases of people convicted of homicide in the year from April 1996 to April 1997, [only] 41 (17%) were found to have symptoms of mental health problems at the time of the offence.

- Contrary to popular belief, the incidence of homicide by people diagnosed with mental health problems is not increasing ... Home Office figures show that in 1996 (the most recent figures available) homicides committed by people with mental health problems were at the lowest level for ten years.

- The fear of random, unprovoked attacks on strangers by people with mental health problems is unjustified. Only 10% of the victims of homicide by people with mental health problems were strangers compared to 26% of the victims of homicide by people with no diagnosable mental health problem (Stewart 1998, p.1).

Mental health service users are more likely to die in the psychiatric system (MIND 1995) or to take their own lives (Stewart 1998) than to kill someone else. Yet those involved in the system of social responsibility continue to make frequent reference to 'dangerousness' and 'risk' in relation to psychiatric system survivors. In view of the long history of neglect, abuse and damaging 'treatment' associated with the psychiatric system, we suggest that it may be more appropriate to apply the concept of 'dangerousness' and the assessment of 'risk' to those who engage in the practice of 'social responsibility'.

It is not difficult to see how the concept of dangerousness could apply to the use of 'psychosurgery', or 'neurosurgery for mental disorder' as it is now known. Psychiatric system survivor Derek Wright-Hutchinson, who himself was subjected to hypothalamotomy in Leeds in 1974, maintains that the 'people who took part in and assisted in this barbaric operation should be seen for what they really are' (Darton 1998, p.7) – rather than 'socially responsible' professionals. The concept of dangerousness also applies when considering the use of electro-convulsive therapy (ECT) – the passing of an electrical current through the brain. According to psychiatrist Max Fink, in order to be effective, 'ECT *needs* to cause a certain amount of brain damage' (cited by Taylor and Butterfield 1995, p.12). Pat Butterfield, herself a recipient of ECT, has likened ECT to physical assault:

If one doctor did this to a patient, the police would prosecute for GBH if not worse.

If a group of doctors did it, the authorities might hesitate but eventually would take some action.

> But when all hospitals do it, the police don't even look their way: the very prevalence is the authority. *The prevalence of the treatment lends it a spurious air of legitimacy.* The sheer scale of the illusion of normalcy blots out the fact that ECT does damage and not merely on the margin. (Taylor and Butterfield 1995, p.12)

ECT has been reported as giving rise to numerous 'side effects', including 'severe memory loss, present and continuing memory problems, asthma, horror and fear of ECT itself so bad that people daren't come forward next time they feel they are in mental distress' (Taylor and Butterfield 1995, p.11). But as Jean Taylor and Pat Butterfield point out, 'the NHS scores the latter cases as a "cure" by ECT, shoring up the notion that the treatment is effective' (Taylor and Butterfield 1995).

Other psychiatric 'treatments' can also be associated with dangerousness. The iatrogenic 'brain disease' tardive dyskinesia 'is a neurological disorder (*sic*) in which patients have abnormal movements over which they have no control, affecting the jaw, tongue and lips, and sometimes other parts of the body. Once established the condition is irreversible' (Thomas 1997, p.62).

Tardive dyskinesia is widely known to be *caused* by the neuroleptic medication used in the 'treatment' of schizophrenia (Thomas 1997). Yet despite this knowledge, there is 'an identifiable trend towards the use of even higher doses of these powerful drugs, and for longer periods of time. The use of extremely high doses is associated with even more serious risk, that of sudden death' (Thomas 1997, p.110). MIND, the mental health charity, estimate that neuroleptic medication is implicated in approximately one death per week in the UK (MIND 1995). Yet patients are rarely given information about medication, so are generally not in a position to weigh up potential benefits and 'side effects', or make an informed choice about whether or not to take medication (Campbell 1996a) – if indeed they have a choice. The potential for dangerousness is even greater given that patients with a diagnosis of schizophrenia are kept on neuroleptic medication for very prolonged periods on the grounds that they 'relapse' when the medication is withdrawn or reduced. Philip Thomas points out that:

> The drug withdrawal explanation for relapse has been overwhelmingly neglected in the psychiatric literature. The implications of this are too frightening for psychiatry to contemplate. It means that for many patients, 'relapse' may be iatrogenic, a consequence of drug treatment and not an inevitable part of the process of a disease. (Thomas 1997, p.121)

That the psychiatric profession is 'in denial' about the effects of its 'treatment' further compounds its dangerousness.

In linking the concept of dangerousness to 'social responsibility', we are not only referring to the effects of psychiatric 'treatment'. Our consideration extends beyond psychiatry to other (non-medical) aspects of social responsibility and their iatrogenic effects. As we have seen, structures of social responsibility play a part in the 'detection' of mental illness. The consequences of a mental illness diagnosis may be full or partial exclusion from mainstream society (Rogers and Pilgrim 1989). This exclusion is, we suggest, policed by those in positions of social responsibility. It is this 'policing' which we point to when we refer to dangerousness and the iatrogenic effects of non-medical social responsibility.

The discrimination experienced by mental health service users and psychiatric system survivors has been clearly documented in recent years (for example Rogers, Pilgrim and Lacey 1993; Baker and Read 1996). It is our contention that much of this discrimination, far from being challenged by those in positions of social responsibility, is actually supported and reinforced by systems of social responsibility. For example, a GP's first responsibility is supposedly to his patient, but he may argue that he also has a responsibility to a patient's prospective employer and/or their family or community. If asked, he may reveal information about psychiatric treatment for 'serious' mental illness to employers or family members. Indeed he may even argue that he has a *duty* to reveal such information without the patient's knowledge or consent. If patients protest about what they had been told were their personal, confidential medical records being disclosed to third parties, they may be met with the response that the records do not belong to the patient but are 'the property of the Secretary of State'. Despite the fact that other parties appear to have a right to the information contained in these records, people with a mental illness diagnosis may be denied access to their own medical records if, 'in the opinion of the practitioner such information would be likely to cause serious harm to the physical or mental health of the individual' (Access to Medical Reports Act 1988, s. 7 (1); Access to Health Records Act 1990, s. 5 (1) (a) (i)). The courts may also support GPs' decisions to withhold information from psychiatric system survivors. For example, Peter Jenkins (1997) cites the case of R. v. *Mid-Glamorgan FSHA* (1993) where the court refused permission for a patient with 'a history of depression and psychological problems' to access her medical records. Without knowing what has been written about them, it is even more difficult for patients to request correction of misleading or inaccurate records or argue their own defence.

Psychiatric system survivors can face similar difficulties if they apply for life insurance, mortgages, visas to travel, study or work abroad or make applications to become registered childminders, foster or adoptive parents (McNamara 1996, p.199), or seek fertility treatment (Steinberg 1997, pp.86–87). The basis of this exclusion appears to be a belief that people can never fully recover from mental or emotional distress. This unsubstantiated myth is perpetuated by those in positions of social responsibility each time they apply the concepts of risk and dangerousness to psychiatric system survivors, without also reflecting on how they may apply to themselves. 'Social responsibility', in these situations, seems to be more concerned with 'covering its own back' at the expense of the future potential of the psychiatric system survivors concerned than with securing its ostensible aims.

As we pointed out earlier, it can be particularly difficult for psychiatric system survivors to cross the divide into positions of social responsibility. For example:

> I had been written off on the basis of the psychiatric history recorded in my medical file. The GP and the medical officer of the social service department had described me as 'fundamentally emotionally unstable and unfit for such work'. 'Such work' was located at a mental health rehabilitation project. If these two medics had decided that I was unfit for such work in the community, then perhaps they were saying that it is not possible to rehabilitate psychiatric patients, current or past. If that was the case, why waste all that public money on the project? (McNamara 1996, p.200)

This 'them' and 'us' of the psychiatric system – and this seems to apply to structures of social responsibility more generally – appears to be one of its defining characteristics. Crossovers and links between the two groups, professionals and patients, are discouraged. One group has control and makes prescriptions for the other: one is cast as capable, expert and effective; the other as incompetent, inadequate and vulnerable.

The impact of iatrogenic social responsibility

The impact of iatrogenic social responsibility can be more damaging than the original distress people experience. Once discharged from hospital or the community-based service system, the individual may struggle to cope with everyday life. The frameworks and supports which the rest of us take for granted may no longer be in place in her life. She may have lost her job and possibly also her home and/or partner. Her friends may shun her, or she may break contact with them herself to avoid their uneasiness in her presence and the difficult, stilted contact which ensues; likewise with relatives and family friends. She may also limit the contact she has with parents and immediate family because of the shame she feels she has brought upon them and because she has little positive to report – no success stories or miracle recovery, just her daily struggle to survive. Most people would find it difficult to survive under these conditions. She may also be struggling with her original distress which may be all the more difficult to cope with if she is living on her own. The neuroleptic medication she has been prescribed may cause strange uncontrollable feelings, perceptions or movements. She may be given further psychoactive medication to counteract these 'side effects'. The medication may numb her emotions and make her feel drowsy and detached from her surroundings. She may sleep most of the day. If she decides to stop taking her medication, she may be given slow-acting injections instead. If she refuses these, this may be taken as further evidence of her mental illness. She may judge her situation intolerable and attempt to take her life. If she is 'unsuccessful', this too will be viewed as further evidence of her mental illness rather than an understandable reaction to intolerable circumstances and her re-entry and stigmatic treatment within social responsibility systems is likely to follow.

'Social responsibility' gives very clear messages to psychiatric system survivors – You are ill. Your 'self' has been damaged. You will never (fully) recover. You cannot be trusted to take responsibility for yourself. We know what's best for you.

The emerging inadequacies of social responsibility

So far we have examined *existing* arrangements for social responsibility. We have identified a number of problems associated with them in the context of the psychiatric system. They are rarely reciprocal, frequently reducing rather than increasing people's capacity to take responsibility for themselves and others. The conceptual models and frameworks upon which they are based are often suspect and are neither clinically nor theoretically justified or validated. Instead of reducing the problems and distress which they are intended to address, through both their process and procedures and their 'treatment', they frequently exacerbate them and create new layers of personal and social problems. They are not properly accountable or democratically constituted.

These arrangements have two further shortcomings which have increasing significance, because they relate to new priorities on political and public agendas. The first is the failure of such arrangements to 'safeguard the public'. As we have indicated, one of the problems of 'social responsibility' is the way in which it has conventionally polarised the rights and interests of its subjects and those of broader publics and society – in the context of psychiatric services, to the disadvantage of its users. The announcement by the new Labour government in 1998 that 'Care in the community is scrapped' (*Daily Telegraph* 1998), followed directly from this concern. Whatever the *principles* of community care, *in practice*, as actually implemented, it is seen conspicuously to have failed, as a system of social responsibility, to take collective action to regulate individuals and related behaviour judged to be inconsistent with the interests of society, as we set out at the beginning of this discussion. It has ironically thus failed to respect individual patients' rights *or* to safeguard those of the 'general public'. The situation in other areas of 'social responsibility' needs to be subjected to rigorous examination before any definitive judgement can be made, but we suspect that similar if less highlighted and visible problems may also be identified there.

The second problem facing systems of social responsibility is their traditional and continuing concern to *exclude*. This has been reflected both in the conceptual distinctions and divisions which they have drawn, as well as in the related efforts they have made to segregate and congregate the groups that they have identified as subjects for attention and intervention. But this is now coming under fundamental challenge because of the new importance of ideas and policies of *social inclusion*. The new UK Labour government has made challenging social exclusion a cornerstone of its social and public policy. The concept of social exclusion is central to its political philosophy. It is at the heart of its health, welfare, economic and employment policies (Beresford and Wilson 1998; Barry and Hallett 1998). While the government's definition of social exclusion seems to be employment-centred and, for some critics, more concerned with economic integration and assimilation than social inclusion (Levitas 1996), it nonetheless represents a clear counter to the direction of many arrangements for social responsibility. These have traditionally removed people from the world of employment, because of fears of their inefficiency and contamination, to a world of non-work or make-work.

It remains to be seen how far traditional approaches to social responsibility are compatible with this new direction in policy. The likelihood is that they will seek to accommodate it by shifting from one form of compulsion – to segregation, control and restriction in a world of non-employment; to another – within the least valued, worst rewarded area of employment. Such a shift is unlikely to represent an improvement for subjects of social responsibility systems and it is also open to question whether it will be any more effective or successful in its ostensible aims than its predecessors.

A new social responsibility

Many psychiatric system survivors are discouraged or prevented from engaging in traditional arrangements for social responsibility, thus denying important and useful perspectives. We believe that there are crucially important lessons to be learnt from people subjected to and targeted by social responsibility systems. We are not, however, arguing for the inclusion of psychiatric system survivors in traditional arenas of social responsibility. As we have already indicated, within such arenas, psychiatric system survivors are hampered by having to hide or minimise their distress, or face increased surveillance if they are open about their psychiatric history. In addition, such survivors usually also have to struggle single-handedly against a system of social responsibility which does not value distress or madness and can seem also to deride or even despise those on the receiving end. For instance:

> I got in a lot of trouble at different agencies that I worked in, for advocating different treatments and respect of people. When I went to staff meetings for instance, I would be horrified at the negative emotional atmosphere – the patient bashing, the jokes and the insulting remarks. I tried to get people to ask themselves how they would like to be talked about like that. For the most part I wasn't very successful in changing anything. It was very, very depressing. (Brendan (Clinical Psychologist) in O'Hagan 1993, p.34)

We are instead arguing for the development of a *new approach to social responsibility* which is owned and controlled by psychiatric system survivors. Such an approach is, in effect, what is already in place within many self-help groups and organisations of psychiatric system survivors. A range of user-controlled self-help alternatives to 'mental health' services are described by Mary O'Hagan (1993) and Vivien Lindow (1994). More specifically, these alternatives include initiatives such as:

- user-controlled crisis centres (for example, Chamberlin 1988, pp.144–159; Jenkinson 1994)

- Local Exchange Trading Schemes (LETS) (for example, Sanders 1995)

- training schemes for user-trainers and user-led training schemes (for example, Lindow 1994, pp.25–54)

- user-led and user-controlled research and evaluation projects (see Beresford and Wallcraft 1997).

All of these are expressions of the emergence of a growing and increasingly powerful movement of psychiatric system survivors, with its own democratically constituted local, regional, national and international organisations, its own history, literature, culture, arts and developing philosophy (Campbell 1996b; Beresford 1999).

This *new social responsibility* differs from traditional versions in a number of crucial ways. Without these differences, it reduces to a social responsibility which labels, defines and excludes those over whom it *assumes* responsibility. Having been on the receiving end of such traditional structures of social responsibility ourselves, we suggest that the following critical differences characterise such new arrangements for social responsibility:

- defining our*selves*, with self-definition based upon our oppression by the psychiatric and social responsibility systems, rather than externally imposed definitions centring around presumed 'pathology'

- challenging the validity of mental illness diagnoses and subjecting them to rigorous examination and critique

- reclaiming our 'symptoms' and developing our own understandings of our distress/madness rather than being subjected to externally imposed explanations or theories

- reclaiming *personal* responsibility and accountability within our own lives

- promoting positive images of ourselves and challenging ideas that our *whole selves are permanently damaged* by temporary episodes of madness or distress

- asserting our right as citizens to full participation in the rights *and responsibilities* of active citizenship

- remaining alert to the dangers of co-option into traditional arenas and versions of social responsibility.

Each of these is a direct response to the damaging and dangerous effects of traditional approaches to social responsibility.

Disabled people's campaigns for full civil rights have highlighted and targeted systems of social control and institutional discrimination *within* welfare services *for* disabled people (see, for example, Barnes 1991; Oliver 1996). Just as the campaign of disabled people challenges and confronts the *additional* disabling barriers created by organised welfare, so too are psychiatric system survivors challenging the 'mental health' services' disabling responses to their distress and madness (see, for example, Chamberlin 1988; Pembroke 1994a; Campbell 1996a; O'Hagan 1996). Our view, as psychiatric system survivors, is that it is this iatrogenic issue which is most pressing in terms of moving towards (full) civil rights for people labelled and defined as 'mentally ill'.

The danger of traditional structures of social responsibility cannot be overestimated, for they underpin disabling, paternalistic welfare approaches to the 'care' and control of people defined as 'mentally ill'. They also create, promote and perpetuate a construction of psychiatric system survivors as 'inferior and damaged goods' who can never, ever achieve the same status, rights or responsibilities as 'the undamaged' – those who remain safely within the limits of the normalcy defined and policed by traditional structures of social responsibility.

Social responsibility is a civil rights issue. The new social responsibility offers the prospect of securing the rights and interests of both psychiatric system survivors and the broader population, highlighting their overlaps and similarities, as well as respecting their differences. It also offers the possibility of psychiatric system survivors and other subjects of social responsibility having the opportunities to fulfil their responsibilities as they would wish to, as full citizens within society.

Note

The pronouns 'he' and 'she' are used interchangeably in the text of this chapter.

References

Baker, S. and Read, J. (1996) *Not Just Sticks and Stones: A Survey of the Stigma, Taboos and Discrimination Experienced by People with Mental Health Problems.* London: MIND Publications.

Banks, S. (1998) 'Professional ethics in social work – what future?' *British Journal of Social Work 28,* 213–231.

Barnes, C. (1991) *Disabled People in Britain and Discrimination: A Case for Anti-Discrimination Legislation.* London: Hurst and Company.

Barry, M. and Hallett, C. (eds) (1998) *Social Exclusion and Social Work: Issues of Theory, Policy and Practice.* Lyme Regis: Russell House Publishing.

Beresford, P. (1999) 'New movements, new politics: Making participation possible'. In T. Jordan and A. Lent (eds) *Storming the Millennium: The New Politics of Change.* London: Lawrence and Wishart.

Beresford, P. and Wallcraft, J. (1997) 'Psychiatric system survivors and emancipatory research: Issues, overlaps and differences'. In C. Barnes and M. Oliver (eds) *Doing Disability Research.* Leeds: The Disability Press.

Beresford, P. and Wilson, A. (1998) 'Social exclusion and social work: Challenging the contradictions of exclusive debate'. In M. Barry and C. Hallett (eds) *Social Exclusion and Social Work: Issues of Theory, Policy and Practice.* Lyme Regis: Russell House Publishing.

Bird, J. and Davies, M. (1996) *Supervision Registers, Social Work Monograph 153.* Norwich: University of East Anglia.

Bracken, P. and Thomas, P. (1997) 'Broken promises, fractured dreams'. *OpenMind 88,* 18.

Brunner, P. (1996) 'A survival story'. In J. Read and J. Reynolds (eds) *Speaking Our Minds: An Anthology.* London: Macmillan.

Campbell, P. (1996a) 'Challenging loss of power'. In J. Read and J. Reynolds *Speaking Our Minds: An Anthology.* London: Macmillan.

Campbell, P. (1996b) 'The history of the user movement in the United Kingdom'. In T. Heller, J. Reynolds, R. Gomm, R. Muston and S. Pattison S. (eds) *Mental Health Matters.* Basingstoke: Macmillan.

Chamberlin, J. (1988) *On Our Own.* London: MIND Publications.

Commission on Social Justice (1993) *Social Justice in a Changing World.* London: IPPR.

Curran, C. and Grimshaw, C. (1996) 'A brief guide to supervised discharge'. *OpenMind 81,* 28.

Curran, C. and Grimshaw, C. (1998) 'The *OpenMind* guide to the Mental Health Act Commission'. *OpenMind 91,* 24.

Daily Telegraph (1998) 'Care in the community is scrapped'. 13 January, 1.

Darton, K. (1998) 'Head games'. *OpenMind 91,* 7.

Davis, L. (1997) 'Constructing normalcy: The bell curve, the novel, and the invention of the disabled body in the nineteenth century'. In L. Davis (ed) *The Disability Studies Reader.* London: Routledge.

Goffman, E. (1961) *Asylums.* Harmondsworth: Penguin.

Hogman, G. (1995) *The Silent Partners: The Needs and Experiences of People who Provide Informal Care to People With a Severe Mental Illness.* Kingston-upon-Thames: National Schizophrenia Fellowship.

Jenkins, P. (1997) *Counselling, Psychotherapy and the Law.* London: Sage.

Jenkinson, P. (1994) 'Crisis houses should not be institutions'. *OpenMind 71,* 18–19.

Jones, K. (1960) *Mental Health and Social Policy: 1845-1959.* London: Routledge and Kegan Paul.

Levitas, R. (1996) 'The concept of social exclusion and the new Durkheimian hegemony'. *Critical Social Policy 16,* 1, Issue 46, 5–20.

Lindow, V. (1994) *Self-Help Alternatives to Mental Health Services.* London: MIND Publications.

Lindow, V. and Morris, J. (1995) *Service User Involvement: Synthesis of Findings and Experience in the Field of Community Care.* York: Joseph Rowntree Foundation.

Lord Chancellor's Department (1997) *Who Decides? Making Decisions on Behalf of Mentally Incapacitated Adults.* Cmd 3803. London: The Stationery Office.

Martin, J. (1984) *Hospitals in Trouble.* Oxford: Blackwell.

McNamara, J. (1996) 'Out of order: madness is a feminist and a disability issue'. In J. Morris (ed) *Encounters with Strangers: Feminism and Disability.* London: The Women's Press.

MIND (1995) Press Release, 17 May. London: MIND Publications.

Monahan, J. (1993) 'Mental disorder and violence: Another look'. In S. Hodgins (ed) *Mental Disorder and Crime.* London: Sage.

O'Hagan, M. (1993) *Stopovers On My Way Home From Mars: A Journey into the Psychiatric Survivor Movement in the USA, Britain and the Netherlands.* London: Survivors Speak Out.

O'Hagan, M. (1996) 'Two accounts of mental distress'. In J. Read and J. Reynolds (eds) *Speaking Our Minds: an anthology.* London: Macmillan.

Oliver, M. (1990) *The Politics of Disablement.* London: Macmillan.

Oliver, M. (1996) *Understanding Disability: From Theory to Practice.* London: Macmillan.

Parker, I., Georgaca, E., Harper, D., McLaughlin, T. and Stowell-Smith, M. (1995) *Deconstructing Psychopathology.* London: Sage.

Pembroke, L.R. (ed) (1994a) *Self Harm: Perspectives From Personal Experience.* London: Survivors Speak Out.

Pembroke, L.R. (ed) (1994b) *Eating Distress: Perspectives From Personal Experience.* London: Survivors Speak Out.

Pilgrim, D. and Rogers, A. (1993) *A Sociology of Mental Health and Illness.* Buckingham: Open University Press.

Plumb, A. (1994) *Distress or Disability.* Manchester: Greater Manchester Coalition of Disabled People.

Potts, M. and Fido, R. (1991) *A Fit Person To Be Removed: Personal Accounts of Life in a Mental Deficiency Institution.* Plymouth: Northcote House.

Race, D. (1995) 'Historical development of service provision. In N. Malin (ed) *Services for People with Learning Disabilities.* London: Routledge, pp.46–78.

Rogers, A. and Pilgrim, D. (1989) 'Mental health and citizenship'. *Critical Social Policy 26*, pp.44–55.

Rogers, A. and Pilgrim, D. (1996) *Mental Health Policy in Britain: A Critical Introduction.* London: Macmillan.

Rogers, A. , Pilgrim, D. and Lacey, R. (1993) *Experiencing Psychiatry: Users' Views of Services.* London: Macmillan/MIND Publications.

Rooke-Matthews, S. (1993) 'Working users'. *Community Care*, 19 August 14–15.

Rooke-Matthews, S. and Lindow, V. (1998) *A Survivor's Guide to Working in Mental Health Services.* London: MIND.

Sanders, C. (1995) 'Let's link up to help'. *Guardian.* 31 May.

Smith, M. (1997) 'Role of the popular media in mental illness'. *Lancet*, 349, 9067, 1779.

Sone, K. (1996) 'What's sauce for the goose'. *Community Care* 12–18 December, 20–21.

Steinberg, D.L. (1997) *Bodies in Glass: Genetics, Eugenics, Embryo Ethics.* Manchester: Manchester University Press

Stewart, G. (1998) *Dangerousness and Mental Health Factsheet.* London: MIND Publications.

Taylor, J. and Butterfield, P. (1995) 'ECT: User perspectives on informed consent'. *OpenMind 78*, 11–13.

Thomas, P. (1997) *The Dialectics of Schizophrenia.* London: Free Association Books.

Thomson, M. (1998) *The Problem of Mental Deficiency: Eugenics, Democracy and Social Policy in Britain c.1870–1959.* Oxford: Clarendon Press.

Wilding, P. (1982) *Professional Power and Social Welfare.* London: Routledge and Kegan Paul.

CHAPTER 10

System Abuse
Social Violence and Families
Sue Amphlett

Introduction

> I sit upon a man's back, choking him and making him carry me, and yet assure myself and others that I am very sorry for him and wish to ease his lot by all possible means – except by getting off his back. (Tolstoy 1935)

Tolstoy's quote was used by a family member to describe to me how distressed and angry he felt about what was happening to him, his wife and his children when he was wrongly thought to be abusing one of his children. This quote depicts so well the anguish and pain expressed by so many other children, parents, family members, carers and others caught in a similar situation. Namely, 'We and our children are being abused by the very system that set out to protect our children – the child protection system. All the time they justify their actions as being in the best interest of our child.' It also crystallises the fundamental differences, of beliefs and perceptions, between those charged with protecting children from abuse and those who might be thought to be the cause of any abuse. During their training, childcare and protection workers are taught the child is their client and their only concern must be to act in the best interests of the child. Consequently the mantra for many of them is, 'We are working in the best interests of your child.' As a consequence, many of them truly believe they cannot be the cause of any harm to a child. The parent of a child who has been wrongly identified as being abused knows only too well the damage and trauma that has been caused to the child and wish only to get social workers off their back. The blinkered attitude of workers, which prevents them from seeing or acknowledging that they can be the cause of significant harm to children, can be likened to what I call the 'Snoopy' syndrome. In a cartoon sequence Snoopy is shown leaving a trail of chaos and devastation behind him in his attempt to assist one of his pals. In the last caption he protests, 'I can't be wrong when I am so sincere!'

This chapter considers the abuse and misuse of power by those in a position of responsibility with regard to the enquiry and investigative process of alleged child abuse and child protection procedures. It views this process from the perspective of PAIN – a charity and a 'user representative' organisation. It sets the scene with a short history of PAIN and it describes 'social violence' and 'system abuse' with their effects and consequences. It describes some of the underlying philosophies and concepts of the childcare system before using anecdotal case history evidence to depict and analyse some of the issues arising from the abuse of power within the system. Finally it makes recommendations for future policies and practices for preventing the abuse of power in the field of social work.

History of PAIN

> PAIN is the unique national charity that specialises in providing advice and support for those who state they are mistakenly involved in investigations of alleged child abuse.

PAIN was set up in 1985 after my husband, our children and I became unnecessarily involved in the child protection system. Our youngest daughter, aged 17 months, sustained a series of fractures and accidental scalds to her feet over a period of six months. We were referred to the social services by a paediatrician. A case conference meeting of a group of multi-agency child protection workers was held; from which we were excluded. Despite our protestations of innocence, our daughter's name, and that of her older sister, were placed on the Child Abuse Register, as it was known as at the time. This was on the basis, according to them, that there was no logical explanation for her injuries. There were indeed explanations for the injuries, such as normal toddler tumbles, but our explanations were rejected as the possible cause of her injuries. Over the following months we lived in constant fear, should there be any more incidents, that our children would be taken from us. During the investigative process that followed, which included me being cautioned and interviewed by the police, we felt powerless, isolated and marginalised. We were not given any information about the process and desperately sought help from outside agencies. We discovered there was no group or organisation that recognised the problem we were facing, that of being *needlessly* caught up in the child protection system. Everyone we spoke to seemed to believe there was 'no smoke without fire'. We discovered that, at national and local levels, the system and its workers refused to accept that families could be needlessly caught up in the system or that, furthermore, such involvement could be significantly harmful to the child and its family alike.

Following months of home monitoring by child care workers, a health visitor and a social worker, it became obvious to them our children were cherished, well-loved and cared for. Our children's names were removed from the register. Two weeks later our youngest daughter sustained another fracture from another minor tumble. Our distress and fear at this stage can only be truly imagined by other parents who have faced a similar situation. Under normal circumstances we are rational and sensible people yet we were ready to flee the country. At this point, however, the doctors said the leg fracture had been caused by a classical twisting injury, commonly sustained by young toddlers. In view of the number of fractures she had sustained we insisted on expert second opinions, which we obtained ourselves. Our daughter was diagnosed as likely to be suffering from mild Brittle Bone disease.

Although we are articulate and literate people who had already coped with a number of difficult and life-threatening incidents, we found the consequences and effects of the investigative process, with all its implications, to be overwhelming. We seemed unable to control our own distress, loss of self-esteem and feelings of inadequacy, even though we knew it was affecting our children badly. This exacerbated our feelings of inadequacy. Our children, young though they were, knew something was badly wrong. They became clingy and withdrawn, which was so unlike their usual happy, confident and outward-going demeanours. Despite this they tried desperately, in their own ways, to comfort us. It was a long time before our family life returned to anything like normality. Sadly, the deleterious effects are sometimes still obvious thirteen years later.

We were concerned that others less fortunate than ourselves were likely to feel even more powerless than we had and were determined some good should come out of our painful experience. We set up the organisation now known as PAIN, whose acronym originated from its full title Parents Against INjustice. We soon discovered that not just parents, but other family members and anyone involved with, working with or caring for children, can find themselves on the receiving end of an allegation or concern about their involvement with a child. For example teachers, nannies, childminders, social workers, residential care workers, school taxi drivers and caretakers, scout leaders, nursery staff and parents assisting on school outings. Accordingly our work has broadened to include these people. A board of trustees determines our policies and we have three main objectives:

1. To provide an advice and support service to children, parents, family members, child care workers and anyone else who state they are mistakenly involved in an investigation of alleged child abuse or neglect.

2. To influence procedure, practice, policy and law, based on information gathered from the case histories.

3. To educate and inform the media and the public about issues arising from investigations and enquiries into alleged child abuse and child protection procedures.

We help and advise approximately 900 new families and others annually, whilst supporting a further 2500 ongoing cases. Over the years we have assisted over 11,000 member families and others, although as will be shown later this number is merely the tip of an iceberg of potential members.

Before considering the question of abuse of power in detail it is necessary to explain what 'parental responsibility' is, the enquiry or investigative process of alleged child abuse, and what happens during an enquiry.

Parental responsibility

The Children Act 1989 brought a new concept, that of 'parental responsibility'. The Department of Health publication, *An Introduction to The Children Act 1989,* states:

> The Act uses the phrase *parental responsibility* to sum up the collection of duties, rights and authority which a parent has in respect of his child. That choice of words emphasises that the duty to care for the child and to raise him to moral, physical and emotional health is the fundamental task of parenthood and the only justification for the authority it confers. (DOH 1989, p.1, s.1.4)

It goes on to say:

> The courts have come to regard parental responsibility as a collection of powers and duties which follow from being a parent and bringing up a child rather than as rights which may be enforced at law. (DOH 1989, p.8. s.2.2)

It continues:

> The value of the term parental responsibility is twofold. First, it unifies the many references in legislation to parental rights, powers and the rest. Secondly, it more accurately reflects that the true nature of most parental rights is of limited powers to carry out parental duties. (DOH 1989, p.9. s.2.3)

The latter comes as a shock to many parents who believe that they do have full rights in relation to their children. This understandable belief is sometimes the cause of immediate misunderstanding, if not conflict, between childcare workers and parents. More needs to be done nationally to inform the public about the legal changes with regard to parental rights and parental responsibility. This could be achieved by, for example: a programme of parenting and social studies in schools; use of the media; and leaflets in antenatal clinics, GP surgeries, hospital clinics and social service departments.

Enquiries and investigations into alleged child abuse: the law and the research

The first Act in England to protect children was passed in 1889 – the Prevention of Cruelty to Children Act. In subsequent years the inspectors of the National Society for the Prevention of Cruelty and Neglect played a large part in protecting children. In the latter part of the 1960s social work was established as a specific occupation and managed at local authority level with guidance from what has now become the Department of Health at a national level. During the 1970s and 1980s there were a number of national Inquiries into child deaths and working practices, including the Cleveland and Orkney Inquiries. The subsequent reports were instrumental in influencing the rewriting of child protection procedures and guidance and the current legislation, the Children Act 1989.

The Children Act 1989 requires a local authority (e.g. social workers) under section 47, or by an 'authorised person' (e.g. NSPCC) under section 44, to make *enquiries* where the local authority has 'reasonable cause to suspect that a child who lives, or is found, in their area is suffering, or is likely to suffer, significant harm.' (s. 47 (1) (b)). Neither the Children Act nor its accompanying guidance defines what is 'reasonable cause' or 'significant harm'. This results in considerable problems for social workers and many of our members because interpretations as to whether there are child protection issues are then left to the interpretation of an individual worker or a group of workers.

In addition it has become obvious that the theory of the Children Act has been misinterpreted when being put into practice. Many families have experienced unnecessary and damaging scrutiny by joint *investigative* teams of police and social workers. Faced with conflict between the requirement to *protect children* (as required under section 47) and/or to provide support and help to *children in need* (defined under section 17), social workers and the police invariably take investigative action. This is in part at least, we believe, to protect them from failing to identify an abused child with all the resultant public vilification. This misinterpretation was identified by the Department of Health research, *Child Protection: Messages from Research*, that reported:

> ... at the time the research was undertaken, the balance between services was unsatisfactory. The stress upon child protection investigations and not enquiries, and the failure to follow through interventions with much needed family support prevented professionals from meeting the needs of children and families. (DOH 1995a, p.55)

Wendy Rose, Assistant Chief Inspector at the Department of Health, described the need for a change of emphasis, at a conference, by stating:

> We have to ask ourselves whether in some cases children in need might be better served by a lighter approach. By this I mean a lesser emphasis on investigating for evidence regarding the alleged incident and a greater emphasis on enquiring and analysing whether family support services are needed. (DOH 1994)

The document *Child Protection: Messages from Research* further states that too much of the work undertaken comes under the banner of child protection. It suggests a different approach:

> A more useful perspective is offered ... Here, much early work is viewed as an enquiry to establish whether the child in need might benefit from services. In only a proportion of cases will the child protection processes be called into play – the outcome of which will be family support or, in a

minority of situations, child welfare for those living away from home. (DOH 1995a, p.54)

So attempts are now being made, in this area at least, to redress the use and misuse of the powers invested in childcare workers. However:

Attempting to redefine this balance is likely to usher in significant changes in social policy in the field of child welfare and protection. Those now involved in the child protection system will experience shock waves for some time to come ... (Shemmings 1996, p.xvi)

We are concerned that a new, less interventionist, system will in itself cause difficulties for families because they will be unsure whether there are concerns relating to possible abuse. If the new system is not provided with clear guidance they are likely to find it even more difficult to hold workers accountable for their actions.

The concept of 'working in partnership', as previously discussed, is now enshrined in the Children Act 1989:

This co-operative working relationship between the helping services and families is essential if the welfare of the child is to be assured. This co-operative partnership is more likely to be achieved if parents are encouraged to take as large a part as possible from the outset in decisions about the protection of their children. (DOH 1995b, p.9, 2.3)

Taken at face value, the above statement is laudable and one would not question the concept of partnership. Examined more closely, however, it appears that assumptions that the children will require protection have already been made. In PAIN's experience it is common for workers to draw this conclusion as soon as families become involved in the system. This behaviour was also seen by Platt and Shemmings (1996) when acting as editors on a book, commissioned jointly by PAIN, the National Institute of Social Work (NISW) and the NSPCC, which included contributions from a range of professionals, practitioners and academics. They commented that it was common sense and good practice for professionals not to automatically assume that mistreatment has occurred. They discovered, however, that this was not the case after the first drafts were circulated to the Steering Committee for comment:

It soon became apparent that whenever terms such as 'suspicion of abuse' or 'allegation' were used, at some stage in their drafts virtually everyone – including the editors in the chapters written by themselves – went on to assume abuse had happened. Such is the nature of preconception, bias and false assumption. (Shemmings 1996, p.xvii)

It will be seen in later sections that preconception, bias and false assumptions are responsible for much of what goes wrong with the system.

The enquiry procedure

Until recent times the word 'investigation' was used to describe the process of determining whether a child had, or had not, been abused. However, as already stated, Department of Health research (DOH 1995a) has recommended a move away from 'investigations' to a lighter approach – to be known as making an 'enquiry'. Unless quoting from a text or referring to the formal investigative process I shall, therefore, use the term 'enquiry'. Despite the DOH's attention to enquiries it has failed to define the procedure. This leads to misunderstanding and different perceptions between workers and families as to what the process is and when it begins or ends. We believe it is important to establish a working definition. The following definition was formulated, during the joint project between PAIN, the NSPCC and the NISW, which led to the publication of the book *Making Enquiries into Alleged Child Abuse and Neglect: Partnership with Families* (Platt and Shemmings 1996).

> Making enquiries into alleged child abuse or neglect is defined as the systematic process by which:
>
> • facts and opinions are collected, recorded and analysed
> • by child care professionals from different agencies
> • from the child, parents or carers, other family members and others from the child's educational and social environment
> • up to and including an appropriate point of resolution such as a child protection conference, court hearing or internal decision to discontinue the process.

Our working definition of the task of an enquiry is as follows:

> The task of an enquiry into alleged child abuse or neglect is:
>
> • to obtain as clear an account as possible of whether abuse or neglect has occurred, and then if appropriate,
> • to assess how and by whom it was caused, and whether the child remains at risk. (Shemmings 1996, p.xviii, xix)

Families should be made aware that an enquiry process has begun but our case histories show that this is often not the case. Workers often make judgements that it is not necessary and better for the family not to know when they make low level enquiries, as it may not go any further. Such enquiries may be to, for example, the health visitor or the GP. Families tell us, almost without exception, that they would rather know, particularly when, as often happens, the situation appears to escalate and some time later a full-blown investigation takes place. They discover that concerns have already been raised and questions have already been asked that they were not able to respond to.

System abuse and social violence

I have briefly described the child protection system and the enquiry process of alleged child abuse, setting it in an historical and recent research context. Before examining the abuse of power in the enquiry and child protection processes I need to explain what we mean by the terms 'system abuse' and 'social violence'.

System abuse

The term 'system abuse' was coined by me in 1988 to describe the cause, effects and consequences experienced by 'non-abused' children and their families when they have been unnecessarily involved in the child protection system (Amphlett 1988, p.2). The term has subsequently been hijacked by childcare social workers to describe other instances of abuse. Namely, the further abuse of children once they have been removed into care; the further abuse of the investigative process when the child has already been abused; abuse by the system when it fails to follow up with support systems after an investigation; and, when carers or family members are convinced a child has been abused but do not receive any services (McGee and Westcott 1996, p.170).

Social violence

Social violence is the root of the problems experienced by those unnecessarily caught up in the system. In the early years of PAIN we spent considerable time and effort trying to understand why children and family members were so traumatised by the investigative process as it was then known. After all, many of the families had been and were coping with a range of problems such as unemployment, poor social and financial backgrounds, marital and relationship breakdowns and bereavements, including the death of beloved children, before their involvement in the system. Some families were well-to-do, with articulate and literate adults, whom one would assume were in a better position to seek help and therefore better able to cope with the alien process arbitrarily thrust upon them. This was not the case. All sections of the community seemed to be equally devastated and to take years, if ever, to recover.

Why was this? It was clear that the support required by them contained elements of grief and bereavement counselling, disaster and trauma counselling and counselling required in marriage and relationship problems – since so many family relationships were under strain as the result of their involvement in the system. We learnt, however, that even with all of these strands we were still not fully helping our members to heal from the system abuse of social violence.

Further investigation led me to the book *Psychosocial Aspects of Disaster* and in particular to the chapter 'Crime, violence and terrorism' by Marlene A. Young. She describes the events that are traumatic to most individuals as those that are: unexpected, random, arbitrary, life or health threatening, take away all or most of the individual's autonomy or control and cause a loss to the individual – whether that loss be of property, values or self (Young 1989, pp.140–153) [see Chapter 5 by Williscroft in this book – *Editor's note*]. It was clear that all of these features were present in our members' situations. In addition, our members were faced with the loss, or threat of the loss, of their child [see Chapter 4 by Heal in this book – *Editor's note*]. Furthermore, Young describes violent victimisation as a traumatic event from which the victims usually suffer a crisis (Young 1989, pp.140–153).

I believe we were witnessing a new form of violence, that of 'social violence' perpetrated by a system or bureaucratic process, namely the child protection system. I have said before:

> The effects felt by our families (and others) are very similar to those subjected to violent victimisation and they undergo the same reactions, stages and emotional turmoil. It is only the cause that is different. (Amphlett 1992, p.28)

Enduring chronic social violence causes repressed anger, particularly if the source must be endured; as, of course it must, when involved in the protection process. For an individual to behave otherwise might further jeopardise the prejudiced and jaundiced perception that many child protection workers will already have. An additional cause of anger and distress is the knowledge that the perpetrator of the crime (as parents perceive it) – the childcare agency or worker who has wrongly identified the child as having been abused – cannot be apprehended or brought to account. At least this is a possibility for the victim of a criminal act of physical violence.

Other feelings may come into play. Fear – the result of being incapable of defending or protecting oneself, or worst still loved ones, including children. People become acutely aware of their vulnerability to harm. Our members are plagued with a 'Why me?' response as they search for a reason for the destruction and disruption to their lives. They experience feelings of guilt and self-blame. They feel a loss of self-control and lose their sense of identity and a sense of the future. Most importantly they experience a loss of a sense of justice. These feelings of inadequacies are compounded by what is described as the 'phenomenon of second assault'. This is caused because the traditional helping agencies (such as social services, doctors, psychiatrists and psychologists), set up by society to help its weak, vulnerable and distressed members, cannot provide a helping role as they are often seen by parents and family members as the cause of the problem in the first place.

Social violence may not be an intentional misuse of power. Any intrusive process, by its very nature, is likely to have detrimental effects. There are a number of areas, however, where power is abused and where action could be taken to redress the balance of power in order to lessen the damaging effects of intervention. For the purposes of this chapter I intend to consider only a few major ones in turn:

1. Gathering of national statistics

2. Decreasing false positives

3. System abuse

4. Reparation

5. Development of a regulatory and accreditation body

6. Implementation of an advocacy service

7. Development of an independent arbitration and complaints body

8. Provision of information

9. Provision of good practice guidelines for enquiries.

1. GATHERING OF NATIONAL STATISTICS

It is incumbent upon a government to develop effective management strategies particularly when its agents are charged with carrying out interventionist procedures. Such strategic management must concern itself with developing policies which recognise that many families find the process of intervention to be traumatic, whatever the outcome. (Amphlett 1998, p.71)

Furthermore, morality and efficiency should underpin organisational strategies, policies and practices as should reparation services, ie services that assist the repair of any effects caused by intervention. Without such underpinning principles it is all too easy, whilst trying to identify and protect the abused child, to victimise the non-abused child who has nevertheless become part of an investigation process.

No one would question the fact that children must be protected from abuse and that in order to do so the family life of some of our citizens will have to be subjected to scrutiny. National guidance from the Department of Health advises workers that this scrutiny must take place 'in partnership with parents and other family members or carers' (DOH 1991, p.43 s.6.11) in part, one assumes, to attempt to redress the balance of power, which is weighted heavily towards the social workers. What the DOH does not do is collate national statistics of the numbers of enquiries carried out annually, nor does it review the outcomes of such enquiries. This is long overdue for the following reasons:

- to know how many investigations are being carried out and what happens to children and families involved in the system

- to effectively manage the human and financial resources required to carry them out in order that we act in the best interests of all children and families, not just in the interest of children who require protection

- to determine what is the level of intervention into family life and whether such intervention was justified

- to decide what action should be taken to decrease unwarranted or unnecessary intervention

- so that we can we determine what are the needs, both short-term and long-term of the child and its family following intervention when the child does not need protection

- to provide appropriate reparation for such an intrusion

- to enable workers to realise that it is more probable than not that the family with which they are about to become involved is more likely 'not to have abused or neglected their child' rather than to 'have abused their child': this reality should be a fundamental tenet of childcare training and it is not. (Amphlett 1994, p.3)

At the time this chapter was being written the DOH published *Child Protection: Messages from Research* (DOH 1995a), a report of a major research programme comprising twenty research studies. Findings from the work of Gibbons, Conroy and Bell (1995) were extrapolated to estimate the number of enquiries carried out in 1992 in England. The estimates were based on the numbers of children whose names were added to the child protection register during the year, namely 24,500. It demonstrated that some 160,000 children had been the subjects of an enquiry during the year. Seventy-five per cent of them were filtered out without a child protection conference being held, and of the 25 per cent of cases that reached the initial child protection conference, only some 15 per cent of the children were registered as requiring child protection action. In other words, in six out of every seven investigations, no protective action is deemed necessary.

When the above extrapolations are applied to the number of children added to the register in 1996, some 29,169, it is probable that 250,000 children were the subjects of an enquiry. (Note the increase from 1992 when the number added to the register was 24,500.) Add to this a conservative estimate of four other family members who will have been involved and somewhere in the region of 1,250,000 children and family members will have been newly involved in the system that year. Multiply this over a ten-year period and a sizeable proportion of the population will have been trawled through the system, with all its implications, ie twelve and a half million people.

We are not suggesting that all of the 85 per cent of non-registered cases are unfounded. As Shemmings says:

> ... the findings of the research suggest that, of the referrals which are *not* placed on a child protection register, some will have been unfounded; some will reflect situations where the concerns are justified (but not to the point where the child is felt to need compulsory intervention); and some will include situations in which the child is at risk – and should have been registered or even removed – but where, for whatever reason, there is not enough evidence to substantiate such a judgement (or where there enough signs but they were misinterpreted). Unfortunately too, some of the names

registered will include children who are not at risk at all and where mistakes have been made – the so called 'false positives'. (Shemmings 1996, p.xiv)

Clearly there is a large investigative and enquiry trawl taking place. What is not clear is how many of the children (and their families) had been needlessly involved in the process. Nowhere has an attempt been made to quantify how many of the cases were deemed unfounded, ie false, without any evidence of abuse or, with clear evidence to the contrary. The closest the research report comes is to state, '… including 25,000 [enquiries] where suspicions of maltreatment or neglect are unsubstantiated' (DOH 1995a, p.25), ie not proven or not confirmed. This interpretation seems to imply that there were problems and it simply was not possible to prove so, rather than that the cases were unfounded.

What is of equal concern is that the figure of 25,000 refers to those filtered out of the system in the very early stage, without it being deemed necessary to visit the child's home. It should be noted, too, 'these families would normally know nothing about the allegation' (Gibbons *et al.* 1995, p.80) – the implication being that once a home visit has been made, no case will ever be deemed unsubstantiated, let alone unfounded. This cannot be so. We have evidence of numerous cases over the years (from what is a very small proportion of those families and others involved nationally, on an annual basis) that demonstrate clear instances of mistaken concerns and allegations. Such cases include: diagnoses eventually being obtained of unrecognised underlying medical conditions, wrongly diagnosed non-accidental injuries; misinterpretation by workers of what children said or were thought to have said; and instances of deliberately false and malicious allegations.

Families have made the following comments to PAIN:

> I never forgot your help and kindness. Life will always be a battle because of our daughter's illness but at least I can sleep at night now that social services have had to recognise her medical condition. No one should have to suffer as we did – a whole year of our lives was taken from us. (PAIN 1995, p.5)

> We experienced years of being treated as guilty but when the investigation finally ended there was no apology, no redress and no offer of help to rebuild the shattered relationships which were once our family unit. (PAIN 1995, p.11)

Please go on telling people about 'system abuse'. Although it became clear that my son's injury was accidental the strain of the past few months has led to the break-up of my marriage. We have had to sell our house and we are now in financial difficulty. My children have become sad and withdrawn. I can no longer cope. (PAIN 1996, p.12)

My daughter has been diagnosed as having a congenitally inherited condition. Even so they are refusing to let us have a letter of exoneration. (PAIN 1997, p.4)

2. DECREASING FALSE POSITIVES

It has been shown that we do not know how many false positives or unfounded cases there are in the system. I know of only one author, Howitt, in this country, who addresses this subject specifically:

> This book is about getting things wrong – making errors that lead to injustice and harm. As such, it is right to raise the question of the value of intervention. The lack of clear answers is the failing of the child protection system and the researchers who provide support for many aspects of child protection work. That the problem of getting things wrong is hardly researched is in itself significant. (Howitt 1992, p.xi)

It would be impossible to ensure that only those who should be in the system are in the system. It will often be necessary to carry out an initial enquiry in order to do so. Nearly all of the families who come to us say they understand that preliminary enquiries needed to be carried out. They do not complain about the enquiry but they do complain about the manner in which it was carried out and of its consequences and effects. Howitt (1992) examined twenty cases and says the following:

> Based on my experience, it would seem that there is a fairly good reason why *initially* child protection services should have become involved with all or virtually all of the families involved in error. There was almost invariably a prima facie case warranting concern and investigation, although sometimes a very trivial one. No doubt this is a sentiment which the families themselves would share more or less unanimously. The problem lies not so much in the investigation itself (though stressful and potentially wasteful of resources), but in the sequence of events which can lead to injustice. (Howitt 1992, p.113)

It should be possible to decrease the numbers of children drawn into the 'net' by paying greater attention to the threshold criteria to be applied to section 47 enquiries, namely that of 'reasonable cause to suspect' and 'significant harm'. Gibbons *et al.* (1995), whose study formed part of the DOH (1995a) research state:

> In summary, we have seen that many children and families were sucked into the child protection system to no apparent purpose. About a quarter of the referred cases were quickly filtered out without any face-to-face interviews. Of the remainder, over 40% were discarded from the system with no apparent need for protective intervention and no offer of other services ... It seems undesirable for two reasons that so many children were drawn into the system apparently unnecessarily. First, the burden of 'unproductive' work represented a waste of the scarce resource of social workers' time. Second, too many families were exposed unnecessarily to investigative interviews and might have been left reluctant to approach social services for help they really needed. (Gibbons *et al.* 1995, pp.67–68)

Gibbons attributes this over-involvement to a number of factors, namely:

1. They were assessed as 'in need of protection', rather than as 'in need'. (p.115)

2. Local authorities with lower rates of children on child protection registers 'did tend to operate child protection procedures in more selective ways and to have higher thresholds for registration'. (p.113)

3. The 'low-rate' ones generally demonstrated a more organised pattern of work and greater compliance with governmental guidance on the role of keyworker. (p.112)

4. The first filter was operated by social work duty staff, often, but not always, in consultation with a senior worker. (p.109)

5. There were some significant differences in practice between the eight authorities, with IL 3 particularly likely to resort to legal protective action. (p.66) [*Author's note*: IL 3 is the identification code for a local authority in inner London.]

6. Some local authorities had a lower threshold for child protection investigations than others. (p. 41)

7. The reported variations in resources, practices and policies had a marked effect on the statistics of children on the register. (p.30)

It should be pointed out that Gibbons draws her conclusions from a detailed study of only eight English local authorities, out of a total of 109 (at that time). What is happening in all the other local authorities in England is still unknown, let alone what is happening in Wales, Scotland and Northern Ireland. It is clear that many children are drawn into the system unnecessarily although, as previously said, nobody knows how many. This situation must be rectified as a matter of urgency.

3. SYSTEM ABUSE

It can be seen that families face the vagaries of individual worker decisions and agendas, differences in supervisory and management practices and different interpretations of thresholds. All of which are crucial in the determination of whether a family will face an enquiry and how far they proceed into the system. In practice these vagaries mean that families with identical stories and circumstances are treated very differently from one area to another. One family may be offered support and services for a child who is determined as being 'in need' whilst another in the same circumstances may find their child's name is put on a child protection register, or indeed, sometimes removed from them. This is an abuse of power by those holding positions of enormous social responsibility.

If the enquiry process were benign then there would be little concern about the effects that it has on children and families; apart perhaps, from the inconvenience caused to individual family timetables. The process, however, is not benign, it is devastatingly intrusive, humiliating, emotionally abusive, demoralising, demeaning and damaging. I have commented previously:

> Make no mistake, the investigative process is traumatic to most children, parents and family members no matter how well and empathetically it may be carried out. It engenders overwhelming feelings of loss of self-esteem and self-respect – which is particularly devastating to those who have little of either to begin with – it makes people feel insecure about their parenting abilities and their ability to protect and care for their children, for years afterwards. (Amphlett 1994, p.8)

Families say:

> I don't think I will ever get over being accused of abusing my own children ... It's been seven months now but I relive the day it started right through to where it finished at least once a day. My son was recently

admitted to hospital with an infection. I had noticed the problem earlier but obviously I now doubt my abilities as a mum and I delayed in taking him to the doctors. If I had taken him sooner he wouldn't have needed to go into hospital. (PAIN 1994, p.2)

As the investigative process progressed we felt more and more that we had been allocated a passive role while others decided the fate of our children. We blamed each other, and our children, sensing the insecurity within the family, had behavioural problems which mimicked signs of abuse which further confirmed the misguided preconceptions of the professionals. (PAIN 1995, p.7)

Isn't it tragic that nobody recognises the harm that is being done to all of us and in particular to our children. (PAIN 1997, p.3)

It cannot be right that the system actually ends up abusing the very children it seeks to protect. Although there is now some recognition that children are needlessly involved in the child protection system, it is worrying that no research has yet been carried out to determine what damage is caused to them and why. What is of equal concern is that there appears to be reluctance, by those working in the area, to recognise that the solution has become the problem.

4. REPARATION

When a child's name is placed on the child protection register the child remains in the system and, hopefully, receives services from the local authority. Those children and families who are weeded out of the enquiry system are totally lost to the local authority and are left without help or support. In recent times, probably because of PAIN's influence, there is an increasing awareness, by social workers, professionals, practitioners and the public, that unnecessary intervention can be significantly harmful. It is clear to us at PAIN that consequences of system abuse are as damaging to children as if they had actually been abused by a human being. It cannot be acceptable to ignore the consequences to these children in the effort to protect abused children and children in need. Furthermore, abuse of parents results in children being affected by that experience too. It seems little or nothing is actually being done to improve this situation. Treating children and their families in this way is an abuse of power by the government and its agencies.

Services should be offered to assist them to put their lives back together again and to minimise the effect of the intervention as much as possible. For example:

- written apologies from social services and other relevant professionals
- counselling for the family
- compensation and reimbursement of legal fees
- destruction of records
- correction of inaccurate records
- assistance to move from an area or to change a child's school if local difficulties have been caused as a result of the investigation.

5. DEVELOPMENT OF A REGULATORY AND ACCREDITATION BODY

Social workers have no professional body. There is no national code of ethical practice or a licence to practice. In recent years there has been an increasing demand for a social work council. The proposals are that the council would have registration and regulation powers. The council would set clear training, qualification and accreditation standards. Such standards would be of immense benefit to the social workers themselves who would be assured of being properly trained to do the job. Currently the minimum training consists of a two-year course only. Workers are expected to take on cases they are ill-equipped to cope with and this is to the detriment of the child and its family:

> ... social workers do not have a regulatory body to whom they are accountable. There is, therefore, no official code of conduct, which specifies the standards of practice and conduct that the public can expect or to which an individual worker can be held accountable. Similarly without such a regulatory body it is difficult to establish a standard level of competence across the country in relation to the practice of social workers. (Amphlett 1998, p. 89)

Families say:

> The professionals had already decided that we were guilty and treated us accordingly. Then things went badly wrong. Instead of working together a 'them' and 'us' situation developed which was to no one's benefit – least of all our children. (PAIN 1995, p.8)

Acting in 'the best interest' of the child vindicated whatever they did and was something parents did not do. (PAIN, NISW and NSPCC 1997, p.18)

It will be seen later that families find it very difficult, and often impossible, to make child protection workers, including medical practitioners and teachers, accountable for their actions. It is an abuse of power to have a system that does not afford proper independent inspection and open accountability to those who are involved and to the public. A social work council would redress some of this misuse of power and authority.

6. IMPLEMENTATION OF AN ADVOCACY SERVICE

DOH research (DOH 1995a, p.31) tells us that in 96 out of every 100 cases the children remain at home with relatives. Thus some 4 per cent are removed into the care system via childcare proceedings. In reality this means that 96 per cent of the families will have to cope with the enquiry process with little or no support or legal advice. This is because legal aid (which pays for the costs of a solicitor and experts, etc) only becomes available to those with parental rights, at the point at which the local authority decides to take *legal proceedings*. Prior to that point, the enquiry is carried out under the auspices of the administrative procedures of local authorities (usually without any review by anybody other than the local authority). The position for families during this time is therefore bleak. Legal aid is available for those on benefits but the amount is often totally inadequate for what is usually weeks, if not months, of an enquiry process. During the process it is likely that interviews will be carried out, medical opinions and psychiatric opinions will be sought, child protection conferences will take place, together with numerous meetings. This is all in the interest of workers gathering evidence for any case that they may instigate in court or use at a child protection conference. For those families not on benefits the position is even bleaker. Unless they have several thousand pounds at their disposal they too will not be able to use the services of a solicitor. Should they have such savings they will have to decide if they will use them to acquire legal advice. In contrast it should be pointed out that workers and their managers have full and ready access to their own legal departments throughout an enquiry process. This is clearly a gross imbalance of power, weighted heavily towards the social workers.

Families have told us in relation to lack of legal aid and legal aid costs:

> We received a full apology from the police and, after several meetings with our MP, a Social Services Appeal and complaints to the Local

Ombudsman, we finally obtained an apology from social services. Although social services did pay us some compensation for the avoidable stress they caused us, this payment did not cover a quarter of the legal fees we incurred (PAIN 1994, p.4). [*Author's note*: Four years later these parents have just finished repaying the debt incurred to protect themselves and their children from 'misguided and over-zealous' professionals.]

We had to re-mortgage our house and use all our savings to help our son when he faced an allegation of abuse against his daughter. Altogether it has cost us over £25,000 in solicitor and barrister's fees and paying for a second medical opinion. Although the allegations were shown to be false we are not entitled to compensation. Now we have no money to care for ourselves in our old age. (PAIN 1996, p. 4)

We were able to take our solicitor to the second conference. The tone was not 'accusative' as was the last time. Also, instead of being asked to leave the building and stand outside whilst the professional discussion took place, we were shown to a private room and supplied with coffee and biscuits. (PAIN, NISW and NSPCC 1997, p.15)

I have said previously:

It surely cannot be right that a parent's ability to ensure that professionals, practitioners and childcare workers are really acting in the best interests of their child is based upon whether or not that parent can afford to pay for legal advice. This is perhaps particularly so when one remembers that in many instances the child has not, in fact, been abused nor is it at risk of abuse. Furthermore a family should not have to use its life-savings or put itself into debt – with the concomitant effects this has on the children – in order to protect itself against the misguided interventions of a government agency. (Amphlett 1998, p.78)

In our view, legal aid should be provided to every parent or person with parental responsibility at the start of the process but, realistically, this is unlikely to happen. Nevertheless it is a misuse of power to do otherwise and seriously disadvantages a large group of children and families. It should be possible, however, to provide independent advice, advocacy and support for families at the start of the process and prior to legal action, if any, being taken. This service should be paid for either centrally or by a local authority. The service should be provided by independent voluntary agencies with no vested interests.

In relation to issues regarding the need for advocacy, families have told us:

Thank you for your reassuring manner and methodical approach to our dilemma – you gave us a great deal of encouragement and confidence. This is the first time anyone has explained to us what is happening. (PAIN 1996, p. 9)

We don't have a telephone and I haven't any money to ring from a phone box. Do you have somebody who could come with me to a (child protection) conference? I want to be there but I am afraid to go on my own. (PAIN 1995, p.9)

Although our problem was over twelve months ago we never forget it and are trying to cope with so many problems as a result. People like us could never survive without you to help us through it. Thank God you are there. (PAIN 1997, p.4)

Being involved with an enquiry or investigative process is daunting even for articulate and literate people. Where does one start to get the information one needs to understand what is happening? What do you do if you cannot read or write, or speak and write English? What do you do if the police suddenly turn up on your doorstep? What do you do if a social worker says they are going to take your child into care? For most people, nothing in their life experiences will have prepared them for this moment. Independent advocacy should be made available, as of right, to children and families at the start and continue throughout the process. An advocate may act directly on someone's behalf, by attending meetings with them for instance, or they may provide someone with the information they need to become self-advocates. Whatever form the advocacy takes it should be appropriate to the needs of the individual, including the use of audio and videotapes and written and translated material where necessary.

7. DEVELOPMENT OF AN INDEPENDENT ARBITRATION AND COMPLAINTS BODY

Technically there is no formal complaint procedure for families wishing to make complaints when they are involved in enquiries. The current complaint or representations procedures, available via either the Community Care Act or Children Act, are for those who receive services. They are not for those who are involved in enquiries or emergency child protection procedures. Under guidance from the DOH, however, families are generally allowed access to these procedures, although there are obvious difficulties and anomalies since the enquiry process is multidisciplinary: involving the agencies of health, education and social services. There is no over-arching complaint body. Families must pursue complaints with the individual agency concerned and spend many hours doing so. Even if their complaint is upheld they find that there is no way to ensure that the recommendations for change are enforced. Why is this? There are a number of reasons, including agencies arguing that they choose not to use their financial resources to carry out the changes. In addition, those complainants involved with the enquiry process will find that the Area Child Protection Committee has no mandate over its constituent multi-agency members. Thus, when an agency's bad practice has impinged on the decisions arrived at, or the actions taken by, the multi-agency team, the complainant finds that there is no body with the power to bring about the changes. A real Catch-22 situation. Additionally, families say their complaints do not get a fair hearing because the process is an internal one, with departments examining their own policies and practices. In two instances that we are aware of, the panel, which is the final stage of the internal complaints procedure, upheld families' complaints. When the report detailing the recommended changes reached the Director of Social Services, he responded by saying, 'there is no money to carry out the recommended changes'. Needless to say, the improvements did not take place.

Families have told us:

> I've just discovered that another family has made the same complaint as we have. They made their complaint three years ago and the local authority upheld their complaints saying they would change the bad practice. Obviously they didn't and we have had to suffer in the same way. Why won't they learn from their mistakes? (PAIN 1997, p.6)

> The Social Services Complaints procedures are not independent. How can they be when they investigate themselves? (PAIN, NISW and NSPCC 1997, p.9)

> Making a complaint – first you write twenty two letters to various people in the hierarchy of social services. It usually takes between three and four weeks to get an answer and then, more often than not, the answer is not to the question you have asked or the person you have written to is not the right one to give you the answer. (PAIN, NISW and NSPCC 1997, p.21)

If the complainant is dissatisfied with the outcome of the internal complaint procedure they may take their complaint to the Local Government Ombudsman. The Ombudsman, however, is only concerned with maladministration of procedure and is not empowered to review any of the decisions that have been made by the local authority. This is of little use to most families, and in any event, when the process is so frustrating and fruitless few of them have the tenacity or the capability to persist to the bitter end.

It is interesting to note that PAIN and its members are not the only ones to raise concerns about continued poor judgement and practice. As this chapter was being written the Senior Counsel for the North Wales Child Abuse Tribunal called for major changes in child care practice. He states, '... there remain significant and worrying defects in the child care system in North Wales.' In particular he argues for a new complaint procedure, stating, 'They are not independent in their investigation or determination, and do not answer repeated criticism of poor judgement and management interference' (Dobson 1998, p.1).

What can a family do if they have exhausted the complaint and Ombudsman procedure, know the wrong decisions have been made and that their legitimate complaints have not been upheld? Under the current system – nothing. It is clear there is an overwhelming case for the system to be open to review by an independent arbitration and complaint body in order to ensure that children and families are afforded natural justice and proper decisions are made about the child. The make-up of such a body would be arrived at following widespread consultation with childcare agencies, user groups, lawyers, advocates and user representatives.

8. PROVISION OF INFORMATION

The commonest complaint we hear from families is that they do not understand what is happening nor why. This is not surprising, since members of the public would not normally be expected to know the law, policies and practices relating to child protection. Many of them are surprised to find that social workers have the statutory power to intervene in their family life and consequently parents and other family members will refuse or resist such intervention. Such defensiveness is often seen as guilt, which is likely to increase the alarm of social services and may precipitate legal action to remove children.

The evidence from our case histories is that the majority of parents and families are still not given any written information about the law, policies, procedures and practice concerning the process with which they have just become involved. Even fewer receive information suitable for their use, such as by tape, video or interpreters or translations in their first language. This last point raises all the additional issues and difficulties for families from ethnic minority groups, for example, cultural differences and child rearing practices or English as a second language.

In relation to this issue families have made the following comments:

> Knowledge is of the utmost importance. You need to know what might happen to your family. When we were under stress it was difficult to take in verbal information – we needed it to be in writing. (PAIN 1995, p.9)

> Thanks for the speedy dispatch of booklets. They are full of information which is comforting to have in writing. Already they have been beneficial. I was told I could not go to the child protection conference but after quoting one of your booklets my daughter and myself are being allowed to attend. (PAIN 1996, p.12)

> Due to the information we received from you we were better equipped to deal with them and learnt some very valued information which made them take notice of us. We don't feel so alone and vulnerable now. (PAIN 1997 p.5)

Working Together Under the Children Act 1989 states:

> Area Child Protection Committees should produce local procedural handbooks, derived from and consistent with this Guide ... The documents should be available to the public, for instance through local libraries, and on special request, to individuals with, if necessary, an appropriate explanation of their purpose. (DOH 1991, p.8 para. 2.18)

> It cannot be emphasised too strongly that the involvement of children and adults in child protection conferences will not be effective unless they are fully involved from the outset in all the stages of the child protection process, and unless from the time of referral there is as much openness and honesty as possible between families and professionals. (DOH 1991, p.43 para. 6.11)

> Local authorities are required by section 26 of the Children Act to establish complaints procedures, and parents should be provided with information about these procedures. (DOH 1991, p.45 para. 6.21)

As previously stated, we find little evidence that families are receiving the information to which they are entitled. We always advise families to ask to see their local Area Child Protection Committee (ACPC) guidelines so that they can understand what should have happened in their particular area. Some social workers claim not to know to what the family is referring. A number of families have been told that the guidelines are a confidential document and therefore they are not allowed access to them. In one infamous instance a father was told, 'There is no point in you seeing them because you wouldn't understand them.'

The current consultation document *Working Together To Safeguard Children: New Government Proposals For Inter-agency Co-operation* places considerable emphasis on involving the community by asking:

> Should revised guidance be more prescriptive about the information which Social Service departments are expected to provide to the public about their services for children in need? What should be the role of ACPCs and their member agencies in educating the wider community about their child protection responsibilities? (DOH 1998a, p.30 para. 4.32)

Whilst this is laudable it does not raise the specific issue about how to ensure that the children, parents and family members directly involved are properly informed. This is despite the Department of Health's statements:

> When enquiries are made in relation to allegations of suspicions of abuse families should be provided with information about the child protection process. (DOH 1995b, p.51 para. 6.8).

> Families should also be supplied with information about the relevant complaints procedures. These procedures should be provided in a form easily accessible to families and they should be advised where they can turn for unbiased advice about their use. It should be made clear to all families that they have the right to complain. (DOH 1995b, p.51 para. 6.10).

In our view it should be stated clearly that social services are *required* to provide – rather than advised to provide – those involved with comprehensive information, at the start and throughout the process, in whatever format is appropriate. Not to do so is once again a misuse of power.

9. PROVISION OF GOOD PRACTICE GUIDELINES FOR ENQUIRIES

Dendy Platt says, 'Comprehensive guidance on the conduct of an enquiry, as an entity on its own, is unavailable' (Platt 1996, p.6). This is despite the fact as we have seen that local authorities have a statutory duty to make enquiries. In 1992 PAIN commissioned an evaluative report of thirty families who claimed to have been falsely accused, which was funded by BBC Children in Need. As far as I am aware this is the only piece of work that relates to those unnecessarily involved in the system. The report expressed concern, as do we, about the way information is recorded and 'how' and 'what' evidence is used. Prosser states:

> Of the 30 cases in our sample 23 mentioned that Social Workers did not appear to have a systematic way of recording information or interviews ... parents reported a large amount of factual inaccuracies ... Initial interactions, observations and events were, they claim, particularly liable to inaccurate recording and reporting. (Prosser 1992, p.10)

He continues:

> There is a requirement for a full account of what evidence has been collected and how that evidence has been interpreted ... If the collection of data is restricted or biased in some way, it inevitably contributes to difficulties in the complex data analysis phase of any investigation carried out. This can lead to misinterpretation or poor evaluation of family circumstances and what might be innocuous evidence. *Our evidence suggests that investigators place too much evidence on prediction through indicators of risk, which are 'indicators' that abuse may have taken place, not evidence of abuse having taken place.* (Prosser 1992, p.12)

The document *Working Together* (DOH 1991) does not give detailed guidance about 'how' the enquiry should be carried out. It is more about the way in which agencies should 'work together'. A practice guide that sets standards that are required when undertaking an enquiry or investigation is well overdue. Without such a guide it is impossible for the families involved to determine 'how' the enquiry should be carried out, thereby making it very difficult to make workers accountable for their actions. The guide would concern itself with informing workers about 'how' to systematically undertake an enquiry. PAIN is currently working jointly with the National Institute of Social Work (NISW) and the NSPCC. One product of this collaboration is the guide *Enquiries into Alleged Child Abuse – Promoting Partnership with Families* (PAIN, NISW and NSPCC 1997). During the production of this guide we consulted widely with children, parents and other family members who had been involved in enquiries. The following words sum up what they told us they want to be afforded during the enquiry process. They want 'competence, honesty, respect, fairness, information, advocacy, influence, accountability, support and reparation.' This guide details how these would be implemented and provides clear guidance on issues such as:

- the way information should be gathered and recorded, ie balanced and accurate (without omissions)
- the need to check the reliability of the sources of information
- the need to work to a time-limited process
- the need to recognise the differences between fact, hearsay, opinion and interpretation
- the need to record accurate minutes of meetings
- ways to fully involve families at relevant meetings
- the provision of ready access to records
- the provision of information, in appropriate forms
- the need to inform families of the procedures relating to enquiries and investigations
- the requirement to inform families of the outcome of enquiries and investigations
- the need to inform families about representation and complaints procedures
- providing families with written apologies when mistakes have been made.

Families make the following comments in relation to some of these issues:

> If you are not allowed to attend meetings or even to see the minutes you have no idea how much misinformation goes into the decision-making process. We were horrified when we finally saw our child's case notes. How could they make the right decision when they were so misinformed? (PAIN 1995, p.10)

> Can you imagine the frustration when the professionals appear to have a preconception that abuse has occurred and seem to be seeking only those facts which will confirm this? (PAIN 1996, p.8)

> If families and professionals are going to work together constructively we, the families, need access to information and the opportunity to give information. We need ongoing support throughout and at the end of an investigation. We need a 'user friendly' and independent complaint procedure. Most importantly we need a system staffed by personnel prepared to acknowledge that an allegation may be without foundation and ones who place more importance on establishing the truth rather than jumping to conclusions. (PAIN 1996, p.10)

The consultation document *Working Together To Safeguard Children* places emphasis on the importance of record-keeping, stating:

> Well kept records are essential to good child care practice. However, we know from Social Service Inspectorate inspection findings ... that record keeping by SSDs often falls below an acceptable standard. This is an issue which needs to be tackled with some urgency. Should guidance be more prescriptive about the content and format of records which are expected to be kept in child protection cases? (DOH 1998a, p.19 para. 3.16)

The answer is, yes. Accurate record-keeping, however, is only a small part of the process of carrying out a proper enquiry or investigation. It is to be hoped that the DOH recognises this and sets the appropriate standards in its next guidance.

Preventing abuses of power

Few people, I suspect, would argue with the fact that in order to protect some children it is necessary, on occasions, to intrude into the family lives of our citizens. *Child Protection: Messages from Research* (DOH 1995a) says:

> Whether professionals offer support services or therapy, remove the child or keep the family together, the benefits of involving the family in decisions about their future emerge clearly in several studies. Partnership with parents is now a feature of legislation and guidance ... Wanting partnership is a step in the right direction but achieving it is difficult. A positive attitude to partnership needs to underpin action. (DOH 1995a, p.37)

It is this last sentence that is crucial to redressing the balance of power and preventing the continuing use of power. Different attitudes, procedures and formal structures will be needed. To summarise, the following two preventative measures are suggested for consideration.

Improved training and accreditation of social workers

The training of workers will need to be considerably improved. Trainers, and those working in child protection, should be accredited to carry out the work. Their training should always include input from the user or client group. They will require supportive management and supervision to enable them to work in a systematic and confident manner. This will enable them to be less fearful of missing something and thereby overreacting.

There needs to be a Social Work Council developed (or a similar professional body), which would be responsible for establishing and monitoring standards and accrediting social workers. Managers and supervisors should be required to undertake ongoing training and meet required standards in order to continue working in a specialist, supervisory role.

During the writing of this chapter Mr Paul Boateng, Health Minister, outlined plans for a General Social Care Council, subsequently set out in a White Paper (DOH 1998b). It would require all social care staff and their employers to sign up to codes of conduct and practice. He stated during a speech to a social service conference:

> It is vitally important that the public and the workforce itself have the clearest possible understanding of what is expected of individual members of staff and to give a basis on which to begin to judge individual performance. I believe that it is through the clear articulation of standards suitably enforced that public confidence can be quickly raised. We will require all staff to sign up to the codes of conduct and practice as a condition of employment. (Cobain 1998, p.3)

Cobain further reported that Mr Boateng said:

> ... the registration of some staff would also improve quality and lift public confidence. It would be based on completion of approved training giving people the skills and knowledge for safe, effective and legal practice. (Cobain 1998, p.3)

This initiative is welcomed. It will go some way to answering some of the concerns and criticisms voiced by family members in addition to raising public confidence.

National statistics and comprehensive research

It is imperative the government collates national statistics in respect of enquiries and that it identifies and recognises unfounded cases. Furthermore, multidisciplinary research is required to assess the needs of these children and families subsequent to the enquiry. Monitoring is required to determine:

- whether there is a decrease in the numbers of enquiries and investigations as the DOH advises there should be following the publication of its report, *Child Protection: Messages from Research* (DOH 1995a)
- the numbers of children and families being filtered out of the system

- the identification of those filtered out – who would otherwise be lost to the system and could not subsequently be part of an evaluative process or research.

Comprehensive research is required into the effects and consequences of children and families filtered out of the enquiry system:

> There are numerous arguments coming from research which suggest how harmful abuse is, but by comparison virtually nothing is to be found on the harm caused by child protection interventions. (Howitt 1992, p.xi)

Without such research it is too easy for workers to justify their actions as being in 'the best interests of the child'. The parents and other family members who are left to pick up the pieces know otherwise.

Independent arbitration and complaint body

When the state intervenes into family life its intervention must be fair and be seen to be fair, not just to the children whom they are seeking to protect, but to all members of the family. An independent body is required to oversee such intervention and to ensure that the power invested in those who intervene is wisely and fairly used. The body will need to be independent of social services and all the childcare agencies. It will also require powers such that it can enforce necessary improvements upon any agency. Considerable discussion and consultation would be required in the determination of its make-up and powers.

Mention was made earlier of the recommendations made by the senior counsel to the North Wales Child Abuse Tribunal. It is interesting to note the common ground between his and my recommendations. The following are some of his recommendations:

- a General Social Work Council to regulate professional standards
- independent national and regional inspectorates should be set up
- separate accreditation for child care social workers procedures should be established
- a national childcare strategy should be formulated by government, with ministerial responsibility
- a complaints procedure independent of local authorities
- every child in care should be allocated to a named social worker, with a designated manager for each child in care. (Dobson 1998, p.1)

We at PAIN endorse these recommendations and add the following:

- national statistics should be collated on the incidence and outcomes of enquiries

- research should be undertaken into 'false positives' and the effects of system abuse

- a regulatory and accreditation body is required

- an independent arbitration and complaints body is required

- independent advice, advocacy and support should be provided at the start of the process

- information should be provided at the start, and throughout, the process

- standards are required for carrying out enquiries and investigations.

Reform of the social services system

As the writing of this chapter came to an end, Frank Dobson, Health Secretary, announced a radical overhaul of the social services system in November 1998 with the publication of the Social Services White Paper, *Modernising Social Services* (DOH 1998b). In brief, the proposed changes in relation to child protection and to this chapter are as follows:

1. Eight regional Commissions for Care Standards (CSS) will be established to take over responsibility for regulating and inspecting care from local authorities, health authorities and the Department of Health.

2. Each Commission will have a Children's Rights Officer to protect children's rights and safety.

3. By January 1999 each authority will be required to assess its performance in a number of key areas and propose action to remedy deficiencies.

4. New child protection guidance is to be issued in the spring of 1999.

5. A more holistic view of the needs of vulnerable children will be taken to ensure that children are not unnecessarily drawn into the child protection and court procedures.

6. A General Social Care Council (GSCC) will be established, which will draw up codes to guide all staff and their employers in a 'common understanding' of conduct and practice requirements.

7. Individual practitioners will be required to sign up to the codes as a condition of their employment and should be personally accountable for their own standards of conduct and practice.

8. Employers will be required to take action to ensure the codes are enforced.

9. The GSCC will replace the Central Council for Education and Training in Social Work in regulating the work of social workers.

10. The GSCC will have a registration function.

11. Posts for the areas of highly specialised children's services, including child protection, will be restricted to individuals who are registered by the GSCC.

12. The GSCC will have powers to deregister individuals for breach of the codes of conduct and practice.

13. There will be a new post-qualifying award for those working in child protection.

14. The GSCC will be an independent statutory body governed by a Council appointed by the Secretary of State. Its membership will include a majority of service users and lay members, with a lay person appointed Chair. (SSPM 1998, pp.1–11)

These changes, if implemented at all, will go some way to meeting our recommendations, thereby improving the investigative process of alleged child abuse. Regrettably, however, we can find no reference to the need to collate national statistics on the incidence of enquiries and investigations, nor to the need to determine what help children, their parents and families require, subsequent to such an event.

Conclusion

Family life, in all its guises, is the cornerstone of our society. It is the nurturing arena for our next generation. Most parents make a good job of carrying out a difficult and demanding task. This is sometimes under very difficult circumstances and usually without any training other than their own childhood experiences, good or bad. Most children are brought up in a caring and loving environment. The balance of power between the state and the family can never be equal. Nevertheless, the state should endeavour to ensure that when it intervenes, it was right to do so, that its intervention is open to scrutiny and that it takes steps to repair any damage it may cause.

References

Amphlett, S. (1988) 'The Parents' Dilemma'. A paper presented at the Sieff conference, Windsor, Cumberland Lodge. Bishop's Stortford: PAIN.

Amphlett, S. (1992) 'System abuse and gatekeeping'. In M. Evans and C. Miller (eds) *Partnership in Child Protection: The Strategic Management Response.* London: Office for Public Management and National Institute for Social Work.

Amphlett, S. (1994) 'Secret suffering or false allegation? Recognizing and appropriate reporting of alleged child abuse'. A paper presented at the National Children's Bureau conference. Bishops Stortford: PAIN.

Amphlett, S. (1998) 'The experience of a watchdog group'. In G. Hunt (ed) *Whistleblowing in the Social Services.* London: Arnold.

Cobain, J. (1998) 'Codes of conduct for social care staff'. *Social Services Parliamentary Monitor,* April 1998, 28, 3. London: Cadmus Newsletters Ltd.

Department of Health (1989) *An Introduction to the Children Act 1989.* London: HMSO.

Department of Health (1991) *Working Together Under the Children Act. A Guide to Arrangements for Inter-agency Co-operation for the Protection of Children from Abuse.* London: HMSO.

Department of Health (1994) 'An overview of the development of services – the relationship between protection and family support and the intervention of the Children Act 1989'. Department of Health paper given at the Sieff Conference in September 1994 by Wendy Rose, Assistant Chief Inspector (Social Services Inspectorate).

Department of Health (1995a) *Child Protection: Messages from Research.* London: HMSO.

Department of Health (1995b) *The Challenge of Partnership in Child Protection: Practice Guide.* London: HMSO.

Department of Health (1998a) *Working Together To Safeguard Children: New Government Proposals For Inter-agency Co-operation.* London: The Stationery Office.

Department of Health (1998b) *Modernising Social Services.* London: The Stationery Office.

Dobson, R. (1998) 'Tribunal QC calls for changes to protect children from future abuse'. *Community Care* 16–22 April.

Gibbons, J., Conroy, S. and Bell, C. (1995) 'Operating the Child Protection System'. London: HMSO.

Howitt, D. (1992) *Child Abuse Errors – When Good Intentions Go Wrong.* London: Harvester Wheatsheaf.

McGee, C. and Westcott, H. (1996) 'System abuse: Towards a greater understanding from the perspectives of children and parents'. *Child and Family Social Work 1*, 169–180.

PAIN (1994) Annual Report. Bishop's Stortford: PAIN.

PAIN (1995) Annual Report. Bishop's Stortford: PAIN.

PAIN (1996) Annual Report. Bishop's Stortford: PAIN.

PAIN (1997) Annual Report. Bishop's Stortford: PAIN.

PAIN, NISW and NSPCC (1997) *Enquiries into Alleged Child Abuse – Promoting Partnership with Families.* Available from PAIN and NSPCC.

Platt, D. (1996) 'Enquiries and investigations: The policy context'. In D. Platt and D. Shemmings (eds) *Making Enquiries into Alleged Child Abuse and Neglect: Partnership with Families.* Pavilion Publishing Limited. Reprinted (1997) Chichester: John Wiley.

Platt, D. and Shemmings, D. (eds) (1996) *Making Enquiries into Alleged Child Abuse and Neglect: Partnership with Families.* Pavilion Publishing Limited. Reprinted (1997) Chichester: John Wiley & Sons Ltd.

Prosser, J. (1992) *Child Abuse Investigations: The Families' Perspectives. A Case Study of 30 Families Who Claim To Have Been Falsely Accused.* Funded by BBC Children in Need Appeal. Commissioned and published by PAIN.

Shemmings, D. (1996) 'Introduction'. In D. Platt. and D. Shemmings (eds) *Making Enquiries into Alleged Child Abuse and Neglect – Partnership with Families.* Pavilion Publishing Limited. Reprinted (1997). Chichester: John Wiley & Sons Ltd.

SSPM (1998) *Social Services Parlimentary Monitor,* Special Supplement 7 December. London: Cadmus Newsletters Ltd.

Tolstoy, L. (1935) *What Then Must We Do?'* Greenbooks Hartlands.

Young, A.M. (1989) 'Crime, violence, and terrorism'. In R. Gist and B. Lubin (eds) *Psychosocial Aspects of Disaster.* Chichester: John Wiley & Sons.

CHAPTER 11

Serial Abuse Within the Medical System

Mary Neville

The following chapter has been written as both a means of therapy for myself and also for others who may have survived similar traumatic experiences at the hands of professionals. These powerful people, under the guise of therapy, have caused me much mental suffering and anguish, through repeated sexual assault, false imprisonment, and constant interference with the way in which people like myself conduct their day-to-day lives. This chapter has not been written to gain retribution for the crimes committed against me. I am quite satisfied that the process of litigation has dealt with that. Although I am still deeply troubled by the people who tried their very best to destroy me even further, it is only now that I finally have the opportunity to begin writing about a period which was to change my life beyond all comprehension. As a result of my experiences during this period of time, I fought an intense legal battle, which I am sure would have tested the endurance of the toughest human being.

I will now relate my background, in summary form, for the reader. I had a reasonably happy time throughout my early days and my teenage years living with my mother, father and elder brother. I took little interest at school with academic subjects, preferring to put my energy into sport and practical subjects like cookery, art and dressmaking. I sailed through school with few cares and with no ambition to achieve. I left in the summer of 1977 with just five CSEs, all fairly low grades.

From leaving school I went straight into employment as a sales assistant in a small company with a chain of forty shops in London and the South-East. I quickly settled down at work. I had enormous interest in all that went on in the shop and an enthusiasm that was to outshine everyone else. Every few months I seemed to achieve a pay rise and a little promotional move until at the age of twenty I was made manager of one of the shops. I have no hesitation in saying I was in love with my job. I was only the second female manager in the company and the youngest ever. I had, by then, built myself a solid foundation for my future career as well as establishing myself as reliable, sensible and mature with a great sense of responsibility, an ability to lead others and with a professional attitude towards my work and the company. I had earned respect from staff, other managers and senior management alike, as well as developing friendships with my colleagues.

At the age of twenty-two there were to be two further developments. First, although I had known for a long time, I finally had to admit my feelings to myself about my sexuality. I was gay. I found the courage to visit a gay disco fairly near to where I lived, and from that evening onward my life really began – it was a world I had only ever dreamed of. The reality was that there were so many other people like me and my homosexual feelings were OK. Second, having done so well at work I was now in a position to purchase a flat. These were two great achievements for me. Life was getting better and better.

Now living about thirty miles from where I was born, I began to get involved with community issues. I became a member of the housing committee where I lived and later started to become involved with local politics. After three-and-a-half years I was in a position to sell my flat and purchase a small house about a quarter of a mile away. At the age of twenty-six I became a special constable.

All in all, at this point my life could not have been happier or more fulfilled. I was doing all the things that I enjoyed most; and, most importantly, I was a respected member of the community.

Little did I know that in my late twenties this was about to change drastically. Through no fault of my own, my life was about to be turned upside-down and inside-out. It would lead to years of pain and misery, to say the very least.

In the late 1980s I became unwell at work. I left early and contacted an on-call GP. After twice refusing a home visit, the doctor saw me in his surgery. I was in fact suffering acute appendicitis. In the early hours of the following day my appendix was removed at the local hospital.

Following this surgery I was in a considerable amount of pain, as one might expect. However, after a six-week period away from work, on my GP's instructions I returned to my full-time job. I was still in considerable pain and did not feel up to carrying out the duties of my job. As time went on and I felt no improvement with the pain I returned on many occasions to my GP, only to be told there was nothing wrong. Several months later, after the scar had at one point begun to split open at work, with the continuing pain I was suffering and with my GP saying nothing was wrong, I finally resigned from my job without giving notice because of how unwell I was feeling. Obviously with this went my salary and my company car. It was not long before I got into arrears with my mortgage and the fact that no one was doing anything about the pain not surprisingly led me into a certain amount of despair.

It was after some eighteen months and twenty-one visits to my GP that I was finally referred for a psychiatric opinion.

An in-patient

After two out-patient appointments and numerous rather strange questions from the consultant I was offered an opportunity to go into hospital for further investigations into the pain at the site of the appendix scar. I felt at last something was going to be done about the pain and therefore agreed to admission to hospital. At this stage I was totally unaware that this consultant psychiatrist was assuming that the pain I was experiencing was psycho-somatic.

After my voluntary admission to hospital in the early 1990s it soon became clear to me that all was not as it ought to be having agreed to admission for pain in the stomach. I was in fact on an acute psychiatric and drug and alcohol detoxification ward – a ward which housed acute psychiatric patients. After having been left sitting around in this environment for a couple of hours I said to one of the staff that I was going to buy a daily newspaper from the hospital shop. Immediately I was told that I could not leave the ward. At that time I did not know that I could challenge this statement.

I spent five-and-a-half weeks on this ward, and by the time I was eventually released I was indeed suffering with psychiatric illness. During this period I had been subjected to repeated sexual assault. My breasts were fondled by a doctor two to three times per week. When I objected and asked for a nurse to be present I was told, 'What's the point of having someone else here, we could kill you.' I had been questioned intimately about my sex life whilst having my breasts fondled and interrogated about sex in front of a ward round which consisted of seven men and no women. I had been put before the ward round dressed only in a dressing gown. I had been given large cocktails of psychiatric drugs over four days until I refused to take any more. I was subjected to inhaling cannabis fumes when it was openly smoked by another patient. I was violently assaulted by another very disturbed patient. I was encouraged to tell my parents about my sexuality in order to rid me of the pain from the appendix scar. My parents were alarmed and ceased to visit me any more. When a friend of mine came to visit me she was told that I was not there and was subsequently sent away without seeing me, but not before she had been detained, as the staff thought she was a patient. She was and is in fact a local magistrate and was later to give evidence. Another friend who visited me was offered cannabis by a patient. She was later to give evidence also.

Despite the so-called treatment that I had received, when I was discharged from the ward I was still suffering with extreme pain at the site of the appendix scar.

This above description has all been very brief, just scraping the surface of the events and the sheer terror and abuse which I suffered during those five-and-a-half weeks. As a result of these events and my unlawful detention I was later diagnosed as suffering with acute and long-term post-traumatic stress disorder. This disorder is now chronic in nature.

During the last few days of my time on this ward I was appointed a social worker, who first spoke to me while I was still an in-patient on the ward. I told her of how ill I had become since being admitted to the ward and also of how the doctor was continually fondling my breasts. It did not seem to bother her. She took no action.

Having now arrived back home in shock and a complete state of chronic anxiety I made contact with a local psychotherapist in private practice. Initially with an inability to communicate with this very kind and gentle lady because of the sheer terror within me, it took some while to establish trust and start to open up about my experiences. On explaining about the pain at the site of my appendix scar she encouraged me to seek another opinion. On returning to my GP after my discharge, I found he was dismissive of my anxiety state and totally unhelpful to me in any way. In fact he told me that he had spent enough time trying to help me and that I should go and find another GP. I then registered with a female GP. I would now hopefully get another opinion about the pain and some support for the state the hospital admission had left me in.

On examination of the scar my new GP immediately referred me to a consultant surgeon at the local hospital. Following the appointment with the surgeon I was advised that an exploratory operation was needed to discover the cause of the pain. I then underwent surgery and it was discovered that I was suffering with adhesions. An amount of fibrous tissue was removed, which led to a vast improvement in the pain I had suffered.

Making a complaint

At the beginning of the same year I attempted to lodge a complaint about the treatment I had received. Little did I know the battle I was about to face. I made contact with the local Ombudsman where I was dealt with initially in a concerned manner.

Because of the background of the abuse I had suffered and the fact that the manager of the Community Health Council was a male I was swiftly placed with a female in order for the telling of my story to be made easier, for which I was extremely grateful. However, the unprofessional way in which she dealt with the matter was to cause me further upset. She was dismissive of the seriousness of the facts and I quickly realised that she was not taking the matter seriously. She left the room for a short while and came back saying that she had 'put a stop to that!' Apparently she had contacted someone at the hospital and told them that I was trying to make a complaint about the sexual abuse I had undergone. I was left feeling empty; this was a further blow to my already low self-esteem. There was no mention of the matter being pursued, though there was an offer of help to deal with the ongoing pain I was in following the original surgery.

Later on that year I made contact with my local MP, who was horrified at what I had been put through. He made contact with the hospital and with my GP in order to get the second operation speeded up, and within five weeks of his intervention I was back in the operating theatre for the removal of the fibrous tissue.

I decided to take the complaint further. I turned to the gay community for help. A 'gay-friendly' firm of solicitors were recommended to me. I made contact with this firm, and fortunately for me the solicitor who dealt with medical negligence cases was a female.

The litigation

Following my second operation I visited the solicitor. As my story unfolded, the solicitor could immediately see the complexity of the case and the difficulty she might have bringing any action. She explained to me that these sort of situations were often reported but it was extremely difficult to do anything as psychiatric patients were deemed 'not credible witnesses'. She felt, however, that I was an 'extremely credible person', and with that offered to make some preliminary investigations, and apply for legal aid to finance the case.

This was the start of a legal battle that was to span seven years and involve numerous appointments and the exchange of documents and correspondence between us and the defendants. Correspondence that at times would prove upsetting to me, to say the very least, and made damaging attacks on my personality. My medical records were the first set of documents which were to be scrutinised and as my solicitor so rightly put to the defendants, the 'very facts themselves were evidence of negligence', referring to the detail of events as noted in the medical records.

As my solicitor set about organising various appointments for me to attend to collect evidence from expert witnesses, so I continued with the private lady therapist I had been seeing since my discharge from the psychiatric unit. She at very best was just trying to hold me together as well as attempting to work with my extreme fear of doctors, hospitals and more generally with authority figures. I began to take tranquillisers prescribed by my GP in order to try and reduce my continuous anxiety state.

When I set about writing this chapter I listed the people who were for me and those against and I was surprised to find that the figures were fairly equal. Throughout my battle I had always felt that there were more against me. Nonetheless, I was to face an enormous amount of rejection and disbelief. Even my friends, like some professionals, found it difficult to support me when they realised the extent of the psychological pain I was enduring. At times, I was so alone, with nobody to reach out to.

Following the second surgery and despite the chronic anxiety, terror and constant headaches I was suffering I made an attempt to return to a full-time job. I became increasingly aware that despite my efforts and tenacity to continue working it simply was not possible for me to hold down a job. I had in fact made four separate attempts at employment when I was eventually struck with a deep and very desperate depression two years later. This depression left me feeling more wretched than I had ever done in my whole life. Now was the time when I had to start taking medication in the form of antidepressants. My GP finally persuaded me to see a newly appointed psychiatrist, who was female. I agreed that she could visit me at home as I was not prepared to venture into the psychiatric department of the local hospital.

After a wait of about two weeks the psychiatrist visited me at home. She spent approximately two hours with me and listened carefully as I began to broadly outline some of the horrors I had experienced. I was unaware at that time that the picture I was painting of my experiences were just confirming what this psychiatrist already knew of her predecessor and the way in which the ward had previously been run. On leaving my house she said she would write a detailed report to my GP, of which I requested a copy. She said she would make herself available to me if I needed help or support. I sat back and waited in anticipation for her report – what would she dare to write in it?

Beyond the never-ending support my solicitor had shown me, this was to be the first of several reports which started to support me positively. Her description of my relating of my experiences read as follows: 'Her recollection of her time on this ward is reminiscent of reading about Muslim/Bosnian slave sex camps where women are repeatedly abused and degraded.' Other parts of the report clearly indicated that it was fairly common knowledge to the authorities that all had not been well on that particular ward with the previous doctors.

It was only a matter of days before this report landed on my solicitor's desk. This, along with two other psychiatric reports, were to give us the medical evidence needed to carry the case. An employment consultant was also instructed by my solicitor to report on loss of earnings as a result of the negligence and trauma I had suffered. Meanwhile the defendants were doing everything they could to cover up, delay proceedings and inflict further damage on me.

Because of the continuing illness I was suffering I was involved with social services, who had been asked by my GP to assist me in the community and offer support. This initially seemed to be helpful, but unbeknown to me the social worker who was on my case was in fact relaying details about me to the defendants. She was also probing me for details about the proceedings to relay back to the defendants.

I was, at this stage, referred by my GP to a trauma clinic at a London hospital where at last I began to get some much-needed professional help. Because of the history it was extremely difficult to begin to trust the doctor, though as time progressed I was able to develop a good doctor/patient relationship with her. However, she left her post some nine months later and again I was without the appropriate support.

My psychotherapist as witness

As my solicitor continued to collect evidence for the now certain court case that was to take place, she approached the kind and gentle lady therapist from whom I had first sought help, and had ceased to work with when I was referred to the London hospital. The therapist refused to enter into any correspondence and stated categorically that it would be outside her code of ethics to give any evidence of details of why I had been seeing her. Not surprisingly, neither my solicitor nor I could understand the unhelpful attitude of someone who had been so kind and willing to offer me help and support for some considerable time, and who had relieved me of a considerable amount of money. The strangest point to me in her refusal to submit evidence was that whilst I was in therapy with her it was not outside of her code of ethics to liaise openly and regularly with my GP, with my consent, as to my psychological condition. My solicitor and I both decided we would not bother with her and were confident we had the evidence that we needed from our expert witnesses.

Later on in the build-up to the court case the most horrendous events were about to take place. This therapist was approached by the defendants and asked for a detailed statement. Along with this request it was pointed out to her that if she refused she would be subpoenaed by the court and, if she still refused, would face a prison sentence. With this threat she then decided to supply a statement. This was by far the most hurtful situation that I had faced on the legal side of the story. In reality now this lady would give evidence in court against me as the defendant's witness. I pondered over the matter for several days and also took some independent legal advice as to my situation. It was at this point that I really had to decide whether or not to continue with legal proceedings. My solicitor and I arranged a meeting to discuss this matter, along with other current issues. I had decided for myself before I met with my solicitor to let the therapist go ahead and side against me. I was confident that if she were to be of any help to the defendants then she would have to lie under oath in court. I had confidence enough in my counsel to know that he would annihilate her in the witness box. I had no hesitation in allowing that to happen. However, her action really was the biggest betrayal of trust one could ever imagine.

With this situation, the therapist quite obviously must have felt very anxious about her dilemma and consequently supplied a written sheet of details which she alleged to have written after my very first session with her. She had submitted a statement that was of no use to the defendants in court, as it did not prejudice me in any way. Consequently in the end she was not called as a witness.

Code of ethics for therapists

I believe very strongly that much consideration should be given to the laws and ethics surrounding therapists when such serious matters arise. Many people who enter therapy must, at some point in their lives, have been a victim of abuse. I believe that these professionals should be prepared to face the fact that they may be asked to provide written evidence in support of their client in court, particularly when asked why the client has sought their help. I would suggest that therapists' governing bodies review and amend their code of ethics to cover these situations. Any therapist who is not prepared to stand up in court should not be allowed to become a member of that professional body. No therapist should display double standards of refusing to support the client but then being prepared to stand against them.

Before the trial

In the last few weeks leading up to the trial the defendants became more and more harassed about the very likely outcome of the case and that there was no let-up from my side on the pressure we were putting upon them. They still, apparently, could not trace the doctor involved in the sexual assault. He was finally tracked down abroad. The defendants began to fish for anything they could to throw at me. First came an amazing piece of rubbish written by the alleged hospital chaplain at the time the abuse took place, who more unbelievably was a woman too and who actually supported the doctor who had sexually assaulted me. This incredible statement did nothing for my faith in religion. Second came a statement from the social worker who had been appointed to me as I was about to be discharged from the ward. She had since left her post. What she had in fact done was to access my personal file (which I had assumed was confidential) from the local social services office via my current social worker and used that information to prepare another statement against me.

A matter of weeks before the trial the doctor was finally traced and produced a statement that was very muddled and difficult to interpret.

Just three weeks before the court case, the inevitable happened: the defendants tried to pay me off in order to silence me. Unfortunately for them it did not work – my legal team and I stood firm and ignored the offer.

The day after the trial my social worker admitted to me that only six days previously she had been at the hospital in conversation with another consultant whom I had never met, discussing the forthcoming case. This again was another clear breach of confidentiality by social services, and a further betrayal of my trust, after she had already divulged details from my file to the social worker who had decided to give evidence against me.

I stayed with a friend the night before the trial and travelled all the way to the Central London court by taxi. I sat with two friends, my solicitor, barrister and had a doctor by my side the whole time while we waited for the 10.30 start. Shortly after I had arrived at court I settled down and was all ready to face the most difficult day of my life, where I was to be cross-examined and have my whole life torn into by the defendants. I was as ready then as I would ever be. Exactly on the stroke of 10.30, when we were just about to enter court, came the big retreat. The defendants were not prepared to defend the case and made another financial offer of settlement. Negotiations took up the next hour and a quarter, and when final decisions had been taken by both parties we entered court before the judge to finalise and seal the agreement. As I left court by taxi with my two friends and the doctor I felt satisfied at the outcome. It had indeed been a great day for victims of sexual abuse, for psychiatric patients, women, and all gay people. My thanks go especially to my solicitor for standing by me for nearly seven years and for successfully bringing the case, as well as to all others involved for standing by me. However, I continue to be deeply troubled and damaged by my experiences and still have not been able to return to full-time paid employment.

Recommendations

It concerns me more and more that there are others out there who are suffering in complete silence because they perhaps are frightened or do not have the ability to fight such a case. The only way to break through this barrier of despicable abuse is to unite and face the authorities head on. I will do anything I feel able to do to support anyone who finds themselves in a similar situation.

I believe that the management of health authorities should more closely supervise, spot-check and monitor their employees to ensure high standards of practice and care in order to eliminate the abhorrent crime of sexual assault. These abusers can only operate freely when a blind eye is turned and, more frighteningly, when they know that the health authority and social services will support them against their victims in legal battles which ensue. This attitude that I came up against only provides better opportunities for serial abusers to operate within the National Health Service. It is essential for the well-being of all patients that the system is changed immediately to eradicate such abuse, which it seems is probably quite widespread.

More attention should be paid to doctors and healthcare professionals in the system who are of very different cultures to the patients they are supposed to be caring for. Judging from my case, it seems that it is particularly unwise in psychiatry to mix cultures.

For myself, I feel strongly that in the future there certainly will be more that needs to be written as I grow in recovery and try to find some sort of understanding as to the reasons I have been treated with such abuse. I believe in the years to come that abuse such as I have experienced will become more and more apparent and that hopefully systems and support services will be set up both to acknowledge and to assist in eradicating it. As I regain my strength I hope very much that I will play some part in that.

I now look to the team of professionals, all of whom are outside of the National Health Service, that are currently helping me to overcome the past and who are helping to heal me. I am confident that with their support and dedication to me I will make a recovery sufficient at least for life to be a little more tolerable than it is at present.

I am a heavy smoker, but for every one of the many, many cigarettes I have smoked, I must have shed at least fifty tears.

Still, I resolve to carry on.

If any reader wishes to correspond with me as a result of reading my personal story, I would like to invite them to do so via the publishers.

List of Organisations

African-Caribbean Family Mediation Service, 49 Effra Road, London SW2 1BZ. 0171 733 0214.

Article 12, 8 Wakley Street, London EC1V 7QE

Asian Family and Marriage Guidance Service, c/o Age Concern, Clarence House, 46 Humberside Gate, Leics LE1 31J. 0116 262 9636.

Association of Child Psychology and Psychiatry, St Savour's House, 39–41 Union Street, London SE1 1SD. 0171 403 7458.

Association of Child Psychotherapists, Burgh House, New End Square, London NW3 1LT. 0181 458 8609.

Association for Shared Parenting, PO Box 2000, Derby, W. Midlands DE1 1YZ. 01789 751157. Promotes rights/views of children following separation/ divorce. Children have the right to be cared for by both parents equally if they so desire.

Association of Family Court Welfare Officers, 9 East Street, Swindon SN1 5BU. 01793 612299.

Association of Lawyers for Children, P.O. Box 2029, Buckhurst Hill IG9 6EQ. 0181 505 3900.

British Association for Social Work, 16 Kent Street, Birmingham B5 6RD. 0121 622 3911.

British Association of Counselling, 1 Regents Place, Rugby, Warwicks CV21 2PJ.

British Association of Lawyer Mediators and Law Wise, The Shooting Lodge, Guildford Road, Sutton Green, Guildford GU4 7PZ. 01483 235000.

British Association of Psychotherapists, 37 Mapesbury Road, London NW2 4HJ. 0181 452 9823.

Central Council for Education and Training in SW, Derbyshire House, St Chad's Street, London WC1H 8AQ. 0171 278 2458.

Child Poverty Action Group, Citizen's Rights Office, 4th Floor, 1–5 Bath Street, London EC1V 9PY. 0171 253 3406.

Child Psychotherapy Trust, 121 Maresfield Gardens, London NW3 5SH. 0171 794 8881.

Childline, 50 Studd Street, Freepost 1111, London N1 0BR. Freephone 0800 1111.

Children's Legal Centre, University of Essex, Wivenhoe Park, Colchester, Essex CO4 3SQ. 01206 873820 (24hr answerphone).

Children's Rights Alliance c/o **Children's Rights Development Unit**, 235 Shaftesbury Avenue, London, WC2H 8EL. 0171 278 8222.

Children's Rights Development Unit, 235 Shaftesbury Avenue, London, WC2H 8EL. 0171 278 8222.

Children's Rights Office, Chancery House, 319 City Road, London EC1 1LJ. 0171 278 8222.

Coram Contact Centre, Thomas Coram Foundation for Children, 48 Mecklenburgh Square, London WC1N 1NU. 0171-278 5708. Unsupervised/ supervised contact centre and mediation services.

Department of Health, Public Enquiry Office. 0171 210 4850.

Divorce Mediation and Counselling Centre, 38 Elbury Street, London SW1. 0171 730 2422.

ECT Anonymous, 14 Western Avenue, Riddlesden, Keighley, W. Yorks BD20 5DJ.

Families and Friends of Lesbians and Gays, PO Box 153, Manchester, M60.

Family and Divorce Centre, 1 Brooklands Avenue, Cambridge CB2 2BB. 01223 576308.

Family Law Bar Association, Queen Elizabeth Buildings, Temple, London EC4Y 9BS. 0171 797 7837.

Family Mediation Scotland, 127 Rose Street, South Lane, Edinburgh EH2 4BQ. 0131 220 1610.

Family Mediators Association, 1 Wyvil Court, Wyvil Road, London SW8 2TG. 0171 720 3336.

Family Rights Group, The Print House, 18 Ashwick Street, London E8 3DL. 0171 923 2628.

General Council of the Bar, 2 Cursitor Street, London EC4A 1NE. 0171 440 4000.

Health Service Commissioner (Ombudsman), 11–13th Floor, Millbank Tower, Millbank, London SW19 4QP. 0171 276 2035.

Hearing Voices Network, Fourways House, 16 Tariff Street, Manchester M1 2FN. 0161 228 3896.

Housing Aid, 40 Birmingham Housing Aid Service 37a Waterloo Street, Birmingham B2 5TJ.

Institute for Family Therapy, 24–32 Stephenson Way, London NW1 2HX. 0171 391 9150.

Institute for Legal Executives, Kempton Manor, Kempston, Bedford, Beds MK42 7AB.

Law Group UK, Orbital House, 85 Croydon Road, Caterham, Surrey CR3 6PD. 01883 341341.

Legal Aid Board, 85 Gray's Inn Road, London WC1X 8AA.

Manic Depressive Fellowship, 8–10 High Street, Kingston Upon Thames, Surrey KT1 1EY. 0181 924 6550.

Mediation in Divorce, Children's Counselling Centre, 13 Rosslyn Road, Twickenham TW1 2AR. 0181 891 3107.

Mediation UK, Alexander House, Telephone Avenue, Bristol BS1 4BS. 0117 904 6661.

MIND (National Association for Mental Health), Granta House, 15/19 Broadway, Stratford, London E15 4BQ. 0181 519 2122.

Mindlink, Granta House, 15–19 Broadway, London E15 4BQ. 0181 519 2122.

Mothers Apart from Their Children (MATCH), Health Care Services Limited, UCL Hospital Trust, 57–67 Chenies Mews, London E6 HX. 0171 388 6564.

NASIYAT, 278 Seven Sisters Road, London N4 2HY. Counselling to divorcing parents, ethnic groups and children.

National and Family Mediation, 9 Tavistock Place, London WC1H 9SN. 0171 383 5993.

National Association for People Abused in Childhood, 42 Curtain Road, London EC2A 3NH.

National Association of Guardians ad Litem and Reporting Officers, Down Lodge, 170 Banstead Road, Carshalton Beeches, Surrey SM5 4DW. 0181 643 8572

National Care Leavers Association, 21 Dorset Road, Guisborough, Cleveland TS14 7DN. 01287 638030. E-mail: ncla@mcmail.com.

National Council for Family Proceeedings, University of Bristol, Wills Memorial Building, Queens Road, Clifton, Bristol BS8 1RJ. 0117 954 5381.

National Health Information Service, 0800 665544.

National Voice, A, PO Box 253, Leeds LS1 3RA. 0113 242 9767.

National Youth Advocacy Service (formerly IRCHIN), 1 Downtown Road South, Heswall, Wirral, Merseyside L60 5RG. 0151 342 7852. Freephone Children in Care 0800 616 101.

Network, 2nd Floor, High Holborn House, 52–54 High Holborn, London, WC1V 6RL. 0171 831 8031.

Official Solicitor's Office, 51 Chancery Lane, London WC2A 1DD. 0171 911 7127.

PAIN, 10 Water Lane, Bishop's Stortford, Herts CM23 2JZ.

Parent Network, Room 2, Winchester House, 11 Cranmer Road, SW9 6EJ. 0171 735 1214.

Psychotherapists and Counsellors for Social Responsibility, 27 Elm Grove, London NW2 3AG.

PEG (The Participation Education Group for Children and Young People) c/o Enable Training and Consultancy Services, 63 Grasmere Street West, Gateshead, Tyne and Wear NE8 2TS. 01914 783030.

POPAN (Prevention of Professional Abuse Network), 1 Wyvil Court, Wyvil Road, London SW8 2TG.

Relate, Herbert Gray College, Little Church Street, Rugby CV21 3AP. 01788 573241.

Relateen, c/o Relate Office (see above).

Royal College of Psychiatrists, 17 Belgrave Square, London SW1X 8PG. 0171 235 2351.

Solicitor's Family Law Association, PO Box 302, Orpington, Kent BR6 8PX. 01689 850227.

Survivors Speak Out, 34 Osnaburgh Street, London NW1 3ND. 0171 916 5472.

The Law Society, 113 Chancery Lane, London WC2A 1PL. 0171 242 1222.

Torbay Child Linkline, 0800 220220. Mediation centre offering counselling for children.

UK College of Family Mediators, 24–32 Stephenson Way, London NW1 2HX. 0171 391 9162.

UKCP (United Kingdom Council for Psychotherapy), Regents College, Regents Park, London NW14 NS. 0171 436 3002. Membership of accredited Psycho-therapists.

United Kingdom Advocacy Network, UKAN office, Suite 462, Premier House, 14 Cross Burques Street, Sheffield S1 2HG. 01142 2728171.

Voice for the Child in Care, Unit 4 Pride Court, 80/82 White Lion Street, London, N1 9PF. 0171 833 5792.

Young Minds: National Association for Multi-professional Work in Child and Family Mental Health, 102-108 Clerkenwell Road, London EC1M 5SA.

List of contributors

Sue Amphlett is a registered general nurse who also holds a part 1 midwifery certificate and a distinction certificate in occupational health nursing. She and her husband were founder members of PAIN - Parents Against INjustice. Prior to becoming the Director of PAIN she served as a flight lieutenant nursing officer in the Princess Mary's Royal Air Force Nursing Service. As director of PAIN she is responsible for presenting papers and workshops at national and international conferences, providing training to multi-agency childcare teams, PAIN's involvement with national working parties and joint project collaborative work, and for responding to consultative documents and liaison with the media. She has appeared on numerous radio and television programmes and is the author of many articles and papers relating to the work of PAIN and the investigative process of alleged child abuse.

Peter Beresford PhD is Professor of Social Policy at Brunel University and Honorary Fellow of the National Institute of Social Work. He works with the Open Services Project and is a member of Survivors Speak Out.

Lois Colling is senior registrar in child and adolescent psychiatry in the child and family department at the Tavistock Clinic.

Roger Green is a principal lecturer in social work and Head of the Centre for Social Work and Community Research at the University of Hertfordshire. He has a background in social work and community work practice in both the voluntary and statutory sectors. He has published widely on community needs research and his recent publications include a report on poverty in East London, and articles on the UK Government's new Social Exclusion Unit and the role of community development as an anti-poverty strategy. He has worked with tenants on the Kingsmead Estate in Hackney, East London for a number of years.

Lee Heal, Service User.

Maggie Lane is an ex-service user and has been an active campaigner for the rights of looked after children for ten years. She has carried out work for a number of organisations concerned with children and young people accommodated by social services departments. She is a committee member of National Voice, the national organisation working on behalf of looked after children.

Brian Littlechild is Director of Social Work Studies at the University of Hertfordshire, following work as a social worker, team leader and courts officer in social services departments in the fields of child care and youth justice. He has particular interests in the rights of children in social work processes and youth justice systems, and violence towards social care staff. He has lectured in a number of countries in these areas and has published a wide range of articles and books. Current research includes evaluation of drug education programmes in prison, the effects of violence on child protection staff, and the development of inter-agency working with disaffected young people.

Mary Neville I was born in 1960 in South East England, I attended school until the age of 16. Following a very successful career in retailing, events that I was to endure at the hands of professionals have led to much unrest within me. I continue to be deeply troubled. Now studying law part time at college and at other times occupied with voluntary work. I live alone, and long for a return to my career.

Helen Payne PhD is Senior lecturer in health and social care at the University of Hertfordshire and visiting fellow at the University of Derby. She is an accredited group and individual psychotherapist and has published several books and numerous articles in this field.

Maria E. Pozzi is a child and adolescent psychotherapist and also an adult psychotherapist. She works in Stevenage Consultation Clinic for Children, Families and Young People and also privately. She is a visiting tutor in Italy, Switzerland, at the Tavistock Clinic and at the London Centre for Psychotherapy as well as in Italy and Switzerland. She has published articles and papers on psychodynamic counselling with under-fives and their families and on children with physical and learning disabilities.

Dr Judith Trowell is consultant child and adolescent psychiatrist at the Tavistock Clinic, Fellow of the Royal College of Psychiatrists and Honorary Senior Lecturer at the Royal Free Hospital Medical School and Institute of Psychiatry. She works as an expert witness in child protection cases and is chair of the Tavistock Clinic Legal Workshop. She is chair of Young Minds and leads an MA in child protection and a new M.Phil programme in psychoanalytical psychotherapy for child and adolescent psychiatrists.

Andy Turner trained as a youth and community worker at St Martins in Lancaster. He has been a community worker at the Kingsmead Kabin, on the Kingsmead Estate, Hackney in London's East End for the past five years. The Kabin is a community project which is developing 'bottom up' innovatory and creative responses to the needs of people on the estate.

Sue Williscroft is a lawyer practising in Bradford. She has been qualified for 19 years and is senior partner of a firm specialising in family law and social welfare work and franchised by the Legal Aid Board. She is a member of the Child Care Panel and Mental Health Panel of the Law Society and sits as a Deputy District Judge. She is actively involved in the local Domestic Violence forum, Solicitors Family Law Association, Contact Centre and Child Care representatives groups.

Anne Wilson is a college lecturer and psychiatric system survivor.

Subject Index

Author Index